Mastering Computer Vision with PyTorch 2.0

Discover, Design, and Build Cutting-Edge High Performance Computer Vision Solutions with PyTorch 2.0 and Deep Learning Techniques

M. Arshad Siddiqui

www.orangeava.com

First Published: January 2025

Published By: Orange Education Pvt Ltd, AVA®

Address: 9, Daryaganj, Delhi, 110002, India

275 New North Road Islington Suite 1314 London,

N1 7AA, United Kingdom

ISBN (PBK): 978-93-48107-08-4

ISBN (E-BOOK): 978-93-48107-48-0

Dedicated To

My Beloved Parents:

Late Mohd Ziauddin Siddiqui
Shamama Siddiqui

and

My Wife Zubia Khan

About the Author

M. Arshad Siddiqui is a distinguished computer vision expert with extensive experience in developing and deploying cutting-edge AI solutions. His career began as a Computer Vision Engineer at Lensbricks, where he developed innovative vision systems for emerging technologies. He then advanced to Big Vision, refining his expertise in tackling large-scale challenges in computer vision and artificial intelligence.

Currently a Principal Engineer in Computer Vision and AI, Arshad has collaborated with over 20 organizations, ranging from dynamic startups to Fortune 500 companies, helping them design and implement robust AI solutions. Over the course of his career, he has worked across diverse industries, including healthcare, retail, autonomous systems, and mobile technology, delivering scalable and production-ready solutions that address real-world problems.

Arshad's technical achievements span the full spectrum of AI innovation. He has designed and optimized AI pipelines to operate efficiently in resource-constrained environments, reduced deployment costs without compromising performance, and deployed advanced computer vision solutions on edge devices such as Android and iOS smartphones. His expertise also includes creating scalable architectures for large-scale AI systems and seamlessly integrating them into production workflows.

In healthcare, he has developed AI-powered diagnostic tools to analyze medical images, aiding early detection and improving treatment outcomes. In retail, he has implemented systems for inventory management and customer analytics. His work in autonomous systems includes designing vision algorithms for self-driving vehicles and drones, focusing on real-time object detection and navigation.

Having worked closely with startups to accelerate innovation and with Fortune 500 companies to scale AI systems, Arshad focuses on bridging the gap between cutting-edge research and practical deployment.

In this book, Arshad shares his extensive expertise, offering readers insights into PyTorch 2.0 and its applications in computer vision, empowering them to create impactful AI solutions for dynamic, real-world challenges.

About the Technical Reviewers

Gursimar Singh is a Senior AI Scientist specializing in Computer Vision, with over six years of experience in research and development. He has been pivotal in developing and deploying advanced computer vision solutions across various industries, including agriculture, automotive and real estate photography, thermal imaging, and video conferencing. His innovative work also extends to generative AI applications for portrait animations.

An active member of the OpenCV organization, Gursimar is contributing to the development of OpenCV5, set for release in 2025. His expertise spans algorithm development, artificial intelligence, computer vision, image processing, and generative AI. He has published a research paper and holds a pending U.S. patent in computational photography, highlighting his commitment to advancing technological frontiers.

Gursimar is deeply passionate about education and advocates for access to quality learning and skill development. He is passionate about disseminating knowledge in AI and computer vision, helping to empower others in these rapidly evolving fields.

Nehaa Bansal is a trailblazing thought leader and data scientist with a deep passion for early innovation. Her extensive experience across diverse sectors including banking, finance, telecom, and insurance has honed her expertise in developing impactful predictive models. She holds top honors in her computer science bachelor's degree and a master's in data science from BITS Pilani, providing a strong foundation for her career.

Nehaa's professional life is guided by core values of ownership, prioritizing people, and understanding the "why" behind every action. She embraces an agile approach, acting quickly, learning from failures, iterating continuously, and prioritizing fairness. Driven by a passion for solving user problems, Nehaa combines her expertise in analytics, product strategy, and leadership to develop innovative solutions that consistently push boundaries. Her unwavering dedication to continuous learning, inclusivity, and collaboration, combined with her dedication and empathy, makes her an inspiring leader driving positive change in technology and data science.

Acknowledgements

The journey of writing this book has been deeply enriching, and I am profoundly grateful to those who made it possible through their guidance, support, and inspiration.

First and foremost, I extend my heartfelt gratitude to my wife and parents for their unwavering encouragement and belief in me. Their support has been my anchor, and I could not have completed this book without their constant motivation.

This book represents the culmination of practical experiences I have gained while working in the field of computer vision and artificial intelligence. The dynamic challenges and opportunities presented by real-world industry projects have significantly shaped my understanding of PyTorch and its applications. I am particularly thankful to my colleagues and mentors for fostering an environment of learning and exploration, enabling me to delve deeper into this fascinating field.

I would like to express my sincere thanks to Mr. Gursimar Singh and Ms. Nehaa Bansal for their meticulous technical review of this book. Their insights and expertise have been invaluable in ensuring that the content is accurate and impactful.

A special mention goes to my team for their understanding and support, giving me the time and flexibility to dedicate myself to this project. The decision to divide this book into sections stems from the realization that image processing is a vast and ever-evolving domain.

Finally, I am immensely grateful to the broader machine learning and computer vision community. The shared knowledge, discussions, and advancements in this space have been a source of inspiration throughout this journey.

This book is as much a product of collaboration as it is of individual effort, and to all who have contributed, directly or indirectly, I offer my deepest thanks.

Preface

The advent of PyTorch has revolutionized deep learning, offering a blend of flexibility and power that caters to both researchers and practitioners. With PyTorch 2.0, the framework has reached new heights, incorporating advanced features and optimizations. This book serves as a comprehensive guide to mastering PyTorch for computer vision tasks, combining foundational concepts with practical applications to empower readers in their journey.

Chapter 1. Diving into PyTorch 2.0: This chapter explores PyTorch's history, evolution, and features, including the key advancements in version 2.0, while guiding you through setup and installation.

Chapter 2. PyTorch Basics: This chapter introduces the fundamental building blocks of PyTorch, such as tensors, operations, and computational graphs, alongside practical examples.

Chapter 3. Transitioning from PyTorch 1.x to PyTorch 2.0: This chapter provides a roadmap for upgrading from earlier versions of PyTorch, highlighting key differences, compatibility solutions, and migration examples.

Chapter 4. Venturing into Artificial Neural Networks: This chapter covers the fundamentals of neural networks and guides you through building and training an image classification model in PyTorch.

Chapter 5. Diving Deep into Convolutional Neural Networks (CNNs): This chapter explains CNNs' architecture and implementation, teaching you how to build, train, and optimize CNNs for vision tasks.

Chapter 6. Data Augmentation and Preprocessing for Vision Tasks: This chapter focuses on improving model performance through data augmentation and preprocessing, with practical implementations in PyTorch.

Chapter 7. Exploring Transfer Learning with PyTorch: This chapter introduces transfer learning and pre-trained models, demonstrating how to leverage them for enhanced model performance.

Chapter 8. Advanced Image Classification Models: This chapter delves into popular architectures such as ResNet, VGG, and Inception, guiding readers through their implementation and performance comparison.

Chapter 9. Object Detection Models: This chapter covers object detection techniques and renowned models such as YOLO, Faster R-CNN, and SSD, with practical implementations.

Chapter 10. Tips and Tricks to Improve Model Performance: This chapter discusses advanced methods such as hyperparameter tuning, dropout, and ensemble techniques to enhance model efficiency.

Chapter 11. Efficient Training with PyTorch Lightning: This chapter explores PyTorch Lightning, showcasing its utility for streamlined training workflows and advanced features.

Chapter 12. Model Deployment and Production-Ready Considerations: This chapter concludes with a focus on model deployment, covering TorchServe, quantization, and considerations for production readiness.

This book bridges the gap between theory and practice, equipping readers with the tools and knowledge to excel in their deep learning journey using PyTorch 2.0.

Get a Free eBook

We hope you are enjoying your recently purchased book! Your feedback is incredibly valuable to us, and to all other readers looking for great books.

If you found this book helpful or enjoyable, we would truly appreciate it, if you could take a moment to leave a short review with a 5 star rating on Amazon. It helps us grow, and lets other readers discover our books.

As a thank you, we would love to send you a free digital copy of this book, and a **30%** discount code on your next cart value on our official websites:

www.orangeava.com

www.orangeava.in (For Indian Subcontinent)

☑ **Here's how:**

Leave a review for the book on Amazon.

Take a screenshot of your review, and send an email to **info@orangeava.com** (it can be just the confirmation screen).

Once, we receive your screenshot, we will send you the digital file, within 24 hours.

Thank you so much for your support – it means a lot to us!

Downloading the code bundles and colored images

Please follow the links or scan the QR codes to download the **_Code Bundles and Images_** of the book:

Github: https://github.com/ava-orange-education/Mastering-Computer-Vision-with-PyTorch-2.0

The code bundles and images of the book are also hosted on ***https://rebrand.ly/edf948***

In case there's an update to the code, it will be updated on the existing GitHub repository.

Errata

We take immense pride in our work at **Orange Education Pvt Ltd,** and follow best practices to ensure the accuracy of our content to provide an indulging reading experience to our subscribers. Our readers are our mirrors, and we use their inputs to reflect and improve upon human errors, if any, that may have occurred during the publishing processes involved. To let us maintain the quality and help us reach out to any readers who might be having difficulties due to any unforeseen errors, please write to us at :

errata@orangeava.com

Your support, suggestions, and feedback are highly appreciated.

DID YOU KNOW

Did you know that Orange Education Pvt Ltd offers eBook versions of every book published, with PDF and ePub files available? You can upgrade to the eBook version at **www.orangeava.com** and as a print book customer, you are entitled to a discount on the eBook copy. Get in touch with us at: **info@orangeava.com** for more details.

At **www.orangeava.com**, you can also read a collection of free technical articles, sign up for a range of free newsletters, and receive exclusive discounts and offers on AVA® Books and eBooks.

PIRACY

If you come across any illegal copies of our works in any form on the internet, we would be grateful if you would provide us with the location address or website name. Please contact us at **info@orangeava.com** with a link to the material.

ARE YOU INTERESTED IN AUTHORING WITH US?

If there is a topic that you have expertise in, and you are interested in either writing or contributing to a book, please write to us at **business@orangeava.com**. We are on a journey to help developers and tech professionals to gain insights on the present technological advancements and innovations happening across the globe and build a community that believes Knowledge is best acquired by sharing and learning with others. Please reach out to us to learn what our audience demands and how you can be part of this educational reform. We also welcome ideas from tech experts and help them build learning and development content for their domains.

REVIEWS

Please leave a review. Once you have read and used this book, why not leave a review on the site that you purchased it from? Potential readers can then see and use your unbiased opinion to make purchase decisions. We at Orange Education would love to know what you think about our products, and our authors can learn from your feedback. Thank you!

For more information about Orange Education, please visit **www.orangeava.com**.

Table of Contents

Chapter 1
Diving into PyTorch 2.0

Introduction

Welcome to the thrilling PyTorch 2.0 learning trip for computer vision. This book's opening chapter, "*Diving into PyTorch 2.0*," lays the groundwork for the rest of the chapters. You will gain a comprehensive understanding of PyTorch, a well-liked and potent open-source machine learning package, in this chapter. We will walk you through the specifics of PyTorch's creation, its development over time, and the main advantages it offers in the field of AI research.

Designed for both beginners and intermediate learners in computer vision and deep learning, this book aims to provide practical and in-depth insights into PyTorch's powerful capabilities. The journey starts with a thorough examination of PyTorch's past, helping readers appreciate how PyTorch's unique architecture and foundational principles have distinguished it in the landscape of machine learning frameworks. This historical context will lay a solid foundation for understanding the unique benefits of PyTorch, making it a tool of choice for many researchers and practitioners in the field.

Structure

In this chapter, the following topics will be covered:

- Brief Overview of Pytorch
- PyTorch and Computer Vision
- Origin and Emergence of PyTorch
- PyTorch's Philosophy and Early Days
- Evolution and Growth of PyTorch
- Adoption of PyTorch
- Installing PyTorch
- Troubleshooting Tips

- Setting Up the Development Environment on Jupyter Notebook
- Dynamic Computation Graphs and the Define-by-Run Paradigm
- The Autograd System
- GPU Acceleration
- Distributed Computing
- Introduction to TorchScript

Brief Overview of PyTorch

PyTorch, at its core, is a free machine-learning framework. It offers two high-level features: deep neural networks constructed using a tape-based autograd system and tensor calculations with excellent GPU acceleration support. To put it simply, PyTorch includes all the tools required to create and train deep learning models.

However, PyTorch's 'Pythonic' aspect sets it apart from other machine learning frameworks. PyTorch is not for binding Python into a rigid C++ framework. It is designed to be tightly linked with Python and uses Python's strength to provide a fluid and adaptable user experience. Nearly the same procedures apply when using PyTorch as when using NumPy. And because PyTorch tensors and NumPy arrays are so similar, you can easily swap between the two.

What makes PyTorch particularly attractive for computer vision is its extensive ecosystem of libraries and tools that specifically cater to vision tasks. TorchVision, a package in PyTorch, has datasets, models (including pre-trained models), and transformation functions for images. This means that PyTorch provides us with ready-to-use tools and functionalities that can help us in a wide array of vision tasks, thereby letting us focus on the unique aspects of our specific problems.

But PyTorch is not just about simplicity and ease of use. It's also about power and control. PyTorch uses a method called "define-by-run" for building computational graphs, in contrast to the "define-and-run" method used in many other frameworks. This means that the computational graph, a series of operations that defines a mathematical model, is defined on the go as the operations occur. This provides a lot of flexibility and lets us do complex things with our models.

And it goes beyond that. PyTorch has improved in both power and usability with version 2.0. The history of PyTorch will be covered in more detail on the next pages, along with instructions on how to install and set up PyTorch and an examination of the main changes and additions made in PyTorch 2.0. We're about to blast off into the realm of PyTorch 2.0 and computer vision, so buckle up!

PyTorch and Computer Vision

PyTorch has positioned itself as a go-to library for Computer Vision tasks. It offers a perfect blend of flexibility and power. The ease with which you can build, train, and tweak deep learning models makes PyTorch an attractive choice for researchers and developers in the field of computer vision. But the appeal doesn't stop at flexibility. PyTorch also provides efficiency and performance allowing it to scale from prototyping stages to large-scale deployment.

One of the primary reasons why PyTorch is widely used in computer vision is its rich ecosystem of libraries and tools explicitly designed for vision tasks. Torchvision, a package in PyTorch, includes an array of pre-processed datasets and pre-trained models, such as ResNet and VGG, which have established benchmarks in various computer vision tasks. It also provides transformation functions to perform image manipulations, a crucial aspect in any computer vision pipeline.

With PyTorch's "define-by-run" paradigm, the dynamic computation graph becomes an excellent fit for the sequence of operations typically found in computer vision tasks. This approach provides researchers and developers with maximum flexibility in designing and experimenting with complex architectures, which is often necessary in the rapidly evolving field of computer vision.

Furthermore, the enhancements brought about by PyTorch 2.0 have strengthened its position even more. Improvements in performance, new APIs, and features like mobile deployment make PyTorch 2.0 a compelling choice for any computer vision task - from image classification and object detection to semantic segmentation and beyond.

In summary, the combination of PyTorch's intuitive design, coupled with its strong performance characteristics, has made it a favorite among the computer vision community. As we move forward in this book, you will get a hands-on experience of using PyTorch for various exciting and impactful computer vision tasks and use cases.

Origin and Emergence of PyTorch

PyTorch has its roots in the Torch library, a machine learning library based on the Lua programming language, and widely used in academia. Torch, however, suffered from the limitations of Lua and lacked the rich ecosystem of libraries that other programming languages provided. To address these challenges, a group of AI researchers at Facebook, Soumith Chintala, the director of AI Research (FAIR), began constructing a brand new deep learning system. They wanted a tool that was just as responsive, adaptable, and user-friendly as Torch while also being tightly connected with a more powerful programming language.

They introduced PyTorch, an open-source machine learning package created for Python, in January 2017. Python, a language that was already a leader in the field of scientific computing and had a strong ecosystem of libraries like NumPy, SciPy, and Matplotlib, was created with the intention of bringing the magic of the Torch library to Python. The machine learning community reacted positively to PyTorch's release, which hastened the adoption of this tool.

PyTorch's Philosophy and Early Days

From the beginning, PyTorch was guided by a Python-first philosophy. It wasn't a binding into a monolithic C++ framework, but a tool built to be deeply integrated with Python. It could leverage the power of Python to deliver a user experience that was smooth, flexible, and intuitive. This was in stark contrast to other machine learning frameworks of the time, which often felt like they were fighting against Python's dynamics, rather than embracing them.

The Python-first design of PyTorch had profound implications. It meant that users could leverage the full power of Python when working with PyTorch, and they could use native Python control flow statements in their models. It also meant that debugging PyTorch models was as straightforward as debugging Python scripts. This was a breath of fresh air for developers who were accustomed to the opaqueness of other frameworks.

Furthermore, PyTorch was designed to be imperative or define-by-run, which means the computational graph, a series of operations that define a mathematical model, is defined on the fly as the operations occur. This was unlike the static, define-and-run computational graphs found in many other frameworks. The dynamic nature of PyTorch provided a lot of flexibility and allowed users to use native Python debugging tools. This was another factor that contributed to PyTorch's rapidly growing popularity.

Despite coming late to a field already dominated by several well-known frameworks, PyTorch soon established itself. Many researchers identified with its design ethos, while developers favored it because it worked well with Python. PyTorch has already established itself as a major force in the deep learning industry by the conclusion of its first year. The PyTorch team, however, was not satisfied with that. They were eager to push the envelope even further, and as a result, PyTorch 2.0 was created. This new version of PyTorch is more potent, effective, and user-friendly than before.

As we move forward, we will delve deeper into the features and enhancements brought by PyTorch 2.0 and explore how they can help us in our journey through the realm of computer vision and artificial intelligence.

Evolution and Growth of PyTorch

The early success of PyTorch was just the beginning. From its inception, PyTorch continually evolved and matured, guided by feedback and contributions from its growing user community.

One of the significant developments in PyTorch's evolution was the release of TorchScript in PyTorch 1.0. TorchScript is a way to separate your PyTorch model from Python, making it portable and optimizable. TorchScript uses PyTorch's JIT compiler to compile Python code into an intermediate representation that can then be run in a high-performance environment such as C++. This was a significant step forward because it made PyTorch models much more scalable and production-ready.

In addition, PyTorch continued to enrich its ecosystem. Libraries such as TorchText for natural language processing tasks and TorchVision for computer vision tasks, provided users with a wealth of resources for their projects. Newer additions such as the Captum for model interpretability, and PyTorch Lightning, a lightweight wrapper for more organized PyTorch code, made PyTorch even more versatile and user-friendly.

Adoption of PyTorch

As PyTorch matured, it also saw significant adoption. The clear syntax, dynamic computation graphs, and strong support for GPUs made it a favorite among researchers and developers alike. Its deep integration with Python and its active, open-source community also contributed to its popularity.

By the end of 2018, just a year after its launch, PyTorch was already one of the most popular deep learning frameworks, widely adopted in both academia and industry. Several notable companies and research institutions started to switch to PyTorch, including Uber's Pyro, HuggingFace's Transformers, and Catalyst, to name a few.

However, what truly cemented PyTorch's place in the pantheon of deep learning tools was its adoption by major AI research labs. For example, OpenAI switched to PyTorch as its primary research platform in 2020, citing PyTorch's ease of use and efficiency as the primary reasons.

PyTorch was adopted outside of the software sector as well. It also made its way into several industries where deep learning began to have an impact, including banking, healthcare, and autonomous vehicles. It was used to create algorithms for health diagnosis, stock price forecasting, and even self-driving cars.

Today, PyTorch is a crucial component of anyone's toolkit who works with machine learning or artificial intelligence. It's a monument to its design principles, functionality, and the thriving user and contributor community that has developed around it.

Improvements and new functionality introduced with PyTorch 2.0 continue to push the envelope of what is possible. We will set up PyTorch 2.0 and explore these fascinating updates in the following part.

The Importance of Virtual Environments and Creating Them

Creating an isolated environment for your Python projects, including PyTorch, is a good practice as it prevents conflicts between dependencies. It also allows you to experiment with different versions of libraries without disrupting your primary Python setup. One common way to create such isolated environments is using virtualenv or Python's built-in venv module.

For Ubuntu

1. If not already installed, install **`virtualenv`** with **`pip`**:

   ```
   pip install virtualenv
   ```

2. Navigate to the directory where you want to create the virtual environment, then run:

   ```
   virtualenv pytorch_env
   ```

3. To activate the environment, run:

   ```
   source pytorch_env/bin/activate
   ```

For Mac

1. If not already installed, install **`virtualenv`** with **`pip`**:

   ```
   pip install virtualenv
   ```

2. Navigate to the directory where you want to create the virtual environment, then run:

   ```
   virtualenv pytorch_env
   ```

3. To activate the environment, run:

   ```
   source pytorch_env/bin/activate
   ```

Once the environment is activated, the name of the environment will appear on the left side of the terminal prompt. This indicates that the environment is ready to use.

Installing PyTorch

With the virtual environment set up, you can now install PyTorch. PyTorch provides pre-built binaries that can be installed via **`pip`** or **`conda`**. In this book, we will use **`pip`**.

For the latest version of PyTorch, run the following command:

```
pip install torch torchvision torchaudio
```

If you need a specific version of PyTorch, for instance, version 2.0, use the `==` operator:

```
pip install torch==2.0 torchvision==0.11.1 torchaudio==0.10.1
```

CPU vs. GPU (CUDA) Installation:

If you have a compatible NVIDIA GPU and want to take advantage of CUDA for faster computation, you can install PyTorch with CUDA support. Here are examples for both CPU-only and GPU (CUDA) installations:

CPU-only Installation:

```
pip install torch torchvision torchaudio
```

CUDA (GPU) Installation (specify the CUDA version if necessary):

```
pip install torch torchvision torchaudio --index-url https://
download.pytorch.org/whl/cu118
```

It's important to note that installing specific versions of PyTorch might be necessary for compatibility reasons. For instance, if you're working with certain libraries or legacy code that doesn't support the latest PyTorch version.

Troubleshooting Tips

Ensure that your pip version is up-to-date. You can upgrade pip using `pip install --upgrade pip`.

1. If you're facing issues with the installation, try creating a new virtual environment and reinstalling PyTorch.
2. If **`pip install`** on a specific version throws any errors, you can try adding a force flag:

   ```
   pip install torch==1.8.0+cu111 -f https://download.pytorch.org/
   whl/torch_stable.html
   ```

Setting Up the Development Environment on Jupyter Notebook

Jupyter notebooks provide an interactive environment that's great for experimenting, documenting, and sharing your work. Here's how to set it up:

1. With your virtual environment activated, install Jupyter Notebook:

   ```
   pip install notebook
   ```
2. To start the Jupyter Notebook, run:

   ```
   jupyter notebook
   ```

3. This will start the Jupyter Notebook server and open your default web browser. You can create a new Python notebook by clicking the **New** button and selecting **Python 3** or the corresponding version.
4. You can ensure PyTorch has been installed correctly by importing it into a new cell:

```
import torch
print(torch.__version__)
```

You are now ready to start developing PyTorch using Jupyter Notebooks!

PyTorch 2.0 is compared to PyTorch 1.x as shown in the following table:

	PyTorch 1.x	PyTorch 2.0
Interface	Provides a clear and Pythonic interface, making it easier to build and debug models	Preserves the Pythonic interface while further enhancing usability and intuitiveness
Dynamic Computation Graph	Supports dynamic computation graphs, enabling users to change the network behavior on the fly	Continues to support dynamic computation graphs and introduces improved tools for better graph visualization and debugging
Deployment	Introduced TorchScript for model deployment in non-Python environments. TorchServe is released for model serving	Continues to support TorchScript and TorchServe. Provides better integration and support for ONNX and introduces more deployment options
Device-Agnostic Code	Offers device-agnostic code. The same code can be run on CPUs or GPUs	Preserves this feature and further optimizes the computation for different hardware, including improved support for accelerators
Distributed Training	Provides basic distributed training capabilities	Enhances distributed training with more robust and scalable solutions
Quantization and Pruning	Supports model quantization and pruning, which are essential for deploying models to edge devices	Offers improved support and additional techniques for model quantization, pruning, and optimization

Ecosystem	Has a growing ecosystem of tools and libraries (such as TorchVision, TorchText, and TorchAudio) developed by the community	The ecosystem grows even more with increased community contributions and improved interoperability with other libraries and tools
Performance	Shows good performance in both research and production settings	Offers performance improvements, faster training. and inference times due to under-the-hood optimizations

Table 1.1: *PyTorch 1.x vs PyTorch 2.0*

Dynamic Computation Graphs and the Define-by-Run Paradigm

In the world of deep learning, there are two main paradigms for defining computation graphs - static (define-and-run) and dynamic (define-by-run).

In a static graph (used by TensorFlow prior to version 2.0), the graph is defined and optimized before running the session. The same graph is then run repeatedly, allowing for certain performance optimizations, but at the cost of flexibility. Modifying the graph requires a complete rebuild, making debugging and dynamic modifications harder.

On the other hand, PyTorch uses the dynamic or define-by-run graph paradigm. Each forward pass defines a new computation graph. Nodes in the graph are Python objects and edges are tensors flowing between them. As operations are carried out, the graph is built on the fly. This provides an immense degree of flexibility, making PyTorch well-suited for models that need to have their architecture changed dynamically during execution, such as recurrent neural networks (RNNs) and models with loops or conditional statements.

```
# PyTorch dynamic graph example
import torch

x = torch.ones(2, 2, requires_grad=True)
print(x)  # tensor([[1., 1.], [1., 1.]], requires_grad=True)

y = x + 2
print(y)  # tensor([[3., 3.], [3., 3.]], grad_fn=<AddBackward0>)
```

In the preceding code, we first define a 2x2 tensor x. Then we perform an operation y = x + 2, building the computation graph dynamically.

The Autograd System

A critical component of PyTorch's dynamic computation graph system is its automatic differentiation engine, autograd. It is responsible for calculating the derivatives, that is, the gradients of tensors involved in the computation, facilitating backpropagation.

When you create a tensor with **requires_grad=True**, PyTorch starts to track all operations on it. After you compute the forward pass, you can **call .backward()** and have all the gradients computed automatically. These gradients are accumulated into the **.grad** attribute of the tensor.

```
# Compute forward pass
z = y * y * 3
out = z.mean()
print(z, out)  # tensor([[27., 27.], [27., 27.]], grad_fn=<MulBack-
ward0>) tensor(27., grad_fn=<MeanBackward0>)

# Compute backward pass
out.backward()
print(x.grad)  # tensor([[4.5000, 4.5000], [4.5000, 4.5000]])
```

In the preceding example, we define z and out as functions of y and compute the forward pass. We then call **out.backward()**, which triggers the computation of gradients, and print **x.grad** to see the gradients of x with respect to out.

Understanding autograd and the dynamic computation graph system is vital for effectively implementing and debugging your deep learning models with PyTorch. Their combination allows PyTorch to provide a flexible and intuitive interface for defining and training neural networks, while automatically taking care of the intricate details of derivatives and backpropagation. This makes it highly popular for complex computer vision tasks where flexibility and customizability of models are essential.

GPU Acceleration

Graphics Processing Units (GPUs) play an integral role in accelerating deep learning tasks. Unlike CPUs, GPUs are designed for high-throughput, parallel computation, making them excellent for tasks involving large-scale matrix operations, which are ubiquitous in deep learning.

PyTorch provides native support for GPU computation, leveraging the CUDA platform. Tensor computations can be seamlessly moved onto the GPU, significantly speeding up the execution. The following is an example of how to run PyTorch tensor operations on the GPU:

```
# Specify device to be used
device = torch.device('cuda' if torch.cuda.is_available() else 'cpu')
```

```
# Create a tensor and move it to GPU
x = torch.ones([3, 3], device=device)

# Perform operations on the GPU
y = x + 2
```

Here, we first create a **torch.device** that's set to '**cuda**' if CUDA is available, and '**cpu**' otherwise. We then create a tensor x on this device, and any operations involving x will also be carried out on this device.

Always remember to move both your model and your data to the GPU. PyTorch won't automatically move your data or model to the GPU. Forgetting to move your data or model to the GPU is a common mistake, and PyTorch will throw an error if you try to perform operations on objects that are on different devices.

```
# Moving model to GPU
model = model.to(device)

# Moving data to GPU
data, target = data.to(device), target.to(device)
```

Distributed Computing

As datasets and models grow in size, distributed computing has become a necessity in deep learning. Distributed computing allows you to parallelize computation across multiple GPUs on a single machine or across multiple machines each with multiple GPUs.

PyTorch provides several packages, such as **torch.nn.DataParallel** and **torch.nn.parallel.DistributedDataParallel**, to facilitate this distributed computing. The **torch.nn.parallel.DistributedDataParallel** is recommended as it provides greater flexibility and efficiency.

Here's a brief example of how to utilize **DistributedDataParallel**:

```
# Import the package
from torch.nn.parallel import DistributedDataParallel

# Assume your model is on the GPU and you are using two GPUs
model = model.to(device)
model = DistributedDataParallel(model, device_ids=[0, 1])

# Now any tensor you pass to model will be split on its first dimension
# and fed to separate GPUs and the outputs are then concatenated
output = model(data)
```

This splits the data across the first dimension (typically the batch size), feeding to separate GPUs. Each GPU computes its part and the outputs are then gathered and concatenated. Remember, the input data should be on the same device as the model.

In addition to these, PyTorch 2.0 has introduced many optimizations to its distributed computing capabilities, enabling even more efficient utilization of resources and improved performance. It includes better support for various backends, better handling of network communication, and advanced algorithms for gradient aggregation and model synchronization.

Being able to effectively use GPU acceleration and distributed computing can drastically speed up the training of your models and allow you to handle larger and more complex tasks, which is especially crucial in the field of computer vision where datasets and models can be quite substantial.

Remember, distributed computing not only helps in scaling the training process across multiple machines but also allows the utilization of mixed-precision training and optimized communication between processes to make the most of your hardware capabilities. This ensures that you can tackle large-scale computer vision tasks efficiently, making PyTorch an ideal choice for such tasks.

Introduction to TorchScript

TorchScript is a way to serialize your PyTorch models, allowing them to be run in a non-Python environment. This is especially important when it comes to deploying PyTorch models in production, where Python may not be available or desirable due to its performance characteristics.

TorchScript uses a static graph representation of a PyTorch model, which can be optimized for specific hardware. This static graph representation is also more amenable to deployment in low-latency, high-throughput production settings as it can be directly loaded into the PyTorch C++ API.

TorchScript provides a seamless transition from eager mode to graph mode via a process known as **tracing** or **scripting**.

Tracing

Tracing allows you to take an existing module and record all the tensor computations it performs during the forward pass into a **`torch.jit.ScriptModule`**.

Here's an example:

```
import torch
import torchvision.models as models

# An instance of your model.
model = models.resnet50()
```

```
# An example input you would normally provide to your model's forward()
method.
example = torch.rand(1, 3, 224, 224)

# Use torch.jit.trace to generate a torch.jit.ScriptModule via tracing.
traced_script_module = torch.jit.trace(model, example)
```

In this example, we first create a ResNet model. Then, we generate an example input tensor, and pass both the model and the example input to **`torch.jit.trace`**, which records the computations performed by the model when run on the example input and returns a ScriptModule that you can save and load in Python or C++.

While tracing is great for straightforward modules that don't involve control flow (like conditionals and loops), it can struggle with modules where the flow of execution depends on the values in tensors. This is because it only captures the operations performed during the single execution used for tracing, not the control flow itself.

Scripting

Scripting, on the other hand, captures the control flow in your model by directly analyzing the Python code of your model. It does this via a decorator, **`@torch.jit.script`**.

Here's an example of how you might script a module:

```
import torch
class MyModule(torch.nn.Module):
    def __init__(self, N, M):
        super(MyModule, self).__init__()
        self.weight = torch.nn.Parameter(torch.rand(N, M))

    def forward(self, input):
        if input.sum() > 0:
            output = self.weight.mv(input)
        else:
            output = self.weight + input
        return output

my_module = MyModule(10,20)
sm = torch.jit.script(my_module)
```

In this example, we define a simple module that uses control flow in its forward method. We then create an instance of this module and pass it to **`torch.jit.script`** to generate a ScriptModule. This module will behave exactly like the eager mode version but also has its Python code serialized in TorchScript format.

In conclusion, TorchScript gives you the power to optimize your models, leverage the PyTorch C++ runtime environment for deployment, and serialize your models for use in different platforms (for example, serving via a Python server, deploying on mobile devices, and so on.). It's an essential tool for any practitioner who wishes to take their PyTorch models beyond the research environment, especially in the field of computer vision, where models are typically complex and computational resources are at a premium.

Conclusion

In this chapter, we have walked through the journey of PyTorch's creation and evolution. We saw how it rapidly rose in popularity due to its developer-friendly approach, flexibility, and strong support for GPU acceleration and distributed computing. We discussed its inherent Python-first philosophy, which ensures that the library integrates smoothly into the Python ecosystem, making it an excellent tool for both research and development.

We then explored the key improvements brought in by PyTorch 2.0, highlighting its robust capabilities in GPU acceleration and distributed computing. We saw how PyTorch facilitates the seamless migration of tensor computations to the GPU, thereby drastically speeding up the training process. Furthermore, we learned how PyTorch supports distributed computing, enabling us to handle large-scale deep-learning tasks effectively.

The chapter also introduced us to the concept of dynamic computation graphs (DCGs), which, by following a define-by-run paradigm, provide PyTorch with a competitive edge, especially when it comes to debugging and prototyping. The AutoGrad system's simplicity and efficiency in calculating derivatives automatically is another significant advantage of PyTorch that we looked into.

Lastly, we delved into TorchScript, a tool that enables PyTorch models to transition from research to production seamlessly. We discovered that it allows for the serialization of models in a form that can be run and optimized in non-Python environments, demonstrating its importance in deploying models at scale in production settings.

All these factors combined make PyTorch an ideal choice for tackling complex tasks in computer vision, driving us towards its use throughout this book.

As we move on to the next chapter titled *PyTorch Basics*, we will start building upon the foundation laid in this chapter. We will dive deeper into the fundamental building blocks of PyTorch - tensors and explore how they are used in various operations and computational graphs. This will provide us with the necessary tools to start creating and manipulating models in PyTorch, propelling us further into our journey of mastering computer vision with PyTorch 2.0.

CHAPTER 2
PyTorch Basics

Introduction

In the realm of machine learning and deep learning, PyTorch stands tall and is revered for its flexibility and capabilities to architect and train intricate neural network architectures. Whether it's a budding AI enthusiast or an established research scientist, many have come across this name, but not everyone delves deep enough to understand the pillars upon which this powerful framework stands. At the heart of Pytorch's prowess lies a seemingly simple yet profoundly powerful concept: tensors.

Structure

In this chapter, we will cover the following topics:

- Introduction to Tensors
- Tensor Operations in PyTorch
- Understanding Computational Graphs in PyTorch
- Automatic Differentiation in PyTorch: The Power of Autograd
- Conclusion

Understanding the Essence of Tensors

In the broadest sense, a tensor is a generalization of scalars, vectors, and matrices. It's a multi-dimensional container that can store data with varying dimensions. Imagine a scalar, a mere number; it's dimensionless–a point. Extend that into a line, and you have a vector–a 1-dimensional sequence of numbers. Push it into a plane, and you have a matrix–a 2-dimensional grid of numbers. Now, imagine stretching this structure into the third, fourth, or even the nth dimension; you are envisioning tensors.

```
# A scalar (0D tensor)
scalar = torch.tensor(5)

# A vector (1D tensor)
vector = torch.tensor([1, 2, 3, 4])
```

```
# A matrix (2D tensor)
matrix = torch.tensor([[1, 2], [3, 4], [5, 6]])
```

For those acquainted with Python, one can think of tensors as somewhat analogous to NumPy arrays. Yet, tensors boast features far beyond array-like data structures in Python. Their seamless adaptability to GPU acceleration is one such superpower, ensuring that data-intensive operations, particularly common in deep learning, aren't bottlenecked by the CPU's computational limits. We will look into tensors in detail in the following sections.

The Imperative Nature of PyTorch

But why does PyTorch place such emphasis on tensors? The answer lies in the very design philosophy of PyTorch. The framework operates in an imperative or define-by-run mode, which means the computations are executed immediately. There is no symbolic graph waiting in the wings; the graph is constructed dynamically, as operations are defined. This approach is in stark contrast to the define-and-run paradigm, where one first defines a computation graph, and then the data is run through it.

Imagine you're following a cooking recipe. There are two ways you can approach it:

- Read the entire recipe first (from ingredients to the final step), prep everything, lay out your tools and ingredients, and then start cooking. This is like the **define-and-run** approach: you're defining everything you need first and then executing.
- Read a step, do the step. Read the next step, do the next step, and so on. You're learning and adjusting as you go along, perhaps even tweaking the recipe based on the ingredients you have at hand. This is like PyTorch's **define-by-run** approach: everything is dynamic and on-the-fly.

PyTorch follows the second method. When it processes data (like our cooking ingredients), it doesn't wait for the entire computational blueprint (our recipe) to be defined upfront. Instead, as soon as you define a computation, it runs it. This makes PyTorch very flexible and adaptable, like a chef who adjusts based on the ingredients in the pantry.

In simpler terms, with some other frameworks, you might first tell the computer as follows: First, I'll do A, then B, then C, and only after you've laid out the entire plan will you start feeding in your data. But with PyTorch, you can tell the computer to do A, and it will do A right away. Then you ask it to do B", and it promptly does B. It's like a conversation with immediate responses.

This dynamic nature is like building with Lego blocks. You can stack a block, decide if it looks good, maybe remove it, or add another type; all without having to plan the entire structure beforehand.

Consider a navigation system. The define-and-run method is like deciding on the entire route before starting your car. You can't change the route once you start driving. On the other hand, PyTorch's method is like a GPS that recalculates the route as you drive, based on real-time traffic data. You can take a different turn, and the system will adapt instantly.

Such flexibility demands a robust, flexible, and efficient container to hold and manage data—enter tensors.

A Foundation for Complex Architectures

To the students just beginning their journey into machine learning, the concept of tensors might feel a bit abstract. Why bother with multi-dimensional entities when the world around us feels so three-dimensional? The reason lies in data representation. As we move deeper into computer vision, a primary focus of this book, we'll encounter data that isn't always conveniently two or three-dimensional. Images, for example, in deep learning models, are often treated as 4D tensors—batch size, channels, height, and width. When delving into video processing, even higher dimensions become relevant.

Moreover, as professionals and AI enthusiasts seek to craft more sophisticated models, the ability to perform mathematical operations on these tensors becomes invaluable. The addition, multiplication, or transformation of these tensors leads to the formulation of neural network architectures, gradient computations, and ultimately, model training and prediction.

```
# A simple tensor operation: Element-wise addition
tensor_a = torch.tensor([1, 2, 3])
tensor_b = torch.tensor([4, 5, 6])
result = tensor_a + tensor_b
print(result)  # Outputs: tensor([5, 7, 9])
```

A Prelude to Deep Exploration

Grasping the nature and utility of tensors is akin to understanding the very DNA of PyTorch. They represent the framework's ability to juggle and process vast amounts of data, enabling the design, training, and deployment of machine-learning models that can comprehend and generate human-like content, recognize intricate patterns, and make intelligent predictions.

As we transition through this chapter, we'll dissect tensors further, understanding their properties, operations, and their relationship with computational graphs—a pivotal concept in understanding how PyTorch automates the gradient calculations fundamental to training neural networks.

For now, let's embark on this journey with a keen sense of curiosity, knowing that every step taken in understanding these foundational concepts solidifies our path forward into the fascinating realm of computer vision with PyTorch 2.0.

Introduction to Tensors

Tensors are fundamental to understanding and working with PyTorch. Let's unpack what they are, piece by piece, by visualizing them in terms of their dimensionality and drawing parallels with structures you might already be familiar with.

Zero-dimensional Tensor: Scalar

A scalar is the simplest form of a tensor, holding just a single number. It has zero dimensions.

```
# PyTorch
import torch
scalar = torch.tensor(7)
print(f"Scalar tensor: {scalar}, Dimension: {scalar.dim()}")
```

Think of a scalar like an individual box that can hold only one item. It's like when you have a single apple, and you label it with its weight. That weight value, just one number, is the scalar.

Scalars in mathematics and physics represent quantities that have magnitude but no direction. In PyTorch, they are akin to Python's basic data types like int or float but wrapped within a tensor's structure.

One-dimensional Tensor: Vector

A vector is a single line of values, akin to a list in Python.

```
# PyTorch
vector = torch.tensor([1, 2, 3, 4])
print(f"Vector tensor: {vector}, Dimension: {vector.dim()}")
```

Visualize a vector as a row of boxes, each holding a value. Like a line of ducklings, where each duckling has a specific color, and their sequence forms a pattern.

In linear algebra, vectors are fundamental building blocks, often used to represent points in space or any ordered collection of data.

Two-dimensional Tensor: Matrix

A matrix has rows and columns, a grid where each cell can contain a value.

```
# PyTorch
matrix = torch.tensor([[1, 2], [3, 4], [5, 6]])
print(f"Matrix tensor: {matrix}, Dimension: {matrix.dim()}")
```

If a vector is a single line of boxes, a matrix is like stacking multiple rows of these boxes on top of each other. Imagine a checkers board: It's a grid where each square can hold a checker piece.

Matrices are pivotal in various mathematical computations. They can represent linear transformations, systems of equations, and much more.

N-dimensional Tensor: Higher-dimensional Entities

As you keep adding dimensions, you get higher-order tensors.

```
# PyTorch
tensor_3d = torch.tensor([[[1, 2], [3, 4]], [[5, 6], [7, 8]]])
print(f"3D tensor: {tensor_3d}, Dimension: {tensor_3d.dim()}")
```

Imagine you have multiple checker boards. Stack them to form a cube. Now, each square in this cube is a cell in a 3D tensor. As you stack more and more boards, you're moving into higher dimensions.

Higher-dimensional tensors are crucial for various applications in deep learning. For instance, image data is often represented as a 3D tensor, with dimensions corresponding to the height, width, and color channels of the image.

Superpower of PyTorch Tensors Over NumPy Arrays

PyTorch tensors share many operations and features with NumPy arrays. However, PyTorch tensors have an ace up their sleeve; they can be offloaded to GPUs for faster computation, which is essential for the large-scale calculations typical in deep learning. This seamless GPU integration is what gives PyTorch tensors their superpower.

```
# Moving a tensor to GPU (if available)
if torch.cuda.is_available():
    tensor_on_gpu = tensor_3d.cuda()
    print("Tensor moved to GPU:", tensor_on_gpu.device)
else:
    print("GPU not available.")
```

Think of GPUs as super-fast calculators. When you have tons of math to do, like when training large neural networks, you may want to use these super calculators. PyTorch allows you to do this with ease!

The ability to offload computations to GPU not only speeds up the forward and backward passes but also the optimization steps, making training deep and complex models feasible in a realistic timeframe.

At first glance, tensors might seem remarkably similar to Numpy arrays. They both handle numerical data in a matrix form and support a wide range of mathematical operations. However, there are some key differences:

- **GPU Support**: Tensors can be effortlessly moved to GPU (Graphics Processing Units) for faster computations, which is essential for handling the extensive computations in deep learning. Numpy arrays, on the other hand, are confined to the CPU.
- **Automatic Differentiation**: Tensors, when combined with PyTorch's autograd system, can automatically compute the gradients or derivatives of functions. This feature is paramount for neural network training using gradient-based optimization algorithms.
- **Dynamic vs. Static Computation Graph**: As discussed, PyTorch has a dynamic computation graph. This allows for more flexibility during model building. In contrast, when using Numpy with certain other frameworks, the computation graph is typically static.

```
# Numpy array
import numpy as np
numpy_array = np.array([1, 2, 3])

# PyTorch tensor
import torch
pytorch_tensor = torch.tensor([1, 2, 3])
```

Tensor Operations in PyTorch

Tensors, the heart of PyTorch, are not just static containers. They're alive, malleable, and offer a plethora of operations that bring the world of deep learning to life. By understanding how to manipulate and compute using tensors, we gain the power to construct complex neural architectures and algorithms. Let's delve into the most common operations and their significance.

Summary of the operations for quick reference:

Operation	Function	Example Code	Output
Addition	Element-wise addition of two tensors	`torch.add(a, b)`	`tensor([5, 7, 9])`
Subtraction	Element-wise subtraction of one tensor from another	`torch.sub(a, b)`	`tensor([-3, -3, -3])`

Multiplication	Element-wise multiplication (not matrix multiplication)	`torch.mul(a, b)`	`tensor([4, 10, 18])`
Division	Element-wise division	torch.div(b, a)	tensor([4., 2.5, 2.])
Matrix Multiply	Matrix multiplication, producing the dot product of two matrices	torch.matmul(A, B)	tensor([[4, 6], [10, 12]])
Transpose	Flips a matrix over its diagonal	`torch.t(matrix)`	`tensor([[1, 4], [2, 5], [3, 6]])`
View	Reshapes tensor without copying data (memory-efficient)	`tensor.view(2, 3)`	`tensor([[1, 2, 3], [4, 5, 6]])`
Reshape	Reshapes tensor; may create a copy if needed	`tensor.reshape(2, 3)`	`tensor([[1, 2, 3], [4, 5, 6]])`
Squeeze	Removes dimensions of size 1	`tensor.squeeze()`	`tensor([1, 2, 3])`
Unsqueeze	Adds a dimension of size 1 at a specified position	`tensor.unsqueeze(dim=0)`	`tensor([[[1, 2, 3]]])`

Broadcasting in PyTorch

Broadcasting allows PyTorch to perform operations on tensors of different shapes, making tensor manipulation more flexible. Rather than requiring identical dimensions, PyTorch uses broadcasting rules to "stretch" smaller dimensions to match larger ones, so that operations like addition, multiplication, or division can be executed.

Broadcasting Rules:

1. **Align dimensions from the right:** PyTorch compares each tensor's dimensions starting from the rightmost side.
2. **Match or Stretch:** For each dimension, two sizes are compatible if:
   a. They are equal, or
   b. One of them is one (the smaller tensor will be "stretched" to match the larger one).

Examples:

1. **Compatible Shapes:**

```
a = torch.tensor([1, 2, 3])          # Shape: (3,)
b = torch.tensor([[1], [2], [3]]) # Shape: (3, 1)
result = a + b                        # Result shape: (3, 3)
```

2. **Non-Compatible Shapes:** If two tensors have different shapes without any dimension of size 1 to stretch, PyTorch will raise an error. For instance, (3, 2) and (3, 3) cannot be broadcast together.

Broadcasting simplifies arithmetic operations across tensors, especially in deep learning, where aligning inputs and outputs across layers is essential. Understanding these rules will make tensor operations smoother and help avoid shape mismatch errors.

Arithmetic Operations

These are foundational mathematical operations that you can perform element-wise on tensors.

Addition

PyTorch supports the addition of two tensors of the same shape.

```
# PyTorch
a = torch.tensor([1, 2, 3])
b = torch.tensor([4, 5, 6])
result = torch.add(a, b)
print(result)  # Outputs: tensor([5, 7, 9])
```

Subtraction

Similar to addition, subtraction is performed element-wise.

```
# PyTorch
a = torch.tensor([1, 2, 3])
b = torch.tensor([4, 5, 6])
result = torch.sub(a, b)
print(result)  # Outputs: tensor([-3, -3, -3])
```

Multiplication

Element-wise multiplication, not matrix multiplication.

```
# PyTorch
a = torch.tensor([1, 2, 3])
```

```
b = torch.tensor([4, 5, 6])
result = torch.mul(a, b)
print(result)  # Outputs: tensor([ 4, 10, 18])
```

Division

Again, this is element-wise division.

```
# PyTorch
a = torch.tensor([1, 2, 3])
b = torch.tensor([4, 5, 6])
result = torch.div(b, a)
print(result)  # Outputs: tensor([4., 2.5, 2.])
```

Think of arithmetic operations as basic calculations you'd perform with a calculator. Each tensor element is paired with its counterpart in the other tensor, and the desired operation (add, subtract, and so on) is executed.

These operations, when paired with broadcasting capabilities, allow for powerful and flexible transformations on tensor data, which is essential for feature engineering and normalization.

Matrix Operations

Tensors, especially 2D ones (matrices), support advanced linear algebra operations fundamental to neural networks.

Matrix Multiplication

Given two matrices, A and B, this operation gives a matrix C where C[i][j] is the dot product of A[i] and B[:,j].

```
# PyTorch
A = torch.tensor([[1, 2], [3, 4]])
B = torch.tensor([[2, 0], [1, 3]])
result = torch.matmul(A, B)
print(result)  # Outputs: tensor([[ 4,  6], [10, 12]])
```

Transpose

Flips a matrix over its diagonal.

```
# PyTorch
matrix = torch.tensor([[1, 2, 3], [4, 5, 6]])
transposed = torch.t(matrix)
print(transposed)  # Outputs: tensor([[1, 4], [2, 5], [3, 6]])
```

Matrix operations can be visualized as transforming a grid of numbers. The transpose, for example, can be imagined as flipping a book's page along its center binding.

Matrix operations are at the core of linear transformations in neural networks. Operations like matrix multiplication become increasingly important in layers like fully connected or dense layers in neural nets.

Reshaping Operations

One of PyTorch's strengths is the flexibility in manipulating tensor shapes, crucial for neural network layers that expect inputs of specific dimensions.

View and Reshape

Both **`view`** and **`reshape`** methods allow you to change the shape of a tensor without altering its data. However, there is a subtle difference between them in terms of memory usage:

`view`: This method returns a reshaped tensor that shares the same memory as the original tensor, which makes it more memory-efficient. It requires the tensor to be contiguous in memory, meaning the elements are stored in an unbroken sequence. If the tensor isn't contiguous, you may need to call **`.contiguous()`** before using **`view`**.

`reshape`: This method can return either a `view` or a copy of the original tensor. If possible, it will return a `view` for efficiency. However, if a contiguous view is not possible, `reshape` will create a copy to achieve the desired shape.

```
import torch

# Original tensor
tensor = torch.tensor([1, 2, 3, 4, 5, 6])

# Using view
reshaped_view = tensor.view(2, 3)
print(reshaped_view)  # Outputs: tensor([[1, 2, 3], [4, 5, 6]])

# Using reshape
reshaped_reshape = tensor.reshape(2, 3)
print(reshaped_reshape)  # Outputs: tensor([[1, 2, 3], [4, 5, 6]])
```

In most cases, both methods will give the same result, but understanding their differences can help you optimize memory usage in your projects.

Squeeze and Unsqueeze

Squeeze removes dimensions with size 1, while unsqueeze adds a dimension.

```
# PyTorch
tensor = torch.tensor([[[1, 2, 3]]])
squeezed = tensor.squeeze()
print(squeezed.dim())  # Outputs: 1
```

Reshaping means rearranging blocks. You have a fixed number of blocks that can be arranged in different patterns like a single line, a square, or even a cube.

Tensor reshaping is vital when designing neural architectures, especially when transitioning between different layer types. Operations like view and reshape are indispensable for flattening operations before fully connected layers or when preparing data for convolutional layers.

Operations on tensors serve as the toolkit for building, training, and manipulating neural networks in PyTorch. A good grasp of these basics ensures that as we delve deeper into more complex architectures and algorithms, we're not held back by the foundational mechanics. The journey into deep learning is, in many ways, a dance of tensors, and knowing the steps by heart empowers the choreography.

Understanding Computational Graphs in PyTorch

At the heart of deep learning frameworks lies the concept of a computational graph, a directed graph where nodes correspond to operations or variables. Computational graphs enable efficient computation of gradients, making them indispensable for training neural networks. In PyTorch, these graphs aren't just static structures but are dynamic, evolving entities built on-the-fly. Let's delve deeper to unravel the mysteries of these graphs.

Computational Graph

A computational graph is a visual representation of mathematical operations laid out in a sequence. Each node in this graph represents an operation, and the edges stand for tensors that flow between them. Think of this as a step-by-step guide, showing how data transforms and moves through your defined operations.

Real-world analogy: Imagine baking a cake. You follow a recipe that dictates the sequence in which ingredients are mixed. The recipe can be thought of as a computational graph, where each step (or node) is an action, for example, "mix" or "bake," and the ingredients (or edges) flow through these steps.

The Dynamic Nature of PyTorch's Graphs

PyTorch stands out because of its define-by-run philosophy. In traditional "define-

and-run" frameworks, you first set the entire computation (define the full recipe) and then pass the data (ingredients). However, in define-by-run frameworks like PyTorch, you can change the computation on-the-go based on the input data, resulting in a dynamic computational graph.

```
# PyTorch
import torch

a = torch.tensor(2.0, requires_grad=True)
b = torch.tensor(3.0, requires_grad=True)
c = a + b
c.backward() # Gradients are computed here
print(a.grad) # Outputs: 1.0 (because dc/da = 1)
```

In the preceding code, as soon as the addition operation is performed, a computational graph is constructed, linking tensors a and b to their resultant tensor c.

Nodes and Edges in Computational Graphs

Nodes: These usually represent operations. Simple operations such as addition or multiplication, or complex ones such as convolution or batch normalization, all find representation as nodes.

Edges: Tensors flow through these edges. When an operation is performed on two tensors, the resulting tensor carries forward information from its ancestors.

```
# PyTorch
import torch
x = torch.tensor(2.0, requires_grad=True)
y = x  2
z = y * 3
```

Visualizing the preceding operations:

```
# PyTorch
x --> [**2] --> y --> [*3] --> z
```

In this graph, [**2]and [*3] are nodes, and x,y, and z are values flowing through the edges.

Autograd and Backpropagation

The true magic of computational graphs in PyTorch is the autograd system. Autograd automatically calculates the gradients or derivatives of each operation, enabling the backpropagation algorithm, which is vital for training neural networks.

When you call `.backward()` on a tensor, PyTorch traverses the computational graph from that tensor all the way back to tensors that have `requires_grad=True`, computing gradients along the way.

```
# PyTorch
z.backward()
print(x.grad) # Outputs: 12.0 (because dz/dx = 2*x*3 for x=2)
```

Real-world analogy: Consider the process of assembling a toy from a manual. If a part doesn't fit or you made an error, you would trace back your steps (backpropagate) to understand where you went wrong and rectify it. The computational graph helps in retracing these steps.

Benefits of Dynamic Graphs

- **Flexibility**: Since the graph is built on-the-fly, PyTorch offers flexibility to change the model architecture dynamically. This is especially useful for models with varying architectures like recursive neural networks or for conditions where decisions depend on data.
- **Debugging**: Debugging becomes intuitive. As operations are executed immediately, errors in your architecture or operations can be caught on-the-go, making PyTorch more Pythonic and interactive.

Memory Implications

While dynamic computational graphs provide flexibility, they are rebuilt from scratch after every `.backward()` call. It means the graph's history is discarded after use, saving memory but requiring the graph to be rebuilt for every forward pass.

Detaching from the Graph

Sometimes, you might want to perform operations on tensors without having them tracked by the computational graph. The `detach()` method comes to the rescue. It creates a tensor that shares the same data but doesn't require gradient computation.

```
# PyTorch
detached_y = y.detach()
w = detached_y * 3 # w won't be part of the computation graph.
```

Understanding computational graphs is akin to grasping the pulse of deep learning frameworks. In PyTorch, this understanding is further elevated by the dynamic nature of these graphs, promoting intuitive and flexible model building. As we proceed deeper into the world of neural networks, this foundational knowledge ensures that we are well-equipped to harness the full power and flexibility of PyTorch.

Automatic Differentiation in PyTorch: The Power of Autograd

In the realm of deep learning, understanding how a model updates and tweaks itself is essential. At its core, this self-adjustment boils down to derivatives or gradients. PyTorch's autograd system takes away the tediousness of manual gradient computations, enabling the magic of learning. Let's unpack this system and recognize its importance.

The Essence of Autograd

Autograd stands for automatic differentiation. At a high level, it's a system to compute the derivatives of tensors with respect to some functions. In the world of deep learning, these derivatives or gradients signify how much a change in the model's parameters will affect the model's output. Hence, by understanding these gradients, models can iteratively reduce their errors.

Real-world analogy: Consider driving a car on hilly terrain. You'd need to adjust your speed based on the incline of the road. Imagine if your car could automatically adjust its speed, recognizing steeper areas, much like cruise control. Autograd does a similar job but for neural networks, tweaking parameters according to the "steepness" of the gradient.

Tracking Operations with `requires_grad`

When a tensor's **`.requires_grad`** attribute is set to True, PyTorch will begin to track every operation involving that tensor. This tracking forms the basis for gradient computation later.

```
# Create a tensor and enable tracking
x = torch.tensor([2.0, 3.0], requires_grad=True)
print(x.requires_grad)  # Outputs: True
```

The Computation Graph and `.backward()`

Each operation on tensors creates a new node in the computational graph. When you call the **`.backward()`** method on a tensor, it computes the gradient of that tensor with respect to every tensor in the graph that has **`requires_grad=True`**.

Here's a simple example:

```
# Compute Gradient
x = torch.tensor([2.0, 3.0], requires_grad=True)
y = x * 2
z = y.mean()
z.backward()  # Compute gradients
print(x.grad) # Outputs: tensor([2., 2.])
```

Accumulating Gradients

Subsequent backward operations will accumulate gradients in the **`.grad`** attribute, rather than overwriting them. This accumulation is crucial for certain types of models and operations.

```
# Accumulating Gradients
y = x * 2
y.backward(torch.tensor([1.0, 1.0]))  # Using a vector for gradient
scaling
print(x.grad)  # Outputs: tensor([2., 2.])

# Doing another operation
y = x * 3
y.backward(torch.tensor([1.0, 1.0]))
print(x.grad)  # Outputs: tensor([5., 5.]) because gradients accumulate
```

Non-Scalar Backward Operations

The **.backward()** operation expects a scalar, that is, a tensor with a single value. If it's not a scalar, you need to specify the `**gradient**` argument, which is a tensor of the same shape, typically representing the gradient of a scalar function with respect to the non-scalar tensor.

```
# Non-Scalar Backward Operations
y = x * 2
# This would raise an error since y is not a scalar:
# y.backward()
# Instead, use:
y.backward(torch.tensor([1.0, 1.0]))
```

Disabling Gradient Tracking

There are scenarios where gradient tracking might be unnecessary, such as during model evaluation. You can locally disable it using **torch.no_grad()**:

```
# Disable Gradient Tracking
with torch.no_grad():
    y = x * 2
    print(y.requires_grad)  # Outputs: False
```

Gradients and Memory

Gradients consume memory. Once they've been used (for example, in an optimization step), it's often a good practice to zero them out to prevent accumulation.

```
# Gradient & Memory
optimizer.zero_grad()  # For models, where optimizer is a defined
optimizer instance
x.grad.zero_()  # For individual tensors
```

Detaching Tensors

In situations where you wish to prevent certain parts of your computation from being tracked, you can use the **.detach()** method.

```
# Detach
y = x.detach()
print(y.requires_grad)  # Outputs: False
```

Autograd is the linchpin of PyTorch's flexibility and ease of use. While the concept of automatic differentiation may seem daunting at first, PyTorch's approach simplifies the process, allowing developers to focus on model design and implementation rather than the intricacies of gradient computation. As you venture deeper into neural networks, always remember that behind every learning process, there's the silent, efficient work of autograd ensuring your model improves with each iteration.

Examples of Basic PyTorch Operations

Diving deeper into PyTorch invariably means working intimately with tensors. These multi-dimensional arrays lie at the heart of the framework and mastering the basic operations on them is crucial. Let's walk through some foundational tensor operations, ensuring you have a toolkit ready to take on more complex deep learning challenges.

Creating Tensors

There are many ways in Python with which we can create tensors.

From Lists:

PyTorch makes it simple to create tensors from Python lists.

```
# Tensor from list
import torch

tensor_from_list = torch.tensor([1, 2, 3, 4])
print(tensor_from_list)
```

From Numpy Arrays:

For those familiar with NumPy, transitioning tensors is a breeze.

```
# Tensor from Numpy array
import numpy as np
import torch

numpy_array = np.array([5, 6, 7, 8])
```

```
tensor_from_np = torch.from_numpy(numpy_array)
print(tensor_from_np)
```

With Specific Data Types:

Sometimes, specifying the data type is necessary.

```
# Tensor with specific data types
import torch

tensor_float = torch.tensor([1, 2, 3, 4], dtype=torch.float32)
print(tensor_float)
```

Zeros, Ones, and Ranges

Often, initializing tensors with specific shapes and values can be handy.

```
# Tensor with specific data types
import torch

tensor_zeros = torch.zeros(3, 3)
tensor_ones = torch.ones(3, 3)
tensor_range = torch.arange(0, 10, 2)
print(tensor_zeros, tensor_ones, tensor_range)
```

Tensor Operations

Tensors give us a wide range of simple and complex operations which can be performed on them.

Arithmetic Operations

Basic mathematical operations are intuitive and straightforward.

```
# Arithmetic operations
import torch


x = torch.tensor([1, 2, 3, 4])
y = torch.tensor([5, 6, 7, 8])

sum_tensors = x + y
product_tensors = x * y
print(sum_tensors, product_tensors)
```

Matrix Operations

Dives into linear algebra operations.

```
# Matrix operations
import torch

x = torch.tensor([[1, 2], [3, 4]])
y = torch.tensor([[5, 6], [7, 8]])

matmul_result = torch.matmul(x, y)
print(matmul_result)
```

Reshaping Tensors

The tensors can be manipulated in several ways to change/reshape them.

View and Reshape

Both methods allow you to change the shape of a tensor.

```
# Reshape tensors
import torch

x = torch.arange(10)
reshaped_tensor = x.view(2, 5)
print(reshaped_tensor)

reshaped_tensor_alt = x.reshape(5, 2)
print(reshaped_tensor_alt)
```

Squeeze and Unsqueeze

Manipulates the dimensions of tensors.

```
# Squeeze & Unsqueeze tensors
import torch

tensor = torch.tensor([[1, 2, 3]])
squeezed_tensor = tensor.squeeze()
print(squeezed_tensor.shape)

unsqueeze_tensor = squeezed_tensor.unsqueeze(dim=0)
print(unsqueeze_tensor.shape)
```

Using CUDA (if available)

PyTorch seamlessly integrates with CUDA for GPU acceleration.

```
# Use CUDA
import torch
```

```
device = torch.device("cuda" if torch.cuda.is_available() else "cpu")
x = x.to(device)
print(x.device)
```

Indexing, Slicing, and Concatenating

Similar to Python lists or Numpy arrays, we can index, slice, and concatenate tensors

Tensor Indexing

Accesses specific elements in a tensor.

```
# Indexing
import torch

x = torch.tensor([0, 1, 2, 3, 4])
print(x[2])
```

Slicing Tensors

Extracts specific parts of a tensor.

```
# Slicing
import torch

print(x[1:4])
```

Concatenating Tensors

Combines tensors along a given dimension.

```
# Concatenating
import torch

y = torch.tensor([5, 6, 7, 8, 9])
concatenated = torch.cat((x, y))
print(concatenated)
```

Cloning Tensors

Ensures that the original isn't altered when you want to duplicate a tensor.

```
# Cloning
import torch

y = x.clone()
y[0] = 100
print(x, y)
```

While PyTorch boasts a myriad of advanced features tailored for deep learning, mastering the basics is equally important. These foundational operations act as stepping stones, propelling you toward more intricate neural network architectures and applications. As you delve deeper, you'll realize that having a strong grasp on these operations is invaluable, offering flexibility, ease, and efficiency.

Conclusion

As we close this chapter on the fundamentals of PyTorch, it's clear how tensors and their associated operations form the building blocks of this powerful deep-learning framework. From the intricacies of computational graphs to the magic of automatic differentiation, we've unraveled the core aspects that make PyTorch both a versatile and intuitive tool for researchers and developers alike. With a solid understanding of these basics, you are better equipped to harness the full capabilities of PyTorch in more advanced applications and neural network architectures.

PyTorch has seen its share of evolutions, improvements, and refinements with the latest being its transition from PyTorch 1.x to PyTorch 2.x. As we venture into the next chapter, we will delve deep into what this transition means for users, both old and new. Whether you're a seasoned PyTorch developer looking to update your knowledge or a newcomer eager to start, the next chapter promises insights, tips, and practical guidance on making the shift seamlessly.

We will demystify the changes, enhancements, and innovations brought by PyTorch 2.0, ensuring you're poised to take advantage of all it has to offer.

CHAPTER 3
Transitioning from PyTorch 1.x to PyTorch 2.0

Introduction

Both the deep learning field and the libraries and tools that support it are constantly changing. The leading library in the field of deep learning, PyTorch, is no different. PyTorch 2.0 has brought with it several new features, improvements, and adjustments aimed at enhancing performance, usability, and efficiency. Though advantageous, these modifications nevertheless necessitate a transition and adaptation period, particularly for individuals accustomed to PyTorch 1.x.

We will walk you through the complex process of migrating from PyTorch 1.x to PyTorch 2.0 in this chapter. Making this switch is essential to taking advantage of the most recent developments and breakthroughs that PyTorch 2.0 offers. To guarantee a seamless transition, we'll analyze the main distinctions between the two versions, offer a thorough upgrade path, and go into compatibility problems and their fixes. In addition, we will look at actual code migration cases and discuss typical problems encountered in this upgrade.

The purpose of this chapter is to equip you with the knowledge and tools necessary to seamlessly migrate from PyTorch 1.x to PyTorch 2.0, while ensuring that you can continue to harness the full potential of PyTorch in your computer vision projects and beyond. So, without further ado, let's embark on this journey of transition and explore the new horizon that PyTorch 2.0 brings forth.

Structure

In this chapter, the following topics will be covered:

- Performance Enhancements in PyTorch 2.0
- Guide to Upgrading from PyTorch 1.x to 2.0
- Common Compatibility Issues and Solutions
- Code Migration - Updating a Simple Model from PyTorch 1.x to 2.0
- Code Migration - Utilizing torch.compile for better performance
- Code Migration - Updating a Classification Model from PyTorch 1.x to 2.0
- Code Migration - Updating a Segmentation Model from PyTorch 1.x to 2.0

Performance Enhancements in PyTorch 2.0

In the realm of deep learning, the speed at which models train and infer is paramount. PyTorch 2.0 brings about notable performance enhancements over its predecessor, PyTorch 1.x, to ensure faster model training and inference. This section elucidates the key performance improvements and explains how they can be leveraged to accelerate your machine-learning projects.

Introduction to Performance Improvements

PyTorch 2.0 is engineered to push the performance boundaries further. One of the hallmark features contributing to this performance boost is the introduction of `**torch.compile**`. This new feature enables the compilation of models, thereby significantly accelerating their training and inference times. The `**torch.compile**` feature is particularly a game-changer as it moves parts of PyTorch from C++ back into Python, marking a substantial new direction for PyTorch.

```
# Example Code for torch.compile
import torch

class SimpleModel(torch.nn.Module):
    def forward(self, x):
        return x + x

model = SimpleModel()
compiled_model = torch.compile(model)
```

Underpinning Technologies of torch.compile

The prowess of **`torch.compile`** emanates from four groundbreaking technologies: TorchDynamo, AOTAutograd, PrimTorch, and TorchInductor. These technologies capture PyTorch programs, generate ahead-of-time backward traces, canonicalize PyTorch operators, and generate fast code for multiple accelerators and backends, respectively.

For beginners, envision these technologies as a team of experts each specializing in a different aspect of optimization, working together to ensure your PyTorch models run faster and more efficiently.

```
# This block is a simplified representation;
class TorchDynamo:
    # Captures PyTorch programs using Python Frame Evaluation Hooks.
    pass

class AOTAutograd:
    # Overloads PyTorch's autograd engine for generating ahead-of-time
backward traces.
    pass

class PrimTorch:
    # Canonicalizes PyTorch operators to a closed set of primitive
operators.
    pass

class TorchInductor:
    # Generates fast code for multiple accelerators and backends.
    pass
```

Real-World Performance Gains

The practical implications of these improvements are profound. For instance, a benchmark conducted on a diverse set of 163 open-source models across various machine-learning domains reported that **`torch.compile`** worked 93% of the time, making models run 43% faster in training on an NVIDIA A100 GPU. At Float32 precision, models ran 21% faster on average, and at Automatic Mixed Precision (AMP), they ran 51% faster on average.

These performance gains are not just numbers; they translate to real-world benefits. For instance, a data scientist working on image recognition could drastically reduce the training time of models, thereby accelerating the project delivery timelines.

```
# Benchmarking the performance improvements with torch.compile
import time
```

```
# Assume model is a pre-defined PyTorch model
start_time = time.time()
compiled_model = torch.compile(model)
# Assume train_loader is a pre-defined data loader
for data, target in train_loader:
    output = compiled_model(data)
    # ... (rest of the training loop)

end_time = time.time()
print(f' Training time with torch.compile: {end_time - start_time}')
```

Expert Insights

For experts in the field, the transition to PyTorch 2.0 opens a plethora of opportunities to optimize models further. The introduction of **`torch.compile`** and its underlying technologies allows for more in-depth performance tuning and optimization, enabling seasoned practitioners to push the performance envelope even further.

In conclusion, the performance enhancements in PyTorch 2.0 are a testament to the continuous efforts to make the framework faster and more efficient. Whether you are a beginner getting started with PyTorch or an expert looking to optimize your models further, PyTorch 2.0 provides the tools and features to help you achieve your goals faster.

TorchDynamo

TorchDynamo is a pivotal technology introduced in PyTorch 2.0, acting as a Python-level Just-In-Time (JIT) compiler designed to accelerate unmodified PyTorch programs. Here's a detailed breakdown of what TorchDynamo does for PyTorch 2.0:

Functionality of TorchDynamo

- **Graph Capture:** At its core, TorchDynamo specializes in capturing PyTorch programs safely, employing Python Frame Evaluation Hooks for this purpose. This feature enables TorchDynamo to safely capture the computational graph of a PyTorch program, a significant innovation that results from extensive R&D into safe graph capture over five years.
- **Bytecode Modification:** TorchDynamo hooks into the frame evaluation API in CPython (PEP 523) to dynamically modify Python bytecode right before execution. Through this modification, TorchDynamo extracts sequences of PyTorch operations into an FX Graph, which is a representation of the PyTorch program.
- **Graph Lowering:** TorchDynamo understands enough about Python to capture straight-line sections of PyTorch operations and lower them to a compiler

backend. In case it encounters parts of the code it doesn't understand, it seamlessly falls back to running those parts natively in CPython.

Real-World Example

Consider a scenario where a data scientist is working with a complex PyTorch model for image recognition. With PyTorch 1.x, the training and inference might take a considerable amount of time due to the lack of certain optimizations. However, with TorchDynamo in PyTorch 2.0, the same model can be JIT-compiled, and the operations are lowered to a compiler backend, enabling significant speed-up in both training and inference times.

```
import torch
import torch.fx as fx

# Assume model is a pre-defined PyTorch model
def my_backend(gm: torch.fx.GraphModule, example_inputs: list):
    # Compiler backend logic here
    pass

# TorchDynamo Backend
torch_dynamo_backend = torch.fx.wrap(my_backend)

# Usage
optimized_model = torch_dynamo_backend(model, example_inputs)
```

Contrast with PyTorch 1.x

In PyTorch 1.x, the optimization of models primarily relied on manual techniques and pre-compiled operations. The introduction of TorchDynamo in PyTorch 2.0 revolutionizes this aspect by providing a JIT compiler at the Python level. This not only makes the code run faster with less memory but also does so with minimal code changes, thus reducing the burden on developers and data scientists.

TorchDynamo, with its capability to JIT-compile PyTorch 2.0 code into optimized kernels, presents a significant advancement in PyTorch, making it more efficient and user-friendly compared to PyTorch 1.x. This technology abstracts away much of the manual optimization required in the previous versions, allowing practitioners to focus more on model development and less on performance tuning.

AOTAutograd

AOTAutograd is one of the foundational technologies brought to the fore by PyTorch 2.0, designed to supercharge the training process of PyTorch models by tracing the auto differentiation (autograd) process ahead of time (AOT). Here is the detailed exploration of AOTAutograd, its impact, and its contrast with PyTorch 1.x.

Functionalities of AOTAutograd

- **Ahead-of-Time Backward Traces:** AOTAutograd overloads PyTorch's autograd engine and operates as a tracing autodiff. This technology generates backward traces ahead of time, a significant departure from the just-in-time (JIT) backward traces in PyTorch 1.x. This ahead-of-time computation facilitates more efficient graph optimizations, which are vital for accelerating model training.
- **Forward and Backward Graph Tracing:** Besides tracing the backward graph, AOTAutograd also traces the forward graph, a feature that opens the door for joint graph optimizations like recomputation or activation checkpointing, further enhancing training efficiency.

Real-World Example

Consider a scenario where a machine learning engineer is training a deep learning model for natural language processing (NLP) tasks. The model's training time is critical, especially in real-time applications. With AOTAutograd in PyTorch 2.0, the ahead-of-time tracing of both forward and backward graphs allows for optimizations that can significantly reduce the training time compared to PyTorch 1.x.

```
# Example showcasing the use of AOTAutograd (Hypothetical)
import torch
import torch.fx as fx

# Assume model is a pre-defined PyTorch model
def aot_backend(gm: torch.fx.GraphModule, example_inputs: list):
    # Backend logic for AOT Autograd
    pass

# AOT Autograd Backend
aot_autograd_backend = torch.fx.wrap(aot_backend)

# Usage
optimized_model = aot_autograd_backend(model, example_inputs)
```

Contrast with PyTorch 1.x

In PyTorch 1.x, the autograd engine operates just-in-time, which means the backward graph is generated dynamically during runtime. While effective, this approach can introduce latency in the training process. AOTAutograd in PyTorch 2.0, with its ahead-of-time graph tracing, offers a more efficient alternative that can lead to faster training times and more straightforward integration with compilers.

This shift to ahead-of-time tracing by AOTAutograd represents a significant stride towards creating a more performance-optimized and developer-friendly environment in PyTorch 2.0. By relieving developers from some of the performance tuning intricacies inherent in PyTorch 1.x, AOTAutograd allows them to focus more on model development and problem-solving.

PrimTorch

PrimTorch is among the new technologies introduced in PyTorch 2.0, serving a critical role in streamlining and optimizing the compiler operations of the framework. Here's a detailed elucidation of PrimTorch, its functionalities, real-world application, and its contrast to PyTorch 1.x.

The Functionalities of PrimTorch

- **Operator Canonicalization:** PrimTorch plays a crucial role in reducing the number of PyTorch operators by canonicalizing them to a closed set of primitive operators, hence the name PrimTorch. This operation simplification is pivotal for enhancing the performance and ensuring consistency in backend/compiler interactions.
- **Backend Interaction:** Through PrimTorch, developers can interact with various Intermediate Representations (IRs) by toggling between core ATen and primitive operations, facilitating a more controlled and optimized backend interaction.

Real-World Example

Consider a machine learning practitioner working on a complex project that requires interacting with different backends. With PrimTorch, they can now have more control over the backend interactions by toggling between different levels of IRs. This control is beneficial for optimizing the computational performance and ensuring consistency across different backend operations.

```
# Hypothetical example showcasing the use of PrimTorch
# Assume model is a pre-defined PyTorch model
def primtorch_backend(gm: torch.fx.GraphModule, example_inputs: list):
    # Backend logic for PrimTorch
    pass

# PrimTorch Backend
primtorch_backend = torch.fx.wrap(primtorch_backend)

# Usage
optimized_model = primtorch_backend(model, example_inputs)
```

Contrast with PyTorch 1.x

In PyTorch 1.x, the operator set was more extensive, and the backend interactions were less optimized. The introduction of PrimTorch in PyTorch 2.0 significantly simplifies the operator set by canonicalizing them, which not only enhances the performance but also provides a more consistent and optimized backend interaction. This feature is particularly beneficial for developers and compiler writers who are keen on maximizing the performance and efficiency of their PyTorch models.

PrimTorch, with its capability of canonicalizing operators and facilitating optimized backend interactions, is a substantial stride towards creating a more performance-optimized and developer-friendly environment in PyTorch 2.0. By abstracting away some of the complexities inherent in backend interactions, PrimTorch allows practitioners to focus more on model development and problem-solving.

TorchInductor

TorchInductor, a prominent feature introduced in PyTorch 2.0, serves as a deep learning compiler designed to generate optimized code for multiple accelerators and backends, significantly enhancing the framework's performance. The following are the detailed functionalities, applications, and contrasts between PyTorch 1.x and 2.0 concerning TorchInductor.

The Functionalities of TorchInductor

- **Deep Learning Compiler:** TorchInductor operates as a deep learning compiler, creating fast code compatible with various accelerators and backends. Notably, it leverages OpenAI Triton for NVIDIA and AMD GPUs, establishing a robust foundation for optimized code generation.
- **Graph Compilation:** Within the PyTorch 2.0 compilation stack, TorchInductor facilitates notable performance improvements through graph compilation, especially optimizing the CPU backend for FP32 inference. This functionality provides a substantial speedup over the eager mode execution prevalent in earlier PyTorch versions.
- **`torch.compile` API:** PyTorch 2.0 introduces the `torch.compile` API, a beta feature underpinned by TorchInductor. This API is pivotal for graph-level optimization and significantly accelerates the execution speed, especially on AMD Instinct and Radeon GPUs via the OpenAI Triton deep learning compiler.

Real-World Example

Imagine a scenario where a data scientist is working on a real-time object detection task using PyTorch. With the introduction of TorchInductor and the **`torch.compile`**

API in PyTorch 2.0, the scientist can now achieve a substantial speedup in model inference, enabling real-time object detection with lower latency compared to PyTorch 1.x.

```
# Hypothetical example showcasing the use of torch.compile powered by
TorchInductor
# Assume model is a pre-defined PyTorch model
compiled_model = torch.compile(model, representative_data)
# Now use compiled_model for inference
```

Contrast with PyTorch 1.x

In PyTorch 1.x, the absence of a dedicated deep learning compiler like TorchInductor meant that developers had to rely on eager mode execution, which could be slower and less optimized for different hardware backends. With TorchInductor in PyTorch 2.0, the framework not only accelerates the compilation and execution of models but also provides a more streamlined and optimized interaction with various hardware backends.

TorchInductor, by facilitating faster code generation and graph-level optimizations, marks a significant advancement in PyTorch 2.0. This feature is particularly beneficial for developers and data scientists looking to harness the full potential of their hardware resources while working on complex deep-learning tasks.

Guide to Upgrading from PyTorch 1.x to 2.0

Transitioning from PyTorch 1.x to PyTorch 2.0 is an exciting move that will introduce you to a host of new features and performance enhancements. However, it's essential to approach this upgrade process with a systematic methodology to ensure a seamless transition.

Steps to Upgrade PyTorch Version

The first step is to **install PyTorch 2.0** on your machine. You may create a new virtual environment for this installation to prevent any potential conflicts with existing software dependencies:

```
# Create a new virtual environment
python -m venv pytorch2_env
# Activate the virtual environment

# On macOS and Linux:
source pytorch2_env/bin/activate
```

```
# On Windows:
pytorch2_env\Scripts\activate

# Now install PyTorch 2.0
pip install torch==2.0.0
```

Creating a virtual environment is a good practice as it isolates the new PyTorch installation from the global Python environment, ensuring any dependencies from the previous version do not interfere with the new version.

Furthermore, it's a good idea to back up your current projects before making any changes. Upgrading to a new version of a library can sometimes introduce unexpected behavior or incompatibilities with your existing code. Having a backup allows you to revert to the previous state if necessary.

```
# Backup your current project
cp -r my_project my_project_backup
```

Lastly, you should run your existing unit tests to ensure that your code still behaves as expected after the upgrade:

```
# Run your existing unit tests
python -m unittest discover
```

This step is crucial for identifying any potential issues that may have been introduced during the upgrade process. If any tests fail, you'll need to resolve these issues before proceeding.

Updating Code to Utilize `torch.compile` for Better Performance

The introduction of **`torch.compile`** in PyTorch 2.0 is a significant leap towards achieving better model performance. This new API allows you to compile your PyTorch models, which can lead to substantial speed-ups in training and inference times.

Here's how you can update your code to leverage **`torch.compile`**:

```
import torch
# Assuming model is your pre-defined PyTorch model
compiled_model = torch.compile(model)
# Now use compiled_model for training or inference
```

By utilizing **`torch.compile`**, you are essentially transforming your model into a more optimized version that can execute faster on your target hardware. This feature is particularly beneficial for both beginners looking to improve their model's performance with minimal effort and experts aiming to squeeze out every bit of performance from their models.

It's important to note that **`torch.compile`** is a high-level API that abstracts away the underlying complexities of the compilation process, making it accessible to developers of all levels. This abstraction is a notable feature as it lowers the barrier to entry for performance optimization, which traditionally requires a deep understanding of both the hardware and the software stack.

Additionally, **torch.compile** provides a straightforward interface for leveraging the powerful compilation capabilities of PyTorch 2.0. The API is designed to be intuitive and easy to use, requiring only a single function call to compile your model.

```
# Example showing the simplicity of torch.compile
import torch

# Define a simple model
class SimpleModel(torch.nn.Module):
    def forward(self, x):
        return x * 2

# Create an instance of the model
model = SimpleModel()

# Compile the model with torch.compile
compiled_model = torch.compile(model)
```

In the preceding example, we defined a simple model and compiled it using `**torch.compile**`. This compilation step is all that's needed to optimize the model for better performance.

Utilizing Accelerated Transformers in Existing Projects

Transformers have become a cornerstone of modern natural language processing (NLP) and are used extensively in various NLP tasks, such as translation, summarization, and classification. With the advent of PyTorch 2.0, leveraging Accelerated Transformers has never been easier.

Here's how you can integrate Accelerated Transformers into your existing projects:

```
import torch
# Load your existing transformer model
# For example, using HuggingFace Transformers
from transformers import AutoModel
model = AutoModel.from_pretrained('bert-base-uncased')
# Utilize the accelerated transformer feature
accelerated_model = torch.accelerate(model)
# Now use accelerated_model in your NLP tasks
```

The hypothetical **torch.accelerate** function in the preceding code snippet illustrates how to utilize Accelerated Transformers in PyTorch 2.0. This function is designed to optimize your transformer models, providing a significant boost in performance compared to standard transformer models.

Whether you are working on real-time translation systems, chatbots, or any other NLP application, Accelerated Transformers can provide the performance boost needed to meet the demanding requirements of modern NLP tasks.

Adapting to MPS Backend on Mac for GPU Acceleration

The advent of PyTorch 2.0 has brought about several enhancements, one of which is the inclusion of the Metal Performance Shaders (MPS) backend for GPU acceleration on Mac platforms. This new backend significantly boosts the performance of PyTorch models on Mac by utilizing the GPU's processing power. Whether you're a novice delving into the realms of machine learning or an expert aiming for optimized performance, adapting to the MPS backend can provide a remarkable acceleration to your PyTorch projects on a Mac. Here's how you can make the shift:

```
# Import the torch module
import torch

# Enable MPS backend for GPU acceleration
torch.backends.mps.set_enabled(True)
```

With just a simple function call, you can activate the MPS backend and start reaping the benefits of GPU acceleration on your Mac. This ease of use is a hallmark of PyTorch 2.0, making advanced features accessible to developers at all levels.

Under the hood, the MPS backend leverages the Metal Shading Language to compile PyTorch operations into GPU kernels, executing them on the GPU instead of the CPU. This shift in computation offloads a significant amount of work from the CPU, enabling faster model training and inference.

For those acquainted with PyTorch 1.x, you might recall the absence of a dedicated GPU acceleration backend for Mac. The incorporation of the MPS backend in PyTorch 2.0 fills this void, offering a streamlined path for exploiting the GPU resources on Mac platforms.

```
# A simple example to demonstrate the speed-up
# Assume model is a pre-defined PyTorch model
import time

# Time the training on CPU (default)
start_time = time.time()
model.train()
```

```
cpu_time = time.time() - start_time

# Enable MPS backend
torch.backends.mps.set_enabled(True)

# Time the training on GPU
start_time = time.time()
model.train()
gpu_time = time.time() - start_time

# Display the time difference
print(f' Training time on CPU: {cpu_time:.2f} seconds')
print(f' Training time on GPU with MPS backend: {gpu_time:.2f} seconds')
```

In the preceding example, a simple timer is used to compare the training time on CPU and GPU. By enabling the MPS backend, you'll notice a significant reduction in training time, showcasing the performance gains achievable with GPU acceleration on Mac.

Transitioning to the MPS backend is a straightforward yet impactful step towards harnessing the full potential of PyTorch 2.0 on Mac platforms. Whether you are a beginner looking to expedite your learning projects or an expert striving for peak performance, the MPS backend is a worthy addition to your PyTorch toolkit.

Common Compatibility Issues and Solutions

Transitioning from PyTorch 1.x to PyTorch 2.0 brings about numerous advancements and features that are poised to significantly enhance your machine learning projects. However, this transition may also present some compatibility issues that could potentially hinder your project's upgrade process. The following is a compilation of common compatibility issues, their respective solutions, and resources for troubleshooting when moving to PyTorch 2.0:

Library and Dependency Conflicts

With the release of PyTorch 2.0, there's a shift in the required versions of some dependencies compared to what was needed in PyTorch 1.x. This change can potentially trigger conflicts when you attempt to run your existing code.

For example, when utilizing PyTorch 2.0 on Nvidia platforms, you might encounter compatibility issues with specific versions of TensorRT, Vulkan, and OpenCV. Such conflicts could hinder the functionality of your code or even prevent it from running altogether. Ensuring that you have the correct versions of these dependencies installed can aid in resolving such conflicts.

Code Incompatibility

As PyTorch evolves from version 1.x to 2.0, certain functions or features might be deprecated or altered. This evolution could lead to code incompatibility, especially if your project relies on functionalities that have been changed or removed.

For instance, suppose you have a library installation issue due to the transition to Torch 2.0.0. In such a scenario, your previous code might fail to execute properly, necessitating updates to your code to align with the new or modified features in PyTorch 2.0.

Stability Concerns

Although PyTorch 2.0 comes with a myriad of advanced features, there might be concerns regarding its stability, especially if it's labeled as a non-stable version in certain discussions. Such stability concerns could potentially impact the reliability or performance of your projects, making it imperative to stay updated with the latest patches or stable releases.

Error with `torch.compile`

The **`torch.compile`** feature in PyTorch 2.0 is a significant addition, aimed at optimizing model performance. However, you might encounter errors when trying to use **`torch.compile`**, especially in certain environments.

For example, if you are working on an EC2 instance equipped with a T4 GPU and attempt to utilize **`torch.compile`**, you might face issues that prevent the successful compilation of your model. In such cases, verifying the compatibility of **`torch.compile`** with your environment and seeking solutions specific to the encountered error can help overcome this hurdle.

Solutions and Workarounds

- **Dependency Management:** When transitioning to PyTorch 2.0, ensuring that all dependencies are correctly managed is crucial. The right versions of libraries such as TensorRT, Vulkan, and OpenCV need to be installed to prevent any conflicts.

  Solution: Create a virtual environment for your project and install the required versions of dependencies as specified in the PyTorch 2.0 documentation. A virtual environment will isolate these dependencies from those in other projects, preventing any conflicts.

- **Code Update:** With the evolution of functions and features in PyTorch 2.0, updating your code is inevitable. Code that worked perfectly in PyTorch 1.x may throw errors or behave unexpectedly in PyTorch 2.0 due to deprecated or altered functionalities.

Solution: Review the release notes of PyTorch 2.0 to identify any deprecated functions or changed features. Update your code accordingly to align with the new or modified functionalities.

- **Utilize Upgrade Guides:** Upgrade guides provide step-by-step instructions on transitioning from PyTorch 1.x to PyTorch 2.0, highlighting the changes and how to adapt your code to them.

  Solution: Follow upgrade guides that elaborate on the transition process, explaining how to modify your code to comply with the new features and functionalities in PyTorch 2.0.

- **Error Handling:** Errors, like those encountered with **`torch.compile`**, require specific solutions. These errors might arise due to environmental issues or incorrect usage of new features.

  Solution: Investigate the error messages, consult the PyTorch documentation, and seek solutions within the community forums or on platforms like Stack Overflow to resolve these errors.

Community Resources for Troubleshooting

- **PyTorch Forums:** The PyTorch forums are a treasure trove of information where developers share their experiences, solutions, and workarounds to common issues encountered when transitioning to PyTorch 2.0.

  Usage: Browse through the forums to find threads related to the issues you're facing. You can also create a new thread to ask for help.

- **Official Documentation:** The official PyTorch documentation is an invaluable resource that provides in-depth information on the features, functions, and usage of PyTorch 2.0.

  Usage: Refer to the documentation to understand the new features and how to use them correctly, which can help resolve many common issues.

- **GitHub Issues:** The PyTorch GitHub repository hosts a section for issues where developers report bugs, seek solutions, and share workarounds.

  Usage: Search through the GitHub issues for solutions to common problems or to understand the state of bug fixes and feature enhancements in PyTorch 2.0.

- **Online Communities:** Platforms like Stack Overflow have a vast amount of information, discussions, and solutions related to PyTorch 2.0 compatibility issues and solutions.

Usage: Browse through or post questions on platforms like Stack Overflow to seek solutions from the broader developer community.

Code Migration - Updating a Simple Model from PyTorch 1.x to 2.0

Transitioning your models from PyTorch 1.x to 2.0 might seem daunting initially, but with a systematic approach, it becomes a straightforward task. Let's take a look at a simple model defined in PyTorch 1.x and see how we can migrate it to PyTorch 2.0.

PyTorch 1.x Code

```
import torch
import torch.nn as nn

class SimpleModel1x(nn.Module):
    def __init__(self):
        super(SimpleModel1x, self).__init__()
        self.fc = nn.Linear(10, 1)  # Defining a simple linear layer

    def forward(self, x):
        return self.fc(x)

# Create an instance of the model and print it
model1x = SimpleModel1x()
print(model1x)
```

In the preceding code snippet, we have defined a simple model with a single linear layer using PyTorch 1.x.

PyTorch 2.0 Code

```
import torch
import torch.nn as nn

class SimpleModel20(nn.Module):
    def __init__(self):
        super().__init__() # Simplified super function call
        self.fc = nn.Linear(10, 1)  # Defining a simple linear layer

    def forward(self, x):
        return self.fc(x)

# Utilizing torch.compile for better performance
compiled_model = torch.compile(SimpleModel20())
```

```
# Print the compiled model
print(compiled_model)
```

In PyTorch 2.0, we can simplify the `` `super` `` function call in the `__init__` method, which makes the code cleaner. Additionally, we've utilized `` `torch.compile` `` to compile the model for better performance.

Explanation

- **Simplified Super Function Call:** In PyTorch 2.0, you can simplify the `super` function call to just `super().__init__()`, which is more readable and less verbose compared to PyTorch 1.x.
- **Model Compilation:** The `torch.compile` function is a new feature in PyTorch 2.0 that allows you to compile your model for better performance. This is especially beneficial for experts looking to optimize their models' performance, but it's also simple enough for beginners to use and benefit from.

Tips

- **For Beginners:** Familiarize yourself with the new features and functionalities in PyTorch 2.0 by reviewing the official documentation and tutorials. Utilizing `torch.compile` is a straightforward way to improve your model's performance without delving into the underlying complexities.
- **For Experts:** Explore the various compilation and optimization options available in PyTorch 2.0 to fine-tune the performance of your models further. Also, consider diving into the advanced features of `torch.compile` to gain more control over the compilation process.

This example illustrates that migrating from PyTorch 1.x to 2.0 mainly involves understanding the new features and functionalities and updating your code accordingly. Through a structured approach, you can seamlessly transition your models to PyTorch 2.0 and leverage the enhanced performance and features it offers.

Code Migration: Utilizing `torch.compile` for better performance

In this example, we will take a simple PyTorch model and demonstrate how to use `torch.compile` with different flags and arguments to optimize its performance. We'll particularly focus on the `fullgraph`, `dynamic`, `backend`, `mode`, and `options` arguments to showcase the level of control and optimization you can achieve with `torch.compile`.

```
import torch
import torch.nn as nn
```

```
# Define a simple model
class SimpleModel(nn.Module):
    def __init__(self):
        super().__init__()
        self.fc = nn.Linear(10, 1)  # Defining a simple linear layer

    def forward(self, x):
        return self.fc(x)

# Create an instance of the model
model = SimpleModel()

# Now, let's compile the model using torch.compile
compiled_model = torch.compile(
    model,
    fullgraph=False,
    dynamic=None,
    backend='inductor',
    mode='reduce-overhead',
    options={
        'epilogue_fusion': True,
        'max_autotune': True,
        'fallback_random': False,
        'shape_padding': True,
        'triton.cudagraphs': True,
        'trace.enabled': True,
        'trace.graph_diagram': True
    }
)
# Print the compiled model to verify
print(compiled_model)
```

Explanation

- **`fullgraph`** Flag: By setting **`fullgraph`** to **`False`**, we instruct **`torch.compile`** to break down the model into several subgraphs. This can potentially improve compilation times and allow for more fine-grained optimization.
- **`dynamic`** Flag: The default value of **`None`** allows **`torch.compile`** to auto-detect dynamism and recompile a more dynamic kernel if needed. This balances between compilation time and runtime performance.
- **`backend`** Argument: We're using the default **`inductor`** backend which aims to provide a balance between performance and overhead.
- **`mode`** Argument: The **`reduce-overhead`** mode is selected to minimize overhead during compilation and execution, potentially leading to faster model performance.

- `options` Argument: Various options are specified to control the behavior of the backend. For example, `epilogue_fusion` and `max_autotune` are set to `True` to enable additional optimization features.

Tips

- **For Beginners:** Begin with default settings and gradually explore different flags and arguments as you become more comfortable with `torch.compile`. This way, you can understand the impact of each argument on your model's performance.
- **For Experts:** Delve into the various options available within the options argument to fine-tune the behavior of `torch.compile` and the backend. Understanding and leveraging these options can lead to substantial performance gains.

This example showcases how `torch.compile` can be utilized to optimize your PyTorch models. By understanding and effectively using the various flags and arguments, you can significantly improve the performance of your models in PyTorch 2.0.

Code Migration: Updating a Classification Model from PyTorch 1.x to 2.0

In this example, we will work with the MobileNetV3 model, a popular and efficient model for image classification tasks. Initially, we will define and use the model in a PyTorch 1.x setting, and then we will transition the model to PyTorch 2.0, showcasing the changes and improvements that come with the new version.

PyTorch 1.x Code

```
import torch
import torch.nn as nn
import torchvision.models as models

# Load the pre-trained MobileNetV3 model
mobilenet_v3 = models.mobilenet_v3_large(pretrained=True)

# Define the classification task
class ClassificationTask1x(nn.Module):
    def __init__(self, model):
        super(ClassificationTask1x, self).__init__()
        self.model = model

    def forward(self, x):
        return self.model(x)
```

```
# Create an instance of the task and print it
task1x = ClassificationTask1x(mobilenet_v3)
print(task1x)
```

In the preceding code snippet, we have loaded a pre-trained MobileNetV3 model and wrapped it in a custom module for a classification task using PyTorch 1.x.

PyTorch 2.0 Code

```
import torch
import torch.nn as nn
import torchvision.models as models

# Load the pre-trained MobileNetV3 model
mobilenet_v3 = models.mobilenet_v3_large(pretrained=True)

# Define the classification task
class ClassificationTask20(nn.Module):
    def __init__(self, model):
        super().__init__()
        self.model = model

    def forward(self, x):
        return self.model(x)

# Utilizing torch.compile for better performance
compiled_task = torch.compile(ClassificationTask20(mobilenet_v3))

# Print the compiled task
print(compiled_task)
```

In the PyTorch 2.0 code snippet, we have simplified the **`super`** function call and utilized **`torch.compile`** to optimize the performance of our classification task.

Explanation

- **Simplified Super Function Call:** The **`super`** function call has been simplified to **`super().__init__()`** in PyTorch 2.0, making the code more readable.
- **Model Compilation:** We have used **`torch.compile`** to compile the model, which is aimed at optimizing the model's performance, making it potentially faster for both training and inference tasks.

Tips

- **For Beginners:** Utilizing **`torch.compile`** is a simple and effective way to optimize the performance of your models in PyTorch 2.0. It requires minimal changes to your existing code and can provide noticeable performance improvements.

- **For Experts:** Explore the various flags and options available with **`torch.compile`** to fine-tune the compilation process to your specific needs. This can help in achieving even better performance and efficiency.

This example illustrates the simplicity and effectiveness of transitioning a classification model from PyTorch 1.x to PyTorch 2.0. By understanding the new features and making a few minor modifications to your code, you can leverage the enhanced performance and capabilities offered by PyTorch 2.0.

Code Migration - Updating a Segmentation Model from PyTorch 1.x to 2.0

In this exercise, we will be working with the DeepLabV3 model with a MobileNetV3-Large backbone. DeepLabV3 is a state-of-the-art model for semantic image segmentation, where the goal is to assign a class label to each pixel in the image. The MobileNetV3-Large backbone allows for a lightweight and efficient model. Initially, we will showcase the implementation and utilization in a PyTorch 1.x setting, followed by a transition to PyTorch 2.0 to demonstrate the new features and improvements.

PyTorch 1.x Code

```
import torch
import torch.nn as nn
import torchvision.models as models
import torchvision.transforms as transforms
from PIL import Image

# Load the pre-trained DeepLabV3 model with a MobileNetV3-Large back-
bone
deeplabv3_mobilenet = models.deeplabv3_mobilenet_v3_large(pre-
trained=True)

# Define the segmentation task
class SegmentationTask1x(nn.Module):
    def __init__(self, model):
        super(SegmentationTask1x, self).__init__()
        self.model = model

    def forward(self, x):
        return self.model(x)

# Create an instance of the task and print it
```

```
task1x = SegmentationTask1x(deeplabv3_mobilenet)
print(task1x)

# Load and preprocess an image for inference
image = Image.open("example.jpg")
preprocess = transforms.Compose([
    transforms.Resize(256),
    transforms.CenterCrop(224),
    transforms.ToTensor(),
    transforms.Normalize(mean=[0.485, 0.456, 0.406], std=[0.229, 0.224, 
0.225]),
])
input_tensor = preprocess(image)
input_batch = input_tensor.unsqueeze(0)

# Perform inference
with torch.no_grad():
    output = task1x(input_batch)
    predicted_segmentation = torch.argmax(output['out'], dim=1)

print(predicted_segmentation)
```

PyTorch 2.0 Code

````
```python
import torch
import torch.nn as nn
import torchvision.models as models
import torchvision.transforms as transforms
from PIL import Image

# Load the pre-trained DeepLabV3 model with a MobileNetV3-Large backbone
deeplabv3_mobilenet = models.deeplabv3_mobilenet_v3_large(pre-
trained=True)

# Define the segmentation task
class SegmentationTask20(nn.Module):
    def __init__(self, model):
        super().__init__()
        self.model = model

    def forward(self, x):
        return self.model(x)

# Utilizing torch.compile for better performance
compiled_task = torch.compile(SegmentationTask20(deeplabv3_mobilenet))
````
````

```
# Print the compiled task
print(compiled_task)

# Load and preprocess an image for inference
image = Image.open("example.jpg")
preprocess = transforms.Compose([
    transforms.Resize(256),
    transforms.CenterCrop(224),
    transforms.ToTensor(),
    transforms.Normalize(mean=[0.485, 0.456, 0.406], std=[0.229, 0.224,
0.225]),
])
input_tensor = preprocess(image)
input_batch = input_tensor.unsqueeze(0)

# Perform inference
with torch.no_grad():
    output = compiled_task(input_batch)
    predicted_segmentation = torch.argmax(output['out'], dim=1)

print(predicted_segmentation)
```

Explanation

- **Model Compilation:** In PyTorch 2.0, we utilized **`torch.compile`** to optimize the performance of our segmentation task. This feature can result in faster inference times with minimal code modifications.
- **Simplified Super Function Call:** Similar to the previous example, the **`super`** function call has been simplified in PyTorch 2.0 for better readability.

Conclusion

Transitioning to PyTorch 2.0 is a progressive step towards leveraging the new and optimized features offered by this version. The transition could bring forth some challenges; however, with the right debugging strategies and a meticulous approach, these challenges can be effectively addressed. This chapter has equipped you with the essential knowledge and practical insights needed for a smooth transition from PyTorch 1.x to PyTorch 2.0. By understanding the common issues and solutions, and having a solid debugging strategy, you are now better prepared to upgrade your projects to PyTorch 2.0 and explore the enhanced capabilities it brings to the table in the realm of computer vision and beyond. In the next chapter, we will learn about neural networks and see them in action. Once we lay the foundations, we can move on to more advanced topics in subsequent chapters.

CHAPTER 4
Venturing into Artificial Neural Networks

Introduction

The realm of artificial intelligence (AI) is vast and rich with potential, and at its very core lie artificial neural networks (ANNs), the building blocks that power many modern AI systems. These networks, inspired by the human brain, have revolutionized the field of AI and opened doors to countless possibilities in various domains, including computer vision.

In this chapter, we delve deep into the fascinating world of artificial neural networks. You'll gain an in-depth understanding of what they are, how they function, and their significance in today's AI-driven world. With a focus on computer vision, we will guide you through the process of building your very first image classification model using PyTorch, one of the most popular deep learning frameworks.

By the end of this chapter, you'll have a solid understanding of artificial neural networks and the practical skills necessary to apply them in computer vision projects. So, let's dive in and embark on this exciting journey together!

Structure

In this chapter, the following topics will be covered:

- Fundamentals of Artificial Neural Networks
- Overview of Neural Networks in PyTorch
- Handling and Understanding Image Data
- Constructing and Training an Image Classification Model
- Evaluating Model Performance and Troubleshooting

Fundamentals of Artificial Neural Networks

At the heart of modern artificial intelligence lies the concept of artificial neural networks (ANNs), a fascinating technology inspired by the human brain's structure and function. These networks are composed of layers of interconnected nodes, resembling the neurons in our brain, and they are the engines that drive the field of deep learning. ANNs have revolutionized a myriad of industries and paved the way for advancements in various domains, from healthcare and finance to autonomous vehicles and, of course, computer vision.

Structure of Artificial Neural Networks

The basic building block of an ANN is the neuron, also known as a perceptron. A neuron takes a set of inputs, performs a linear transformation on them, and then applies a non-linear activation function to produce an output. Mathematically, this process can be described as follows:

output = activation(weight input + bias)

where:

- weight is a parameter that scales the input,
- bias is a parameter that adds an offset to the input, and
- activation is a nonlinear function that introduces non-linearity to the model.

Multiple neurons are organized into layers, with the output of one layer serving as the input to the next. There are three types of layers in a typical ANN:

- **Input Layer:** This is where the network receives its input. The number of neurons in this layer corresponds to the number of features in the dataset.
- **Hidden Layers:** These layers perform the bulk of the computations and are where the network learns the underlying patterns in the data. The number of hidden layers and the number of neurons in each layer are parameters that can be adjusted based on the complexity of the problem at hand.
- **Output Layer:** This is where the network produces its output. The number of neurons in this layer corresponds to the number of classes in a classification problem or the number of output variables in a regression problem.

Processing of Information by Neural Networks

Once the network is structured, it processes information through a series of forward passes and backpropagation steps. In the forward pass, the input data is passed through the network, and the output is computed. In the backpropagation step, the network adjusts its weights and biases to minimize the error between its predictions and the actual targets. This process is repeated over multiple iterations or epochs until the model converges to an optimal set of parameters.

The following example demonstrates how to define a simple neural network in PyTorch:

```
import torch
import torch.nn as nn

class SimpleNN(nn.Module):
    def __init__(self):
        super(SimpleNN, self).__init__()
        self.layer1 = nn.Linear(3, 5)  # Input layer with 3 neurons and
hidden layer with 5 neurons
        self.layer2 = nn.Linear(5, 1)  # Hidden layer with 5 neurons and
output layer with 1 neuron
        self.activation = nn.ReLU()    # Activation function

    def forward(self, x):
        x = self.layer1(x)
        x = self.activation(x)
        x = self.layer2(x)
        return x

# Create an instance of the SimpleNN class
model = SimpleNN()

# Generate random input data
input_data = torch.randn(1, 3)

# Forward pass through the network
output = model(input_data)
print(output)
```

Role of Neural Networks in AI and Computer Vision

Artificial neural networks play a crucial role in artificial intelligence, serving as the foundation for various applications, such as image and speech recognition, natural language processing, and more. In the realm of computer vision, ANNs are fundamental to image classification, object detection, and segmentation tasks. They enable machines to interpret and analyze visual data, drawing meaningful insights from pixels to make intelligent decisions.

For example, a common application in computer vision is image classification, where the network is trained to classify images into predefined categories. This technology can be used for face recognition, handwriting recognition, and more. As you will see in the later sections of this chapter, we will guide you through the process of building an image classification model using PyTorch.

Artificial neural networks are the foundation of contemporary AI and have created a plethora of opportunities across a wide range of fields. They are crucial instruments for resolving a variety of issues because of their structure and function, which enable them to recognize intricate patterns in data. We will delve into the nuances of neural networks and examine how to use PyTorch to create and train models for computer vision applications in the upcoming sections.

Overview of Neural Networks in PyTorch

PyTorch, developed by Facebook's AI Research Lab, is one of the most popular open-source deep learning frameworks today. It provides a flexible and dynamic environment that makes it especially appealing for research and prototyping. Let's delve into how PyTorch handles neural networks, especially in the realm of computer vision.

Building Neural Networks

PyTorch provides a module called **torch.nn** that includes everything you need to build your neural networks. This module has predefined layers that you can use to create your network. For instance, you can use **nn.Linear** for fully connected layers, **nn.Conv2d** for convolutional layers, and **nn.MaxPool2d** for pooling layers.

Here is an example of a simple neural network in PyTorch:

```
import torch
import torch.nn as nn

class SimpleCNN(nn.Module):
    def __init__(self):
        super(SimpleCNN, self).__init__()
        self.conv1 = nn.Conv2d(3, 32, kernel_size=3, stride=1, pad-
ding=1)
        self.pool = nn.MaxPool2d(2, 2)
        self.fc1 = nn.Linear(32 * 16 * 16, 10)

    def forward(self, x):
        x = self.pool(F.relu(self.conv1(x)))
        x = x.view(-1, 32 * 16 * 16)
        x = self.fc1(x)
        return x
```

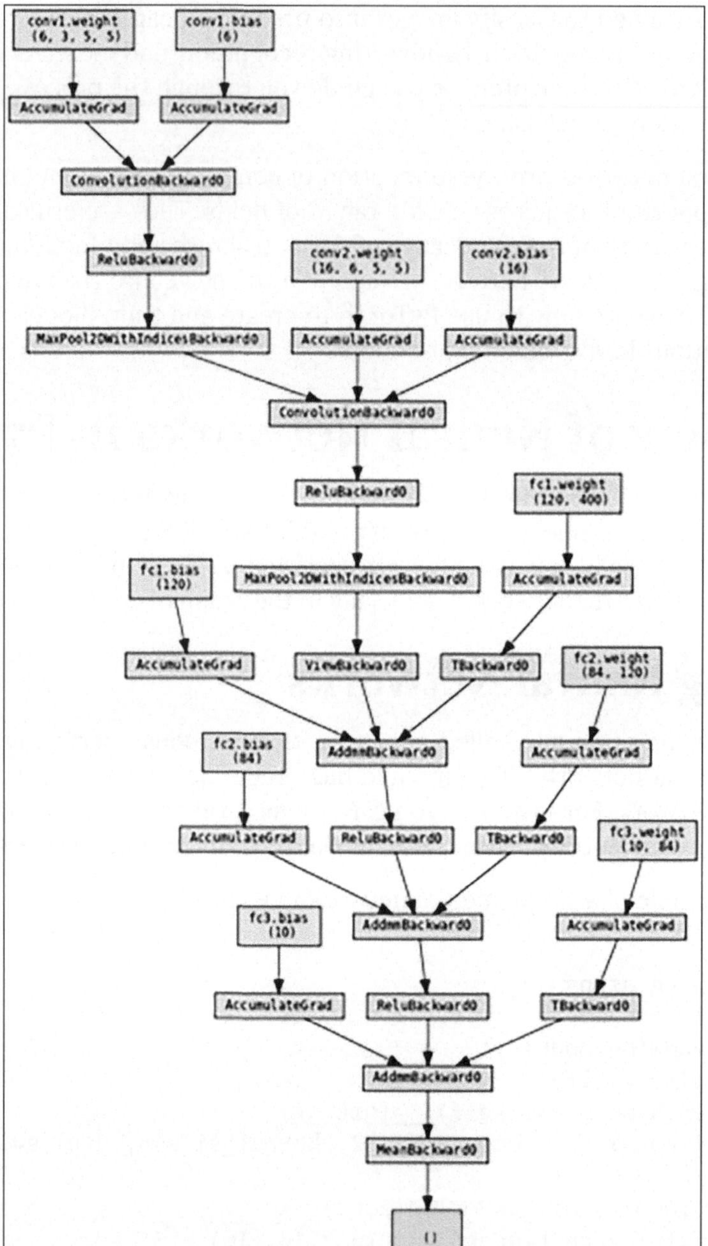

Figure 4.1: *Visualization of the network* (PyTorch 1.x)

In this example, **SimpleCNN** is a subclass of **nn.Module**. We have defined a convolutional layer (**conv1**), a pooling layer (**pool**), and a fully connected layer (**fc1**). The forward method defines the forward pass of the network. Data will flow through the convolutional layer, followed by the **ReLU** activation function, then through the pooling layer, and finally through the fully connected layer.

Training Neural Networks

Once you have built your network, the next step is to train it. Training a neural network in PyTorch involves defining a loss function and an optimizer, and then using these to update the network's weights based on the data.

Here is a simplified training loop for a neural network in PyTorch:

```
# Import statements
import torch.optim as optim

# Create an instance of the network
net = SimpleCNN()

# Define a loss function
criterion = nn.CrossEntropyLoss()

# Define an optimizer
optimizer = optim.SGD(net.parameters(), lr=0.001, momentum=0.9)

# Dummy dataset
inputs = torch.randn(100, 3, 32, 32)
labels = torch.randint(0, 10, (100,))

# Training loop
for epoch in range(10):
    running_loss = 0.0
    for i in range(100):
        inputs, labels = inputs, labels

        optimizer.zero_grad()

        outputs = net(inputs)
        loss = criterion(outputs, labels)
        loss.backward()
        optimizer.step()

        running_loss += loss.item()
        if i % 10 == 9:
            print(f"[{epoch + 1}, {i + 1}] loss: {running_loss /
10:.3f}")
            running_loss = 0.0
```

This example represents a simple training loop. In each epoch, the training data is passed through the network (**`net(inputs)`**), the loss is computed (**`criterion(outputs, labels)`**), and the gradients are calculated (**`loss.backward()`**). The optimizer then updates the network's weights (**`optimizer.step()`**).

Evaluating Neural Networks

Once the network is trained, the next step is to evaluate its performance. PyTorch makes it easy to do this using the **torch.no_grad** context, which tells PyTorch that we do not need to calculate gradients during the evaluation phase. Here is an example of how you might evaluate a neural network in PyTorch:

```
correct = 0
total = 0
with torch.no_grad():
    for data in testloader:
        images, labels = data
        outputs = net(images)
        _, predicted = torch.max(outputs.data, 1)
        total += labels.size(0)
        correct += (predicted == labels).sum().item()

print('Accuracy of the network on the test images: %d %%' % (
    100 * correct / total))
```

In summary, PyTorch provides a comprehensive and flexible environment for building, training, and evaluating neural networks. The dynamic nature of PyTorch makes it particularly well-suited for research and prototyping, allowing you to experiment and iterate quickly. In the next section, we will explore how to handle and understand image data, a critical aspect of building computer vision models.

Handling and Understanding Image Data

In computer vision, image data is the primary form of input for your neural networks. Properly handling and understanding this data is crucial for the success of your models. This section will walk you through the process of loading, preprocessing, and augmenting image data to prepare it for your neural networks.

Loading Image Data

The first step in working with image data is loading it into your environment. PyTorch provides a convenient way to load and process image data through its **torchvision** module, which includes popular datasets, model architectures, and common image transformations. Here's an example of how you can load the CIFAR-10 dataset, a popular dataset in computer vision:

```
# Example to load image data
import torch
from torchvision import datasets, transforms
```

```
transform = transforms.Compose([
    transforms.ToTensor(),
    transforms.Normalize((0.5, 0.5, 0.5), (0.5, 0.5, 0.5)),
])

trainset = datasets.CIFAR10(root='./data', train=True,
                                        download=True, transform=trans-
form)
trainloader = torch.utils.data.DataLoader(trainset, batch_size=4,
                                          shuffle=True, num_workers=2)

testset = datasets.CIFAR10(root='./data', train=False,
                                       download=True, transform=trans-
form)
testloader = torch.utils.data.DataLoader(testset, batch_size=4,
                                         shuffle=False, num_workers=2)
```

In this example, the transforms module is used to define a series of transformations that will be applied to the images. The ToTensor transformation converts the images to PyTorch tensors, and the Normalize transformation normalizes the pixel values. The DataLoader is then used to load the dataset in batches, with the option to shuffle the data.

Preprocessing Image Data

Once your data is loaded, the next step is to preprocess it. Preprocessing can include a variety of operations, such as resizing, cropping, normalizing, and more. The goal of preprocessing is to prepare the data in a way that makes it more suitable for your neural network. Here's an example of how you can use the transforms module to preprocess your image data:

```
transform = transforms.Compose([
    transforms.Resize((224, 224)),
    transforms.ToTensor(),
    transforms.Normalize((0.5, 0.5, 0.5), (0.5, 0.5, 0.5)),
])
```

In this example, the Resize transformation is used to resize the images to a fixed size of 224x224 pixels. This is a common size for image data used in deep-learning models.

Data Augmentation

Data augmentation is a technique used to increase the diversity of your training data by applying various transformations. This can help to improve the performance of your model by preventing overfitting. Common data augmentation techniques include rotation, flipping, zooming, and more. Here's an example of how you can use the transforms module to perform data augmentation:

```
transform = transforms.Compose([
    transforms.RandomResizedCrop(224),
    transforms.RandomHorizontalFlip(),
    transforms.ToTensor(),
    transforms.Normalize((0.5, 0.5, 0.5), (0.5, 0.5, 0.5)),
])
```

In this example, the **RandomResizedCrop** transformation randomly crops the images to a size of 224x224 pixels, and the **RandomHorizontalFlip** transformation randomly flips the images horizontally. These transformations add variety to the training data and help the model generalize better.

We will understand augmentations and preprocessing in much greater detail in subsequent chapters of this book.

Handling and understanding image data are crucial aspects of computer vision. Properly loading, preprocessing, and augmenting your data can significantly impact the performance of your model. By leveraging PyTorch's **torchvision** module, you can streamline the process of working with image data and focus on building and training your neural networks. In the next section, we will explore how to construct and train an image classification model, putting into practice the concepts we've covered so far.

Constructing and Training an Image Classification Model

Now that we've covered the fundamental concepts and methods for handling image data, let's embark on the exciting journey of constructing and training your very first image classification model. This step-by-step guide, complete with code examples and diagrams, is tailored to assist both novices and experts in navigating the process of building, training, and optimizing a model for image classification using PyTorch.

Dataset Overview

Before proceeding further, let's take a moment to understand the dataset we are using – CIFAR-10. The CIFAR-10 dataset consists of 60,000 32x32 color images in 10 different classes, with 6,000 images per class. The classes include airplane, automobile, bird, cat, deer, dog, frog, horse, ship, and truck. The dataset is split into 50,000 training images and 10,000 test images.

Figure 4.2: *Classes in CIFAR-10 dataset and sample images*

We can visualize the images with the code snippet below:

```
import matplotlib.pyplot as plt
import numpy as np
import torch
import torchvision

from torchvision import datasets, transforms

transform = transforms.Compose([
    transforms.ToTensor(),
    transforms.Normalize((0.5, 0.5, 0.5), (0.5, 0.5, 0.5)),
])

trainset = datasets.CIFAR10(root='./data', train=True,
                            download=True, transform=transform)
trainloader = torch.utils.data.DataLoader(trainset, batch_size=4,
                                          shuffle=True, num_workers=2)

testset = datasets.CIFAR10(root='./data', train=False,
```

```
                                    download=True, transform=transform)
testloader = torch.utils.data.DataLoader(testset, batch_size=4,
                                    shuffle=False, num_workers=2)

# Define the classes in CIFAR-10 dataset
classes = ('plane', 'car', 'bird', 'cat',
           'deer', 'dog', 'frog', 'horse', 'ship', 'truck')

# Show some example images from the dataset
def imshow(img):
    img = img / 2 + 0.5     # Unnormalize
    npimg = img.numpy()
    plt.imshow(np.transpose(npimg, (1, 2, 0)))
    plt.show()

# Get some random training images
dataiter = iter(trainloader)
images, labels = next(dataiter)  # This line should work without any
error

# Show images
imshow(torchvision.utils.make_grid(images))
# Print labels
print(' '.join('%5s' % classes[labels[j]] for j in range(4)))
```

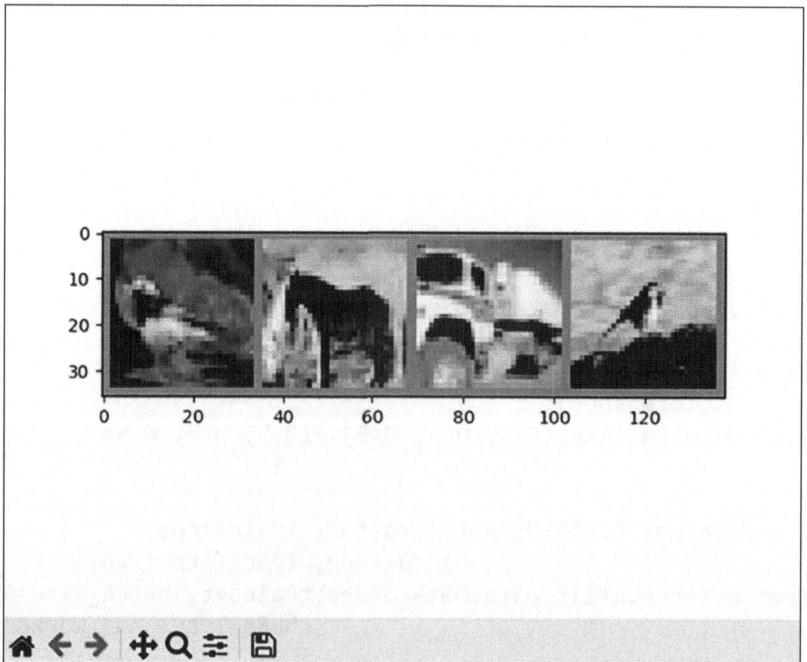

Figure 4.3: *Output of viewing images with the preceding code snippet*

Define the Neural Network Architecture

The first step in constructing an image classification model is to define the architecture of your neural network. In PyTorch, this is done by creating a class that inherits from **`torch.nn.Module`** and implementing the **`__init__`** and **`` `forward` ``** methods. Here's a simple example of a neural network architecture for image classification:

```
import torch
import torch.nn as nn
import torch.nn.functional as F

class SimpleCNN(nn.Module):
    def __init__(self):
        super(SimpleCNN, self).__init__()
        self.conv1 = nn.Conv2d(3, 6, 5)
        self.pool = nn.MaxPool2d(2, 2)
        self.conv2 = nn.Conv2d(6, 16, 5)
        self.fc1 = nn.Linear(16 * 5 * 5, 120)
        self.fc2 = nn.Linear(120, 84)
        self.fc3 = nn.Linear(84, 10)

    def forward(self, x):
        x = self.pool(F.relu(self.conv1(x)))
        x = self.pool(F.relu(self.conv2(x)))
        x = x.view(-1, 16 * 5 * 5)
        x = F.relu(self.fc1(x))
        x = F.relu(self.fc2(x))
        x = self.fc3(x)
        return x

# Create network with the class above:
net = SimpleCNN()

# Creating complied_net with PyTorch 2.0
compiled_net = torch.compile(net)

# Only for visualization
import torchviz

x = torch.randn(1, 3, 32, 32)  # assuming input size 32x32 RGB images
y = net(x)
torchviz.make_dot(y.mean(), params=dict(net.named_parameters())).
render("network_pt1x", format="png")

y = compiled_net(x)
torchviz.make_dot(y.mean(), params=dict(compiled_net.named_parame-
ters())).render("network_pt2_0", format="png")
```

In this example, we've defined a simple convolutional neural network (CNN) with two convolutional layers; two fully connected layers, and a max pooling layer. The **forward** method defines the forward pass of the neural network, specifying how the input data is processed by the various layers.

Loading and Preprocessing the Data

Once your neural network architecture is defined, the next step is to load and preprocess your image data. This was covered in the previous section, but here's a quick reminder:

```
transform = transforms.Compose([
    transforms.Resize((224, 224)),
    transforms.ToTensor(),
    transforms.Normalize((0.5, 0.5, 0.5), (0.5, 0.5, 0.5)),
])

trainset = datasets.CIFAR10(root='./data', train=True, download=True,
transform=transform)
trainloader = torch.utils.data.DataLoader(trainset, batch_size=4,
shuffle=True, num_workers=2)

testset = datasets.CIFAR10(root='./data', train=False, download=True,
transform=transform)
testloader = torch.utils.data.DataLoader(testset, batch_size=4,
shuffle=False, num_workers=2)
```

Defining Loss Function and Optimizer

Next, you'll need to define a loss function and an optimizer for your neural network. The loss function calculates the difference between the predicted output and the actual target, while the optimizer adjusts the weights of the network to minimize the loss. Here's an example:

```
criterion = nn.CrossEntropyLoss()
optimizer = torch.optim.SGD(compiled_net.parameters(), lr=0.001,
momentum=0.9)
```

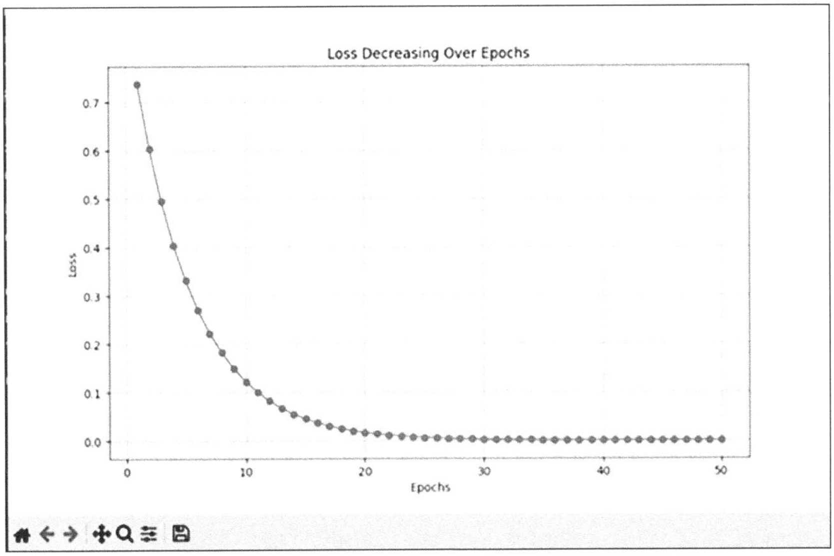

Figure 4.4: *Visualization of loss convergence*

In this example, we've chosen cross-entropy loss as our loss function and stochastic gradient descent (SGD) as our optimizer.

Training the Neural Network

Now, we're ready to train our neural network. This is done by passing the input data through the network, calculating the loss, and updating the weights using the optimizer. Here's an example of how you can train your neural network for a single epoch:

```
for epoch in range(1):  # loop over the dataset multiple times

    running_loss = 0.0
    for i, data in enumerate(trainloader, 0):
        inputs, labels = data
        optimizer.zero_grad()
        outputs = net(inputs)
        loss = criterion(outputs, labels)
        loss.backward()
        optimizer.step()
        running_loss += loss.item()
        if i % 2000 == 1999:    # print every 2000 mini-batches
            print('[%d, %5d] loss: %.3f' %
                  (epoch + 1, i + 1, running_loss / 2000))
            running_loss = 0.0

print('Finished Training')
```

Evaluating the Neural Network

Once your neural network is trained, the next step is to evaluate its performance on the test data. This is done by calculating the accuracy of the model, which is the percentage of correctly classified images. Here's an example:

```
correct = 0
total = 0
with torch.no_grad():
    for data in testloader:
        images, labels = data
        outputs = net(images)
        _, predicted = torch.max(outputs.data, 1)
        total += labels.size(0)
        correct += (predicted == labels).sum().item()

print('Accuracy of the network on the 10000 test images:
 100 * correct / total))
```

Fine-tuning and Optimization

Finally, you can fine-tune and optimize your neural network by adjusting various hyperparameters, such as the learning rate, batch size, and number of epochs. You can also experiment with different architectures, loss functions, and optimizers to find the best combination for your specific dataset.

Output and Testing on an Image

Once your model is trained, the output will be a tensor of shape (**batch_size**, **num_classes**), where **num_classes** is the number of classes in your dataset. Each row of the tensor contains the predicted scores for each class. The class with the highest score is considered the predicted class.

To test your model on a new image, you first need to load the image, preprocess it, and then pass it through the model. Here's an example of how to test your model on a single image:

```
from PIL import Image
from torchvision.transforms import ToTensor
import torchvision.transforms as transforms

# Load the image
# Change 'path/to/your/image.jpg' with actual path to image on your
system
image = Image.open('path/to/your/image.jpg').convert('RGB')
```

```
# Preprocess the image
transform = transforms.Compose([
    transforms.Resize((32, 32)),
    transforms.ToTensor(),
])
image = transform(image).unsqueeze(0)

# Pass the image through the model
output = compiled_net(image)

# Get the predicted class
_, predicted = torch.max(output.data, 1)
print('Predicted class: %s' % classes[predicted[0]])
```

***Figure 4.5:** Output of inference code from the preceding snippet*

This example assumes that the image is a color image with three channels (RGB). If your image is a grayscale image with a single channel, you may need to adjust the preprocessing steps accordingly.

Complete Training Code and Inference

```
import torch
import torchvision
import torchvision.transforms as transforms

# Set up the transform to normalize the data
transform = transforms.Compose([
    transforms.ToTensor(),
    transforms.Normalize((0.5, 0.5, 0.5), (0.5, 0.5, 0.5)),
])

# Load the CIFAR-10 dataset
trainset = torchvision.datasets.CIFAR10(root='./data', train=True, down-
load=True, transform=transform)
trainloader = torch.utils.data.DataLoader(trainset, batch_size=4, shuf-
fle=True)

testset = torchvision.datasets.CIFAR10(root='./data', train=False,
download=True, transform=transform)
testloader = torch.utils.data.DataLoader(testset, batch_size=4,
shuffle=False)

classes = ('plane', 'car', 'bird', 'cat', 'deer', 'dog', 'frog',
'horse', 'ship', 'truck')
```

```
# Define the neural network
import torch.nn as nn
import torch.nn.functional as F

class SimpleCNN(nn.Module):
    def __init__(self):
        super(Net, self).__init__()
        self.conv1 = nn.Conv2d(3, 6, 5)
        self.pool = nn.MaxPool2d(2, 2)
        self.conv2 = nn.Conv2d(6, 16, 5)
        self.fc1 = nn.Linear(16 * 5 * 5, 120)
        self.fc2 = nn.Linear(120, 84)
        self.fc3 = nn.Linear(84, 10)

    def forward(self, x):
        x = self.pool(F.relu(self.conv1(x)))
        x = self.pool(F.relu(self.conv2(x)))
        x = x.view(-1, 16 * 5 * 5)
        x = F.relu(self.fc1(x))
        x = F.relu(self.fc2(x))
        x = self.fc3(x)
        return x

net = SimpleCNN()

# Compile the model with torch.compile for PyTorch 2.0
compiled_net = torch.compile(net)

# Set up the loss function and optimizer
import torch.optim as optim

criterion = nn.CrossEntropyLoss()
optimizer = optim.SGD(compiled_net.parameters(), lr=0.001, momentum=0.9)

# Train the network
for epoch in range(5):  # Loop over the dataset multiple times
    running_loss = 0.0
    for i, data in enumerate(trainloader, 0):
        inputs, labels = data
        optimizer.zero_grad()
        outputs = compiled_net(inputs)
        loss = criterion(outputs, labels)
        loss.backward()
        optimizer.step()
        running_loss += loss.item()
        if i % 2000 == 1999:    # Print every 2000 mini-batches
```

```
            print('[%d, %5d] loss: %.3f' %
                  (epoch + 1, i + 1, running_loss / 2000))
            running_loss = 0.0

print('Finished Training')

# Test the network on the test data
correct = 0
total = 0
with torch.no_grad():
    for data in testloader:
        images, labels = data
        outputs = compiled_net(images)
        _, predicted = torch.max(outputs.data, 1)
        total += labels.size(0)
        correct += (predicted == labels).sum().item()
print('Accuracy of the network on the 10000 test images: %d %%' % (100 *
correct / total))
```

Output

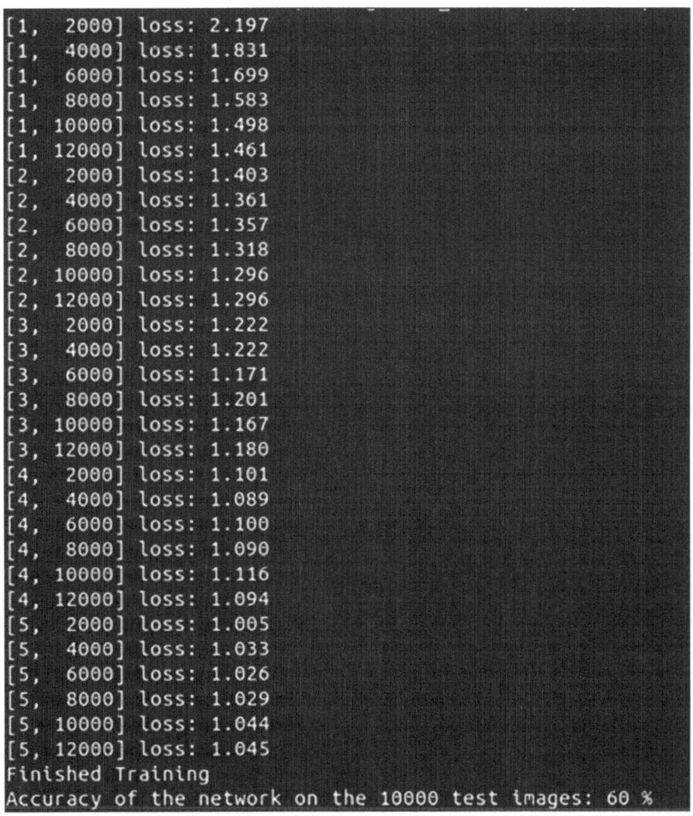

Figure 4.6: *Output of training code with accuracy after five epochs*

You can modify the architecture to see how it affects the accuracy; you can also change other parts like batch size and number of epochs to see how the loss and accuracy converge.

By following these steps, you should have a solid foundation for constructing and training your image classification model using PyTorch. Remember to experiment and fine-tune your model to achieve the best performance on your specific dataset. As always, feel free to refer back to previous sections for more detailed information on specific topics.

Evaluating Model Performance and Troubleshooting

Once your image classification model is constructed and trained, the next crucial step is to evaluate its performance and troubleshoot any issues that may arise. In this section, we'll explore different methods for assessing your model's effectiveness and ways to identify and address potential problems.

Evaluating Model Performance

A robust evaluation is essential to understand the model's accuracy and generalization ability.

Accuracy

Accuracy measures the number of correct predictions made by the model divided by the total number of predictions. It's a good starting point for evaluation.

```
correct = 0
total = 0
with torch.no_grad():
    for data in testloader:
        images, labels = data
        outputs = net(images)
        _, predicted = torch.max(outputs.data, 1)
        total += labels.size(0)
        correct += (predicted == labels).sum().item()

print('Accuracy of the network on the 10000 test images: %d %%' % (100 * correct / total))
```

Figure 4.7: Output of the accuracy calculation snippet

Confusion Matrix

A confusion matrix can help you understand which classes are often confused with each other.

```
from sklearn.metrics import confusion_matrix
import seaborn as sns
import matplotlib.pyplot as plt
y_pred = []
y_true = []
with torch.no_grad():
    for data in testloader:
        images, labels = data
        outputs = net(images)
        _, predicted = torch.max(outputs.data, 1)
        y_pred.extend(predicted.numpy())
        y_true.extend(labels.numpy())
cm = confusion_matrix(y_true, y_pred)
sns.heatmap(cm, annot=True, fmt='d')
plt.ylabel('Actual')
plt.xlabel('Predicted')
plt.show()
```

```
Confusion Matrix:
 [[599  21  86  17  17  11  16   8 156  69]
 [ 27 667  11  11   6  13  18   1  69 177]
 [ 56   8 557  54  91  81  79  18  34  22]
 [ 27   6 108 380  70 188 129  40  15  37]
 [ 30   3 140  53 507  45 146  39  26  11]
 [ 13   2 115 182  71 477  70  41  14  15]
 [  5   1  79  49  27   9 807   6   9   8]
 [ 16   3  55  49 133  97  32 568   7  40]
 [ 62  35  29  21   5   8  12   3 791  34]
 [ 30  62  15  21  11  11  14  13  63 760]]
```

Figure 4.8: *Output of confusion matrix*

Precision, Recall, and F1 Score

These metrics provide a more comprehensive evaluation of your model, especially in imbalanced datasets.

```
# Prepare for metric calculation
all_labels = np.array([])
all_preds = np.array([])
all_outputs = np.array([])
```

```
# Test the network on the test data
with torch.no_grad():
    for data in testloader:
        images, labels = data
        outputs = compiled_net(images)
        _, predicted = torch.max(outputs.data, 1)

        # Store predictions, labels and output scores for metrics
        all_labels = np.append(all_labels, labels.numpy())
        all_preds = np.append(all_preds, predicted.numpy())
        all_outputs = np.append(all_outputs, outputs.numpy())

# Calculate precision, recall, and F1 score
precision, recall, f1, _ = precision_recall_fscore_support(all_labels,
all_preds, average='weighted')
print(f' Precision: {precision:.2f}, Recall: {recall:.2f}, F1 Score:
{f1:.2f}')
```

```
Precision: 0.62, Recall: 0.61, F1 Score: 0.61
```

Figure 4.9: *Output of code snippet from calculating Precision, recall and F1 score*

ROC-AUC Curve

The Receiver Operating Characteristic - Area Under Curve (ROC-AUC) is a performance measurement for classification problems at various threshold settings. The higher the AUC, the better the model is at distinguishing between the positive and negative classes.

By carefully evaluating your model's performance and systematically addressing any issues that arise, you'll be well on your way to developing a highly effective image classification model. Remember that developing machine learning models is an iterative process, and continuous monitoring and tweaking are necessary to achieve the best results.

```
# Prepare for metric calculation
all_labels = np.array([])
all_outputs = np.array([])
# Test the network on the test data
with torch.no_grad():
    for data in testloader:
        images, labels = data
        outputs = compiled_net(images)
        _, predicted = torch.max(outputs.data, 1)

        # Store predictions, labels and output scores for metrics
        all_labels = np.append(all_labels, labels.numpy())
```

```
        all_outputs = np.append(all_outputs, outputs.numpy())

# One-hot encode labels for ROC-AUC
one_hot_labels = np.eye(10)[all_labels.astype(int)]
roc_auc = roc_auc_score(one_hot_labels, all_outputs.reshape(-1, 10),
multi_class='ovr')
print(f'ROC-AUC: {roc_auc:.2f}')
# Plot ROC curve for each class
fpr = dict()
tpr = dict()
roc_auc = dict()
for i in range(10):
    fpr[i], tpr[i], _ = roc_curve(one_hot_labels[:, i], all_outputs.
reshape(-1, 10)[:, i])
    roc_auc[i] = auc(fpr[i], tpr[i])

plt.figure()
for i in range(10):
    plt.plot(fpr[i], tpr[i], label=f'ROC curve of class {classes[i]}
(area = {roc_auc[i]:.2f})')
plt.plot([0, 1], [0, 1], 'k--')
plt.xlim([0.0, 1.0])
plt.ylim([0.0, 1.05])
plt.xlabel('False Positive Rate')
plt.ylabel('True Positive Rate')
plt.title('ROC-AUC curve per class')
plt.legend(loc="lower right")
plt.show()
```

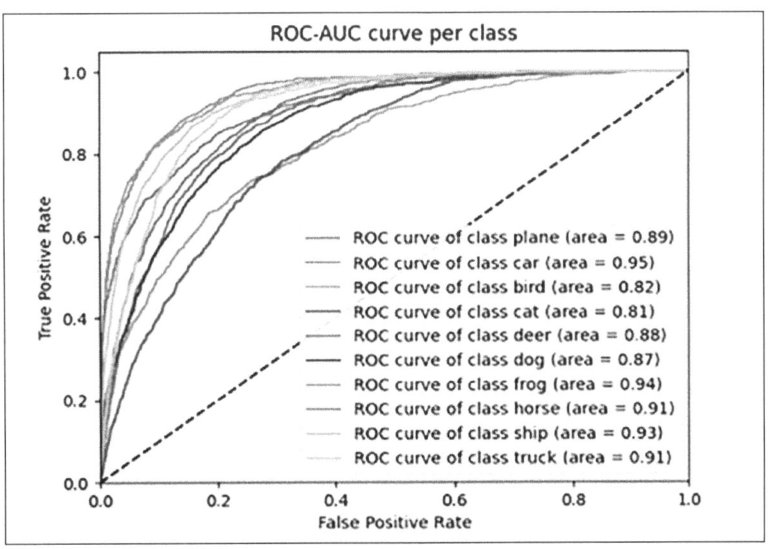

Figure 4.10: *ROC-AUC curve from the trained model*

Conclusion

In this chapter, we've explored the fascinating world of artificial neural networks and their implementation in PyTorch, providing a solid foundation in the principles and practices of constructing, training, and evaluating a basic image classification model. With the knowledge and skills gained, you are well-equipped to take on more complex challenges in the realm of computer vision.

As we wrap up our journey through the basics of neural networks, it's time to venture deeper into the world of Convolutional Neural Networks (CNNs), a class of deep neural networks that have proven to be incredibly effective for analyzing visual imagery. In the upcoming chapter, *Chapter 5, Diving Deep into Convolutional Neural Networks* (CNNs), we will delve into the underlying theory, structure, and implementation of CNNs, exploring how they are uniquely suited to handle image data. We'll also cover the best practices for building and training CNNs, providing you with the knowledge and tools needed to take your computer vision models to the next level.

We'll take a closer look at the architecture of CNNs and learn how to construct and train these powerful models using PyTorch. By the end of the next chapter, you'll have a comprehensive understanding of CNNs and be equipped with the practical skills to apply them to real-world computer vision problems. Moreover, we will see how we can improve the model we created in this chapter, aiming for higher accuracy and better performance. So, let's get ready to dive deep and unlock the full potential of convolutional neural networks in the fascinating world of computer vision!

CHAPTER 5

Diving Deep into Convolutional Neural Networks (CNNs)

Introduction

We have established the foundation required to delve further into the intriguing field of Convolutional Neural Networks (CNNs) in the preceding chapters. You should now be well-versed in the concepts of artificial neural networks, handling and processing picture data, and the tools and capabilities available in PyTorch for constructing neural networks. We may now investigate Convolutional Neural Networks (CNNs), a class of deep neural networks that excel at processing visual imagery since we have these foundations in place.

Convolutional Neural Networks (CNNs) are a crucial component in the field of computer vision, which seeks to enable computers to interpret and understand the visual world. CNNs are designed to automatically and adaptively learn spatial hierarchies of features from input images. These networks have been the driving force behind the success of numerous real-world applications, such as image classification, object detection, and image generation.

Structure

In this chapter, the following topics will be covered:

- Understanding the Layers of a CNN
- Deep Dive into Filters and Kernels
- Advanced CNN Architectures

Understanding the Layers of a CNN

Convolutional Neural Networks (CNNs) are a class of deep learning models specifically designed to process and interpret visual data. CNNs are composed of several layers; each layer plays a crucial role in extracting features and making predictions. In this chapter, we will explore each of these layers in detail, including their functions, how they are implemented in PyTorch, and real-world examples of their usage.

Convolutional Layer

The convolutional layer is the core building block of a CNN. It applies a series of filters to the input image to create feature maps that highlight specific features in the image, such as edges or textures.

Theory

The convolutional layer uses a small, square filter that slides over the input image. At each position, the filter performs a dot product operation with the underlying image data, producing a single value representing the presence of a specific feature.

PyTorch Implementation

```
conv_layer = nn.Conv2d(in_channels=1, out_channels=32, kernel_size=3,
stride=1, padding=1)
```

Explanation

The **`nn.Conv2d`** function creates a 2D convolutional layer. This layer filters the input image to create feature maps that highlight specific features like edges, corners, and textures.

- **`in_channels`**: Number of input channels (or depth). For a grayscale image, this would be 1; for a color image, this would be 3.
- **`out_channels`**: Number of output channels. This also represents the number of filters the layer will learn.
- **`kernel_size`**: Size of the filter. It can be a single number or a tuple (height, width).
- **`stride`**: The step size the filter takes while moving across the image. It can be a single number or a tuple (height, width).
- **`padding`**: Number of pixels added to the border of the input image. It helps the filter cover the edges of the image.

Example

In an image classification task, a convolutional layer might be used to detect edges in an image, which are then used to identify the object in the image.

Activation Functions

Activation functions introduce non-linearity to the model, allowing the network to learn complex patterns.

Theory

An activation function takes the output of a neuron and transforms it based on a specific rule. Common activation functions include ReLU (Rectified Linear Unit) and Sigmoid.

PyTorch Implementation

```
relu = nn.ReLU()
```

Explanation

The **`nn.ReLU`** function applies the rectified linear unit activation function, which replaces all negative values in the input with zero, allowing the network to learn complex patterns.

Example

In a face recognition task, an activation function might be used to highlight the features that distinguish one person's face from another.

Pooling Layer

The pooling layer reduces the spatial dimensions of the feature maps, thus reducing the computational load for the network.

Theory

The pooling layer takes small regions of the feature map and performs a down-sampling operation, such as taking the maximum or average value.

PyTorch Implementation

```
pool = nn.MaxPool2d(kernel_size=2, stride=2, padding=0)
```

Explanation

The **nn.MaxPool2d** function performs max pooling, which down-samples the input by taking the maximum value in a filter of a specific size and stride.

- **kernel_size:** Size of the filter.
- **stride:** The step size the filter takes while moving across the image.
- **padding:** Number of pixels added to the border of the input image.

Example

In an object detection task, a pooling layer might be used to reduce the size of the feature maps, making it easier to detect objects in different positions of the image.

Fully Connected Layer

The fully connected layer is used to make predictions based on the features extracted by the convolutional layers.

Theory

The fully connected layer takes the output of the previous layers and connects each neuron to every neuron in the next layer. The output is then used to make predictions.

PyTorch Implementation

```
fc = nn.Linear(in_features=32 * 14 * 14, out_features=10)
```

Explanation

The **nn.Linear** function creates a fully connected layer that connects each neuron to every neuron in the next layer.

- **in_features:** Number of input features.
- **out_features:** Number of output features.

Example

In a handwritten digit recognition task, a fully connected layer might be used to classify the digit based on the features extracted by the convolutional layers.

Batch Normalization

Batch normalization is a technique used to improve the training of neural networks.

Theory

Batch normalization normalizes the output of each layer to have a mean of 0 and a standard deviation of 1, which helps to speed up training and reduce the sensitivity to the initial weights.

PyTorch Implementation

```
batch_norm = nn.BatchNorm2d(num_features=32)
```

Explanation

The **`nn.BatchNorm2d`** function normalizes the input to have a mean of 0 and a standard deviation of 1. It helps to speed up training and reduces sensitivity to initial weights.

- **`num_features`:** Number of features in the input.

Example

In an image segmentation task, batch normalization might be used to normalize the output of each layer.

Dropout

Dropout is a regularization technique used to prevent overfitting in neural networks.

Theory

Dropout randomly drops out a proportion of the neurons during training, which helps to prevent the model from relying too heavily on any one feature.

PyTorch Implementation

```
dropout = nn.Dropout(p=0.5)
```

Explanation

The **`nn.Dropout`** function randomly drops out a proportion of neurons during training to prevent overfitting.

- **`p`:** Probability of dropping out a neuron. It is a value between 0 and 1, where 0 means no dropout and 1 means all neurons are dropped out. In the preceding examples, `p=0.5` means 50% probability of dropout.

Example

In an image classification task, dropout might be used to prevent overfitting to the training data.

In conclusion, the layers of a CNN play a crucial role in extracting features and making predictions. Each layer has a specific function and is implemented using different tools and features in PyTorch. By understanding the theory behind each layer and seeing how they are implemented in PyTorch, you can gain a deeper understanding of how CNNs work and how to use them effectively in your computer vision projects.

Diving Deep into Filters and Kernels

Filters and kernels are integral to the functioning of Convolutional Neural Networks (CNNs). They are small, square-shaped matrices that move across the input data to extract features, such as edges, textures, and patterns. By doing so, filters help the network recognize complex patterns in the data.

Filters and CNNs

A filter or kernel convolves across the input data to produce a transformed version known as the feature map. This process helps to highlight specific features in the data, such as edges, corners, or textures. The process of convolution involves the dot product between the filter and the overlapping section of the input data.

PyTorch Implementation

```
import torch
import torch.nn as nn

# Define a convolutional layer with a single filter of size 3x3
conv_layer = nn.Conv2d(in_channels=1, out_channels=1, kernel_size=3,
stride=1, padding=1)
```

Here, **`nn.Conv2d`** is a 2D convolutional layer in PyTorch. The parameters **`in_channels`** and **`out_channels`** represent the depth of the filter and the number of filters respectively. The **`kernel_size`** parameter specifies the height and width of the filter, and **`stride`** and **`padding`** control the step size and the amount of zero-padding applied to the input data.

Selecting the Right Size and Number of Filters

Choosing the right filter size and number is crucial for capturing the right features from the data. Small filters like **`3x3`** or **`5x5`** can capture fine-grained details, while larger filters like **`7x7`** or **`11x11`** capture more abstract features. The number of filters determines the number of unique features the network can extract.

PyTorch Implementation

```
# Define a convolutional layer with multiple filters of size 3x3
conv_layer = nn.Conv2d(in_channels=1, out_channels=32, kernel_size=3,
stride=1, padding=1)
```

This layer will have 32 filters, each of size 3x3, meaning the network can detect 32 unique features from the input data.

Code Examples in PyTorch

Filters are defined in the **nn.Conv2d** function in PyTorch. Let's go through some examples to understand how filters are used in real-world models.

Example 1: Single Filter of Size 3x3

```
conv_layer = nn.Conv2d(in_channels=1, out_channels=1, kernel_size=3,
stride=1, padding=1)
```

This single filter will produce one feature map highlighting a specific feature in the data.

Example 2: Multiple Filters of Size 3x3

```
conv_layer = nn.Conv2d(in_channels=1, out_channels=32, kernel_size=3,
stride=1, padding=1)
```

Here, **32** filters will produce 32 feature maps, each highlighting a different feature in the data.

Example 3: Using Filters in a Real Model

```
class MyModel(nn.Module):
    def __init__(self):
        super(MyModel, self).__init__()
        self.conv1 = nn.Conv2d(in_channels=1, out_channels=32, kernel_
size=3, stride=1, padding=1)
        self.conv2 = nn.Conv2d(in_channels=32, out_channels=64, kernel_
size=3, stride=1, padding=1)
        self.fc = nn.Linear(64*28*28, 10)

    def forward(self, x):
        x = self.conv1(x)
        x = self.conv2(x)
        x = x.view(x.size(0), -1)
        x = self.fc(x)
        return x
```

In this example, the model has two convolutional layers. The first layer has 32 filters of size 3x3, and the second layer has 64 filters of size 3x3. The output from the second layer is flattened and passed through a fully connected layer to produce the final output.

In summary, filters and kernels are essential components of CNNs that help the network recognize patterns in the data. The size and number of filters should be carefully selected based on the specific features you want to extract from the data. PyTorch provides a convenient way to define filters using the `nn.Conv2d` function and real-world models can have multiple convolutional layers with varying numbers of filters to extract a wide range of features.

Advanced CNN Architectures

In this chapter, we'll explore some popular Convolutional Neural Networks (CNN) architectures that have revolutionized the field of computer vision. We will delve deep into the workings of VGG and ResNet, two of the most influential CNN architectures. By understanding these architectures, you'll be equipped to make informed decisions when choosing a network for your computer vision project.

Overview of Popular CNN Architectures

Here, we will discuss the two architectures and understand them in detail.

VGG (Visual Geometry Group) Network

VGG, developed by the Visual Geometry Group at Oxford, was a breakthrough in demonstrating that depth is a critical component for achieving good performance in CNNs. It consists of 16 to 19 weight layers and is known for its simplicity and homogeneity, with all convolutional layers using small 3x3 filters.

Residual Network (ResNet)

ResNet, introduced by Microsoft Research, was revolutionary for using skip connections or shortcuts to jump over some layers. This architecture addresses the vanishing gradient problem and allows the training of extremely deep networks. Standard ResNets consist of 50, 101, or 152 layers.

Comparing Different Architectures

Comparing the architectures of CNNs is an essential step in understanding the evolution and innovation in the field of deep learning. It also helps in selecting the right architecture for your specific task.

VGG (Visual Graphics Group) Network

- VGG Network is known for its simplicity and depth. It uses 3x3 convolutional layers stacked on each other in increasing depth.
- It does not focus on reducing the spatial dimensions of the image too soon.
- It is easy to implement and understand.

ResNet (Residual Network)

- ResNet introduced the concept of skip connections or shortcut connections.
- These connections allow the output of one layer to be used as input to another layer, skipping some intermediate layers.
- This helps to solve the vanishing gradient problem and enables the training of very deep networks (even 1000 layers deep).
- ResNet is more complex than VGG but has significantly improved performance on various tasks.

Key Differences

- **Depth:** VGG networks are relatively shallower compared to ResNet. ResNet can go up to 152 layers, while VGG has a maximum of 19 layers.
- **Parameters:** VGG has more parameters compared to ResNet due to its fully connected layers. ResNet uses global average pooling which significantly reduces the number of parameters.
- **Skip Connections:** ResNet uses skip connections which helps to train very deep networks. VGG does not have this feature.
- **Training Time:** Training a VGG network is generally faster than training a ResNet, but the performance gain with ResNet is significant.
- **Performance:** ResNet performs better in various tasks and competitions compared to VGG.

VGG or ResNet

- The choice between VGG and ResNet depends on your specific task and the computational resources available.
- If you are working on a simple task and want a straightforward model, then VGG might be the right choice.
- If you need a high-performance model and have the resources to train a deep network, then ResNet is the way to go. It is also worth exploring other architectures and recent innovations in the field of deep learning to select the best model for your task.

Implementing Popular Architectures in PyTorch

Now, let's look at the different architectures.

VGG in PyTorch

```
import torch
import torch.nn as nn

class VGG(nn.Module):
    def __init__(self, num_classes=1000):
        super(VGG, self).__init__()
        self.features = nn.Sequential(
            # 1st block
            nn.Conv2d(3, 64, kernel_size=3, padding=1),
            nn.ReLU(inplace=True),
            nn.Conv2d(64, 64, kernel_size=3, padding=1),
            nn.ReLU(inplace=True),
            nn.MaxPool2d(kernel_size=2, stride=2),
            # 2nd block
            nn.Conv2d(64, 128, kernel_size=3, padding=1),
            nn.ReLU(inplace=True),
            nn.Conv2d(128, 128, kernel_size=3, padding=1),
            nn.ReLU(inplace=True),
            nn.MaxPool2d(kernel_size=2, stride=2),
            # 3rd block
            nn.Conv2d(128, 256, kernel_size=3, padding=1),
            nn.ReLU(inplace=True),
            nn.Conv2d(256, 256, kernel_size=3, padding=1),
            nn.ReLU(inplace=True),
            nn.Conv2d(256, 256, kernel_size=3, padding=1),
            nn.ReLU(inplace=True),
            nn.MaxPool2d(kernel_size=2, stride=2),
            # 4th block
            nn.Conv2d(256, 512, kernel_size=3, padding=1),
            nn.ReLU(inplace=True),
            nn.Conv2d(512, 512, kernel_size=3, padding=1),
            nn.ReLU(inplace=True),
            nn.Conv2d(512, 512, kernel_size=3, padding=1),
            nn.ReLU(inplace=True),
            nn.MaxPool2d(kernel_size=2, stride=2),
            # 5th block
            nn.Conv2d(512, 512, kernel_size=3, padding=1),
            nn.ReLU(inplace=True),
```

```
            nn.Conv2d(512, 512, kernel_size=3, padding=1),
            nn.ReLU(inplace=True),
            nn.Conv2d(512, 512, kernel_size=3, padding=1),
            nn.ReLU(inplace=True),
            nn.MaxPool2d(kernel_size=2, stride=2),
        )
        self.classifier = nn.Sequential(
            nn.Linear(512 * 7 * 7, 4096),
            nn.ReLU(inplace=True),
            nn.Dropout(),
            nn.Linear(4096, 4096),
            nn.ReLU(inplace=True),
            nn.Dropout(),
            nn.Linear(4096, num_classes),
        )

    def forward(self, x):
        x = self.features(x)
        x = x.view(x.size(0), -1)
        x = self.classifier(x)
        return x
```

VGG in PyTorch: Detailed Explanation

Let us understand the different building blocks of the VGG network implemented with PyTorch.

nn.Conv2d

The **nn.Conv2d** function in PyTorch is used to perform the convolution operation, which is the core of a convolutional layer.

- **in_channels**: Number of channels in the input image.
- **out_channels**: Number of filters (kernels).
- **kernel_size**: Size of each filter.
- **Stride**: The step size while sliding the filter across the image.
- **Padding**:The number of pixels added to the border of the image.

nn.ReLU

ReLU (Rectified Linear Unit) is an activation function that outputs the input for positive values and zero for negative values.

- **Inplace**: If set to True, it modifies the input directly and saves memory.

nn.MaxPool2d

Max pooling is a pooling operation that selects the maximum value from a set of values within a filter.

- **kernel_size**: Size of the pooling filter.
- **Stride**: Step size while sliding the filter.

ResNet in PyTorch

```
import torch
import torch.nn as nn

class ResidualBlock(nn.Module):
    def __init__(self, in_channels, out_channels, stride=1, downsample=-
None):
        super(ResidualBlock, self).__init__()
        self.conv1 = nn.Conv2d(in_channels, out_channels, kernel_size=3,
stride=stride, padding=1)
        self.bn1 = nn.BatchNorm2d(out_channels)
        self.relu = nn.ReLU(inplace=True)
        self.conv2 = nn.Conv2d(out_channels, out_channels, kernel_
size=3, stride=1, padding=1)
        self.bn2 = nn.BatchNorm2d(out_channels)
        self.downsample = downsample

    def forward(self, x):
        residual = x
        if self.downsample is not None:
            residual = self.downsample(x)
        out = self.conv1(x)
        out = self.bn1(out)
        out = self.relu(out)
        out = self.conv2(out)
        out = self.bn2(out)
        out += residual
        out = self.relu(out)
        return out

class ResNet(nn.Module):
    def __init__(self):
        super(ResNet, self).__init__()
        self.in_channels = 64
        self.conv1 = nn.Conv2d(3, 64, kernel_size=7, stride=2, pad-
ding=3)
        self.bn1 = nn.BatchNorm2d(64)
        self.relu = nn.ReLU(inplace=True)
        self.maxpool = nn.MaxPool2d(kernel_size=3, stride=2, padding=1)
        self.layer1 = self.make_layer(64, 2)
        self.layer2 = self.make_layer(128, 2, 2)
        self.layer3 = self.make_layer(256, 2, 2)
```

```
        self.layer4 = self.make_layer(512, 2, 2)
        self.avgpool = nn.AdaptiveAvgPool2d((1, 1))
        self.fc = nn.Linear(512, 10)

    def make_layer(self, out_channels, blocks, stride=1):
        downsample = None
        if stride != 1 or self.in_channels != out_channels:
            downsample = nn.Sequential(
                nn.Conv2d(self.in_channels, out_channels, kernel_size=1,
stride=stride),
                nn.BatchNorm2d(out_channels),
            )
        layers = []
        layers.append(ResidualBlock(self.in_channels, out_channels,
stride, downsample))
        self.in_channels = out_channels
        for _ in range(1, blocks):
            layers.append(ResidualBlock(out_channels, out_channels))
        return nn.Sequential(*layers)

    def forward(self, x):
        out = self.conv1(x)
        out = self.bn1(out)
        out = self.relu(out)
        out = self.maxpool(out)
        out = self.layer1(out)
        out = self.layer2(out)
        out = self.layer3(out)
        out = self.layer4(out)
        out = self.avgpool(out)
        out = out.view(out.size(0), -1)
        out = self.fc(out)
        return out
```

ResNet in PyTorch: Detailed Explanation

Let us understand the different building blocks of the ResNet network implemented with PyTorch.

Residual Block

A residual block is the building block of a ResNet network, which includes a skip connection that allows the input to skip some layers and be added to the output.

- **`in_channels`**: Number of channels in the input image.
- **`out_channels`**: Number of filters in the convolutional layers.
- **`Stride`**: Step size for the convolutional layers.

- **Downsample**: A downsample operation to match the dimensions of the input and output.

nn.AdaptiveAvgPool2d

Adaptive average pooling is a pooling operation that performs average pooling to generate an output of a specified size.

- **(1, 1)**: The target output size.

By understanding these functions and components, you can gain insights into how these popular architectures work and how they can be customized for your specific needs.

Regularization and Optimization in CNNs

Overfitting occurs when a model learns the training data too well, capturing noise along with the underlying pattern, and performs poorly on new, unseen data. In the context of CNNs, this can happen when the network is too complex relative to the amount and complexity of the training data. To mitigate overfitting in CNNs:

Data Augmentation

Increase the size and diversity of the training dataset by applying transformations, such as rotation, flipping, cropping, and more, to the images. We will learn about data augmentations in detail.

```
from torchvision.transforms import Compose, RandomHorizontalFlip,
RandomRotation

transforms = Compose([
    RandomHorizontalFlip(),
    RandomRotation(10),
])
```

Regularization

Add regularization terms such as L1 or L2 to the loss function to penalize large weights.

```
import torch.nn as nn
model = nn.Sequential(
    nn.Conv2d(in_channels=1, out_channels=32, kernel_size=3),
    nn.ReLU(),
    nn.MaxPool2d(kernel_size=2),
    nn.Flatten(),
    nn.Linear(32 * 14 * 14, 10),
)
criterion = nn.CrossEntropyLoss() + 0.01 * torch.norm(model.
parameters(), p=2)
```

Dropout

Randomly set a fraction of input units to 0 at each update during training, which helps prevent overfitting.

```
nn.Dropout(p=0.5)
```

Early Stopping

Stop training once the validation loss starts to increase to prevent overfitting.

Hyperparameter Tuning and Grid Search

Hyperparameter tuning means searching for the optimal set of hyperparameters that maximizes the model's performance. Grid search is a technique to perform hyperparameter tuning by exhaustively trying every combination of predefined hyperparameter values.

```
from sklearn.model_selection import GridSearchCV
from skorch import NeuralNetClassifier

params = {
    'lr': [0.01, 0.001],
    'max_epochs': [10, 20],
}
net = NeuralNetClassifier(model, criterion=criterion, optimizer=torch.
optim.Adam)
gs = GridSearchCV(net, params, refit=False, cv=3, scoring='accuracy')
gs.fit(X_train, y_train)
```

Transfer Learning and Fine-tuning

Transfer learning is a technique where a pre-trained model (typically on a large and general dataset) is used as a starting point for a new task. Fine-tuning refers to updating the pre-trained model's weights based on the new task's data.

```
from torchvision import models

# Load pre-trained model
model = models.resnet18(pretrained=True)

# Fine-tune the last layer
for param in model.parameters():
    param.requires_grad = False
model.fc = nn.Linear(model.fc.in_features, num_classes)
```

Practical Tips for Improving Model Performance

Some of the tips are:

- **Learning Rate Schedule:** Adjust the learning rate during training, typically reducing it as the training progresses.

  ```
  from torch.optim.lr_scheduler import StepLR
  scheduler = StepLR(optimizer, step_size=30, gamma=0.1)
  ```

- **Batch Normalization:** Use batch normalization to normalize the input layer by adjusting and scaling the activations.

  ```
  nn.BatchNorm2d(num_features)
  ```

- **Weight Initialization:** Properly initialize the weights of the network to prevent vanishing or exploding gradients.

  ```
  nn.init.xavier_uniform_(layer.weight)
  ```

- **Cross-Validation:** Use cross-validation to assess how the model's performance generalizes across different subsets of the dataset.

  ```
  from sklearn.model_selection import cross_val_score
  cross_val_score(net, X_train, y_train, cv=3)
  ```

Conclusion

In conclusion, understanding the various architectures of Convolutional Neural Networks is crucial for any deep learning practitioner. From the simple yet effective VGG networks to the more complex and deeper ResNet architectures, each has its own advantages and use cases. By learning how to implement these networks in PyTorch, we have equipped ourselves with the knowledge to tackle several computer vision tasks.

As we move forward, we must also consider the quality and nature of the data that we feed into our models. The chapter 6, *Data Augmentation and Preprocessing for Vision Tasks*, will delve into essential techniques to improve our model's performance by transforming and pre-processing our dataset. In this chapter, we will explore the various data augmentation techniques specific to vision tasks and understand how to apply these techniques using PyTorch. Additionally, we will examine the impact of data augmentation on model performance and highlight best practices to ensure our data is well-prepared for training high-performing models.

Thus, the journey from understanding the intricacies of neural network architectures to mastering data augmentation and preprocessing will further enhance our skills and knowledge in the field of computer vision. By the end of the next chapter, we will be well-equipped to handle a myriad of challenges presented by diverse datasets and one step closer to developing robust and effective computer vision models using PyTorch

CHAPTER 6
Data Augmentation and Preprocessing for Vision Tasks

Introduction

Data augmentation and preprocessing are essential techniques in the field of computer vision and machine learning. They play a crucial role in enhancing the performance of models by providing them with better, varied, and cleaner data. By augmenting and preprocessing data, we can ensure that models are trained on high-quality data that accurately represents the problem at hand, leading to improved model accuracy and generalization.

Data augmentation is the process of artificially increasing the size of your dataset by creating new data points through various transformations of the existing data. In the context of computer vision, this can include flipping, rotating, zooming, and color adjustments, among other transformations. By augmenting data, we can provide the model with more varied examples, helping it learn to recognize objects or patterns regardless of their orientation, size, or color. This ultimately leads to a more robust and accurate model.

For instance, consider a model trained to recognize cats in images. If the dataset only contains images of cats in a specific orientation, the model may struggle to recognize cats in different orientations. However, by augmenting the data to include images of cats in various orientations, we can help the model learn to recognize cats regardless of their orientation.

Data preprocessing, on the other hand, involves cleaning and transforming raw data into a format that can be easily and effectively used by machine learning models. In computer vision, this can include normalizing pixel values, resizing images, and handling missing data, among other transformations. By preprocessing data, we can ensure that the model receives data in a consistent format, improving its ability to learn from the data.

For example, consider a dataset of images with different sizes. If the images are not resized to a consistent size, the model may struggle to learn from them, as the size of the objects in the images will vary. By resizing the images to a consistent size, we can help the model learn to recognize objects regardless of their size in the image.

The importance of data augmentation and preprocessing in improving model performance cannot be overstated. By providing the model with high-quality, varied data, we can help it learn to recognize patterns and objects more accurately, leading to better performance. Furthermore, by ensuring that the data is in a consistent format, we can prevent issues that may arise from inconsistencies in the data, further improving model performance.

Structure

In this chapter, the following topics will be covered:

- Understanding Data Preprocessing
- Data Augmentation Techniques for Vision Tasks
- Applying Data Preprocessing and Augmentation in PyTorch
- Impact of Data Augmentation on Model Performance
- Best Practices for Data Augmentation and Preprocessing

Understanding Data Preprocessing

Data preprocessing is a fundamental step in the data preparation process for machine learning models. It involves cleaning, transforming, and organizing raw data into a structured and usable format. The main objective of data preprocessing is to enhance the quality of the data, making it more suitable for feeding into machine learning algorithms. This helps improve the model's performance, leading to more accurate predictions and insights.

Data Preprocessing

Data preprocessing is the process of preparing and cleaning data to make it suitable for a machine-learning model. This involves a range of activities, such as handling missing values, normalizing data, and converting categorical data into a format that can be understood by the algorithms. The primary goal of data preprocessing is to improve the quality and reliability of the data, thereby enhancing the performance of the machine learning models.

Definition and Purpose

- **Definition:** Data preprocessing is the technique of cleaning and organizing raw data to make it suitable for a machine learning model.
- **Purpose:** The main purpose of data preprocessing is to improve the quality of data, thereby enhancing the performance and accuracy of machine learning models.

Types of Data Preprocessing

Data preprocessing encompasses a variety of techniques and methods, each serving a specific purpose. Here are some of the most common types of data preprocessing:

- **Cleaning Data:** Cleaning data involves handling missing values, outliers, and errors in the dataset. This ensures that the data is accurate and reliable.

Example in PyTorch:

```
import pandas as pd

# Load dataset
data = pd.read_csv('dataset.csv')

# Handle missing values
data.fillna(0, inplace=True)

# Handle outliers
data = data[(data['value'] > lower_bound) & (data['value'] < upper_
bound)]
```

- **Normalization and Standardization:**

Normalization and standardization are techniques used to scale features so that they are in a similar range, which can improve a model's performance by preventing large values from disproportionately affecting training. Although often used interchangeably, these techniques differ in their approach and impact.

  - **Normalization:** This technique scales the data to a fixed range, typically `[0, 1]` or `[-1, 1]`. Normalization is useful when you need to constrain values within a specific boundary, which is common for inputs to neural networks.
  - **Standardization:** This technique scales data to have a mean of 0 and a standard deviation of 1, transforming it to a standard normal distribution. Standardization is preferred when your data contains outliers or follows a Gaussian distribution, as it centers the data, which can stabilize and accelerate training.

Example in PyTorch:

```
from sklearn.preprocessing import StandardScaler

# Load dataset
data = pd.read_csv('dataset.csv')

# Standardize features
scaler = StandardScaler()
data_scaled = scaler.fit_transform(data)
```

- **Handling Missing Data:**

Handling missing data is essential as missing values can affect the performance of the machine learning model. Common techniques include imputation and removal of missing values.

Example in PyTorch:

```
# Handle missing values
data.fillna(method='ffill', inplace=True)
```

- **Feature Engineering:**

Feature engineering involves creating new features from the existing data to enhance the model's performance. This can include creating polynomial features, interaction features, and more.

Example in PyTorch:

```
# Create polynomial features
from sklearn.preprocessing import PolynomialFeatures

poly = PolynomialFeatures(degree=2)
data_poly = poly.fit_transform(data)
```

Importance in Computer Vision

In computer vision, data preprocessing is crucial as it helps improve the quality of image data. Common preprocessing techniques in computer vision include image resizing, normalization, and data augmentation. These techniques help ensure that the model receives consistent and high-quality data, leading to better performance.

Example in PyTorch:

```
from torchvision import transforms
# Define transformations
transform = transforms.Compose([
    transforms.Resize((256, 256)),
    transforms.ToTensor(),
    transforms.Normalize((0.5, 0.5, 0.5), (0.5, 0.5, 0.5)),
```

```
])

# Load dataset and apply transformations
dataset = datasets.ImageFolder(root='data', transform=transform)
```

Tools and Libraries

There are various tools and libraries available for data preprocessing in Python. Some of the most popular ones include:

- **Pandas**: A powerful data manipulation library that provides functions for cleaning and organizing data.
- **Scikit-learn**: A machine learning library that offers functions for normalization, standardization, and other preprocessing techniques.
- **OpenCV**: A library that provides functions for image processing, including resizing, cropping, and more.
- **PyTorch**: A deep learning library that includes functions for transforming image data, such as normalization and data augmentation.

By utilizing these tools and libraries, you can streamline the data preprocessing process and improve the performance of your machine-learning models. We will use PyTorch for all the preprocessing tasks.

Data Augmentation Techniques for Vision Tasks

Data augmentation is a technique in which we create new training samples by applying various transformations to the original images, such as rotating, flipping, and changing the brightness. This helps in improving the performance and accuracy of the model by providing more diverse training data.

- **Definition:** Data augmentation is a process of creating new training samples from the original dataset by applying different types of transformations to the images.
- **Purpose:** The main purpose of data augmentation is to increase the diversity of the training dataset, which helps in improving the performance and accuracy of the model.

Transforms and Compose in PyTorch

In PyTorch, data augmentation can be performed using the transforms module from torchvision. The transforms module provides a variety of transformation functions that can be chained together using **transforms.Compose** to create a pipeline of transformations to be applied to the images.

```
from torchvision import transforms

transform_pipeline = transforms.Compose([
    transforms.RandomHorizontalFlip(),
    transforms.ToTensor(),
])
```

Here, **transforms.Compose** takes a list of transformation functions and chains them together. In this example, the image will first be flipped horizontally with a 50% probability and then converted to a tensor.

List of Augmentations Possible in PyTorch

There are many augmentations possible in PyTorch for computer vision tasks; let's walk through some of those:

RandomHorizontalFlip

```
transforms.RandomHorizontalFlip(p=0.5)
```

Flips the image horizontally with a given probability.

- **p:** Probability of the image being flipped.

RandomVerticalFlip

```
transforms.RandomVerticalFlip(p=0.5)
```

Flips the image vertically with a given probability.

- **p:** Probability of the image being flipped.

ColorJitter

```
transforms.ColorJitter(brightness=0, contrast=0, saturation=0, hue=0)
```

Randomly changes the brightness, contrast, saturation, and hue of an image as listed here:

- **brightness:** The factor by which to jitter brightness.
- **contrast:** The factor by which to jitter contrast.
- **saturation:** The factor by which to jitter saturation.
- **hue:** The factor by which to jitter hue.

RandomRotation

```
transforms.RandomRotation(degrees, resample=False, expand=False, center=None, fill=None)
```

Rotates the image by a random angle as listed here:

- **degrees**: Range of degrees to select from.
- **resample**: An optional resampling filter.
- **expand**: Optional expansion flag.
- **center**: Optional center of rotation.
- **fill**: Pixel fill value for the area outside the rotated image.

RandomResizedCrop

```
transforms.RandomResizedCrop(size, scale=(0.08, 1.0), ratio=(3. / 4., 4. / 3.), interpolation=2)
```

Crops the given image to a random size and aspect ratio as listed here:

- **size**: The expected output size of each edge.
- **scale**: Range of size of the origin size cropped.
- **ratio**: Range of aspect ratio of the origin aspect ratio cropped.
- **interpolation**: Desired interpolation.

RandomAffine

```
transforms.RandomAffine(degrees, translate=None, scale=None, shear=None, resample=False, fillcolor=0)
```

Applies random affine transformations to the image as listed here:

- **degrees**: Range of degrees to select from for rotation.
- **translate**: Tuple of maximum absolute fraction for horizontal and vertical translations.
- **scale**: Scaling factor interval.
- **shear**: Range of degrees to select from for shear.
- **resample**: An optional resampling filter.
- **fillcolor**: Pixel fill value for the area outside the transformed image.

GaussianBlur

```
transforms.GaussianBlur(kernel_size, sigma=(0.1, 2.0))
```

Blurs the image with a Gaussian filter as follows:

- **kernel_size:** Size of the Gaussian kernel.
- **sigma:** Standard deviation of the Gaussian kernel.

RandomCrop

```
transforms.RandomCrop(size, padding=None, pad_if_needed=False, fill=0,
padding_mode='constant')
```

Crops the given image at a random location in the following ways:

- **size:** Desired output size of the crop.
- **padding:** Optional padding on each border of the image.
- **pad_if_needed:** If True, pad the image if smaller than the desired size.
- **fill:** Pixel fill value for constant fill.
- **padding_mode:** Type of padding. Should be either '**constant**', '**edge**', '**reflect**', '**symmetric**'.

RandomErasing

```
transforms.RandomErasing(p=0.5, scale=(0.02, 0.33), ratio=(0.3, 3.3),
value=0, inplace=False)
```

Randomly erases a rectangle region in an image as follows:

- **p:** Probability that the Random Erasing operation will be performed.
- **scale:** Range of proportion of erased area against input image.
- **ratio:** Range of aspect ratio of erased area.
- **value:** Erasing value.
- **inplace:** If True, the transform will be in place.

RandomPerspective

```
transforms.RandomPerspective(distortion_scale=0.5, p=0.5, interpola-
tion=3)
```

Performs a random perspective transformation of the image with a given probability as listed here:

- **distortion_scale:** The degree of distortion.
- **p:** Probability of the image being transformed.
- **interpolation:** Desired interpolation.

`CenterCrop`

`transforms.CenterCrop(size)`

Crops the given image at the center as follows:

- **`size`**: Desired output size of the crop.

These are just a few of the many augmentations available in PyTorch. You can combine these transformations using **`transforms.Compose`** to create a transformation pipeline for your images.

Applying Data Preprocessing in PyTorch

Let us now look at some examples of data preprocessing and augmentation in PyTorch that are often used in computer vision.

Overview of PyTorch's Data Processing Libraries

PyTorch offers a range of tools and libraries to facilitate data processing for deep learning models, including **`torchvision`**, **`transforms`**, and **`DataLoader`**. Here is an explanation of some of these tools:

- **`torchvision`**: A package in the PyTorch library that contains datasets, model architectures, and common image transformations for computer vision.
- **`transforms`**: A module within **`torchvision`** that provides common image transformations, such as rotation, flipping, normalization, and so on.
- **`DataLoader`**: A module in PyTorch that provides an efficient and easy way to load and handle data in batches, taking care of shuffling, batching, and multiprocessing automatically.

Diving Deep into PyTorch's Data Processing Libraries

`torchvision`: PyTorch's **`torchvision`** is a package that provides access to popular datasets, model architectures, and common image transformations for computer vision. The **`torchvision.datasets`** module contains loaders for several benchmark datasets, such as CIFAR10, CIFAR100, and MNIST, among others. These datasets are instrumental in training and testing computer vision models.

In addition to datasets, **`torchvision`** also offers a range of pre-trained models, such as ResNet, VGG, and GoogLeNet, which can be used for various computer vision tasks, including image classification, object detection, and more. These pre-trained models can serve as a starting point for building custom models tailored to specific tasks.

Moreover, **torchvision** includes a range of common image transformations that can be used for data augmentation and preprocessing. These transformations include operations, such as resizing, cropping, flipping, and rotating images, as well as converting images to PyTorch tensors and normalizing pixel values.

transforms: The transforms module in **torchvision** is a powerful tool for image preprocessing and augmentation. It provides a range of transformations that can be applied to images to improve model training and performance. These transformations can be composed together using **transforms.Compose**, allowing for a seamless and efficient way to preprocess data.

Some common transformations include:

- **transforms.Resize**: Resizes the image to the given size.
- **transforms.CenterCrop**: Crops the center of the image.
- **transforms.RandomHorizontalFlip**: Randomly flips the image horizontally.
- **transforms.ToTensor**: Converts the image to a PyTorch tensor.
- **transforms.Normalize**: Normalizes the pixel values of the image.

DataLoader:

The **DataLoader** in PyTorch is an essential tool for loading and handling data in batches. It provides an efficient way to handle large datasets by automatically shuffling, batching, and multiprocessing. The **DataLoader** works with a PyTorch dataset and provides an iterable over the dataset, allowing easy integration with training loops.

Implementing Data Preprocessing in PyTorch

Data preprocessing is crucial in preparing data for feeding into neural networks. It helps improve the model's performance and generalization. In PyTorch, data preprocessing can be easily implemented using the transforms module in **torchvision**.

Here is an example of implementing data preprocessing in PyTorch:

```
import torchvision.transforms as transforms
from torchvision.datasets import ImageFolder
from torch.utils.data import DataLoader

# Define the data preprocessing transformations
transform = transforms.Compose([
    transforms.Resize((224, 224)),
    transforms.ToTensor(),
    transforms.Normalize(mean=[0.485, 0.456, 0.406], std=[0.229, 0.224,
0.225]),
])
```

```
# Load the dataset
dataset = ImageFolder(root='path/to/dataset', transform=transform)

# Create a DataLoader
dataloader = DataLoader(dataset, batch_size=32, shuffle=True, num_
workers=4)
```

In the preceding example, the **transforms.Compose** is used to combine multiple image transformations. The image is first resized to 224x224 pixels, then converted to a PyTorch tensor, and finally normalized using the mean and standard deviation values. The **ImageFolder** class is used to load the dataset, and the **DataLoader** is used to create an iterable over the dataset with a batch size of 32, shuffling enabled, and 4 worker processes for loading data.

Data preprocessing is a crucial step in preparing data for training neural networks, and PyTorch provides a range of tools and libraries to facilitate this process. By leveraging **torchvision**, transforms, and **DataLoader**, you can easily implement data preprocessing and augmentation in PyTorch, ultimately improving the performance of your deep learning models.

Applying Data Augmentation in PyTorch

Data augmentation is a strategy to increase the diversity of data available for training models without actually collecting new data. This technique helps to prevent overfitting and allows the model to generalize better to new data. PyTorch's **`torchvision`** library provides an easy-to-use interface for data augmentation through the transforms module.

To demonstrate data augmentation in PyTorch, let's start by applying transformations to a sample image named test.png.

Figure 6.1: *Our input image for visualizing augmentations*

RandomHorizontalFlip

```
# Flips the image horizontally with a given probability (p=1 in this
example).
import matplotlib.pyplot as plt
from torchvision import transforms
from PIL import Image
# Load image
image = Image.open('test.png')

# RandomHorizontalFlip
random_horizontal_flip = transforms.RandomHorizontalFlip(p=1)
h_flipped_image = random_horizontal_flip(image)

# Display
plt.imshow(h_flipped_image)
plt.title('RandomHorizontalFlip')
plt.show()
```

Figure 6.2: *HorizontalFlip augmentation*

RandomVerticalFlip

```
# Flips the image vertically with a given probability (p=1 in this exam-
ple).
import matplotlib.pyplot as plt
from torchvision import transforms
from PIL import Image

# Load image
image = Image.open('test.png')
```

```
# RandomVerticalFlip
random_vertical_flip = transforms.RandomVerticalFlip(p=1)
flipped_image = random_vertical_flip(image)

# Display
plt.imshow(flipped_image)
plt.title('RandomVerticalFlip')
plt.axis('off')
plt.show()
```

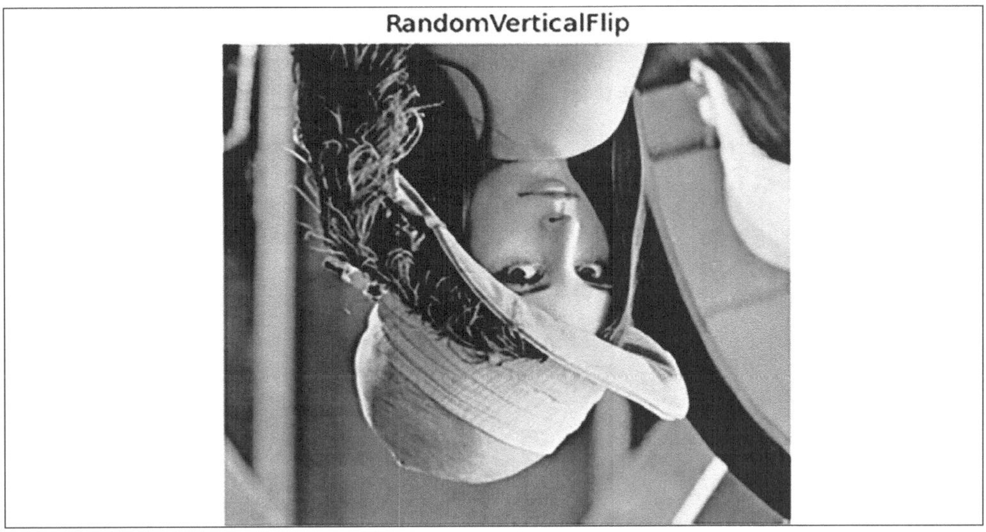

Figure 6.3: *VerticalFlip augmentation*

ColorJitter

```
# Randomly changes the brightness, contrast, saturation, and hue of an
image.
import matplotlib.pyplot as plt
from torchvision import transforms
from PIL import Image
# Load image
image = Image.open('test.png')
# ColorJitter
color_jitter = transforms.ColorJitter(brightness=0.5, contrast=0.5,
hue=0.5)
jittered_image = color_jitter(image)
# Display
plt.imshow(jittered_image)
plt.title('ColorJitter')
plt.show()
```

Figure 6.4: *ColorJitter augmentation*

RandomRotation

```
# Rotates the image by a random angle.
import matplotlib.pyplot as plt
from torchvision import transforms
from PIL import Image

# Load image
image = Image.open('test.png')
# RandomRotation
random_rotation = transforms.RandomRotation(degrees=(0, 180))
rotated_image = random_rotation(image)

# Display
plt.imshow(rotated_image)
plt.title('RandomRotation')
plt.axis('off')
plt.show()
```

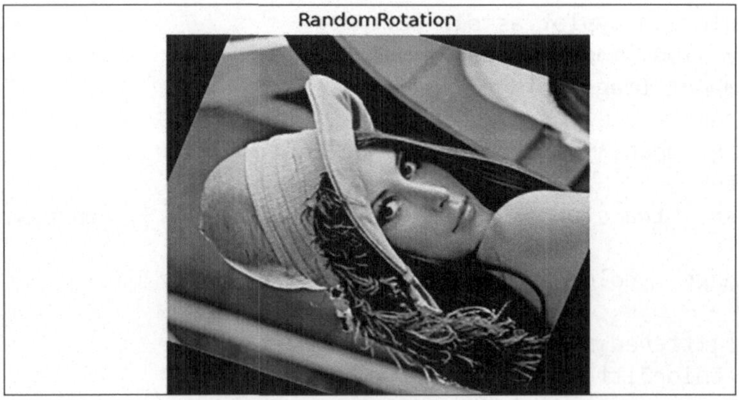

Figure 6.5: *RandomRotation augmentation*

RandomResizedCrop

```
# Crops the given image to a random size and aspect ratio.
import matplotlib.pyplot as plt
from torchvision import transforms
from PIL import Image

# Load image
image = Image.open('test.png')

# RandomResizedCrop
random_resized_crop = transforms.RandomResizedCrop(size=(224, 224))
resized_cropped_image = random_resized_crop(image)

# Display
plt.imshow(resized_cropped_image)
plt.title('RandomResizedCrop')
plt.axis('off')
plt.show()
```

Figure 6.6: *RandomResizedCrop augmentation*

RandomAffine

```
# Applies random affine transformations to the image.
import matplotlib.pyplot as plt
from torchvision import transforms
from PIL import Image
# Load image
image = Image.open('test.png')
# RandomAffine
random_affine = transforms.RandomAffine(degrees=(0, 360), translate=(0.1,
0.1), scale=(0.7, 1.3), shear=(0, 20))
affine_image = random_affine(image)
```

```
# Display
plt.imshow(affine_image)
plt.title('RandomAffine')
plt.axis('off')
plt.show()
```

Figure 6.7: *RandomAffine augmentation*

GaussianBlur

```
# Blurs the image with a Gaussian filter.
import matplotlib.pyplot as plt
from torchvision import transforms
from PIL import Image
# Load image
image = Image.open('test.png')

# GaussianBlur
gaussian_blur = transforms.GaussianBlur(kernel_size=(5, 9), sigma=(0.1,
5))
blurred_image = gaussian_blur(image)

# Display
plt.imshow(blurred_image)
plt.title('GaussianBlur')
plt.axis('off')
plt.show()
```

Figure 6.8: *GaussianBlur augmentation*

RandomCrop

```
# Crops the given image at a random location.
import matplotlib.pyplot as plt
from torchvision import transforms
from PIL import Image
# Load image
image = Image.open('test.png')

# RandomCrop
random_crop = transforms.RandomCrop(size=(100, 100))
cropped_image = random_crop(image)

# Display
plt.imshow(cropped_image)
plt.title('RandomCrop')
plt.axis('off')
plt.show()
```

Figure 6.9: *RandomCrop augmentation*

RandomErasing

```
# Randomly erases a rectangle region in an image.
import matplotlib.pyplot as plt
from torchvision import transforms
from PIL import Image

# Load image
image = Image.open('test.png')

# Convert to tensor for RandomErasing
to_tensor = transforms.ToTensor()
image_tensor = to_tensor(image)

# RandomErasing
random_erasing = transforms.RandomErasing(p=1, scale=(0.1, 0.33),
ratio=(0.3, 3.3), value='random')
erased_image_tensor = random_erasing(image_tensor)

# Convert back to image to display
to_pil = transforms.ToPILImage()
erased_image = to_pil(erased_image_tensor)

plt.imshow(erased_image)
plt.title('RandomErasing')
plt.axis('off')
plt.show()
```

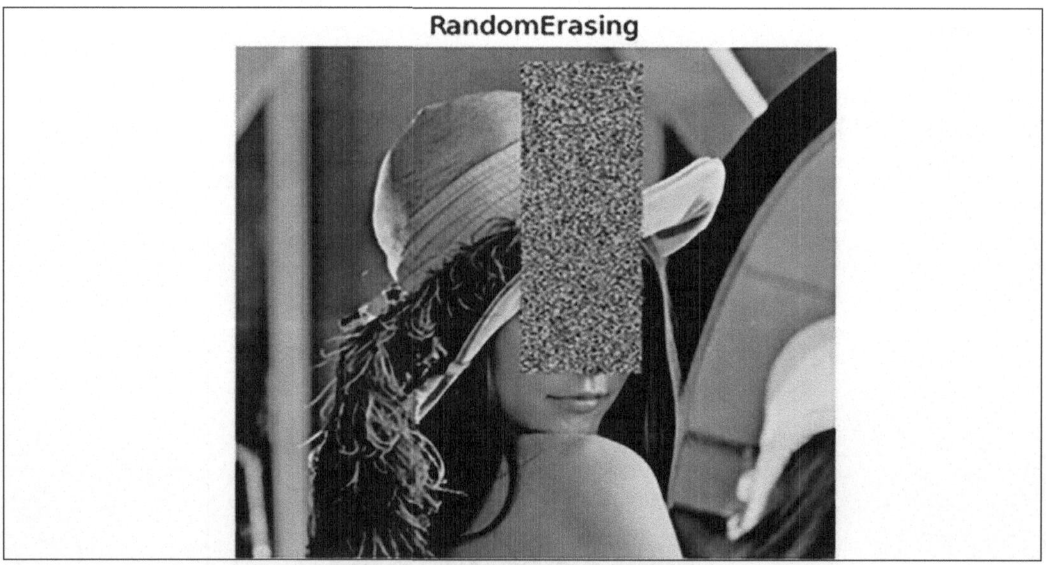

Figure 6.10: *RandomErasing augmentation*

RandomPerspective

```
# Performs a random perspective transformation of the image with a given
probability.
import matplotlib.pyplot as plt
from torchvision import transforms
from PIL import Image

# Load image
image = Image.open('test.png')

# RandomPerspective
random_perspective = transforms.RandomPerspective(distortion_scale=0.6,
p=1, interpolation=3)
perspective_image = random_perspective(image)

# Display
plt.imshow(perspective_image)
plt.title('RandomPerspective')
plt.axis('off')
plt.show()
```

Figure 6.11: *RandomPerspective augmentation*

CenterCrop

```
# Crops the given image at the center.
import matplotlib.pyplot as plt
from torchvision import transforms
```

```
from PIL import Image

# Load image
image = Image.open('test.png')

# CenterCrop
center_crop = transforms.CenterCrop(size=(100, 100))
cropped_image = center_crop(image)

# Display
plt.imshow(cropped_image)
plt.title('CenterCrop')
plt.axis('off')
plt.show()
```

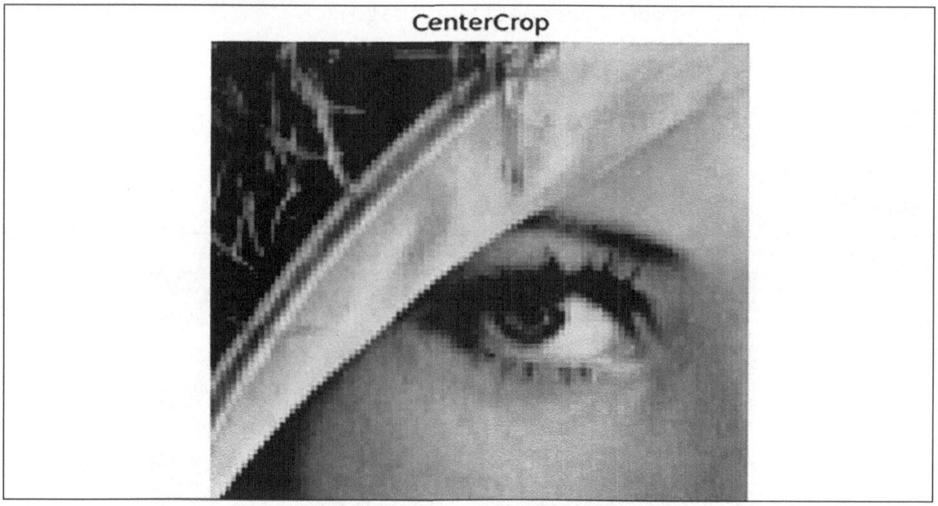

Figure 6.12: *CenterCrop augmentation*

Complete Example

```
# Let's now use all the augmentations together to generate different
images from a single input image
import matplotlib.pyplot as plt
from torchvision import transforms
from PIL import Image

# Load image
image = Image.open('test.png')

# Combined Augmentations
all_augmentations = transforms.Compose([
    transforms.CenterCrop(size=(100, 100)),
```

```
    transforms.RandomPerspective(distortion_scale=0.6, p=1,
interpolation=3),
    transforms.RandomApply([transforms.GaussianBlur(kernel_size=(5, 9),
sigma=(0.1, 5))], p=0.5),
    transforms.RandomAffine(degrees=(0, 360), translate=(0.1, 0.1),
scale=(0.7, 1.3), shear=(0, 20)),
    transforms.RandomResizedCrop(size=(224, 224)),
    transforms.RandomRotation(degrees=(0, 180)),
    transforms.ColorJitter(brightness=0.5, contrast=0.5, saturation=0.5,
hue=0.5),
    transforms.RandomVerticalFlip(p=0.5),
    transforms.RandomHorizontalFlip(p=0.5),
    transforms.ToTensor(),
    transforms.RandomErasing(p=0.5, scale=(0.1, 0.33), ratio=(0.3, 3.3),
value='random'),
])

# Function to display images
def show_augmented_images(image_path, num_images=5):
    image = Image.open(image_path)
    plt.figure(figsize=(15, 3))

    for i in range(num_images):
        augmented_image = all_augmentations(image)
        ax = plt.subplot(1, num_images, i + 1)
        ax.imshow(transforms.ToPILImage()(augmented_image))
        ax.axis('off')
    plt.show()

show_augmented_images('test.png')
```

The type of augmentation and the extent to which their range and probability can be increased depend on the problem we are trying to solve with our model. It also depends on the data.

With the correct augmentations, we can achieve accuracy a lot higher than without any augmentation.

It also makes our model generalized to predict the correct output even when the inference data is slightly or very different from our training data.

Figure 6.13: *Random images generated from running the combined snippet with all augmentations*

Impact of Data Augmentation on Model Performance

Data augmentation is a powerful technique in the arsenal of machine learning practitioners, especially in the field of computer vision. It involves creating new training samples from existing ones by applying random jitters and perturbations, such as rotating, flipping, scaling, or cropping. The intent is to expand the dataset and introduce a level of variation that helps the model generalize better, new, and unseen data.

Case Studies: Real-World Applications

Let us look at some real-world examples where augmentations could help us in improving performance.

Facial Recognition in Varying Conditions

A common application of computer vision is facial recognition. Models trained for this task must be robust to a variety of conditions, such as different lighting, facial expressions, and orientations. Without data augmentation, a model might perform well in controlled environments but poorly in natural, diverse settings. A real-world example is a security system that uses facial recognition to grant access to employees. If trained only on well-lit, front-facing images, the system might struggle to identify employees in different lighting or when they're not facing the camera directly. By incorporating augmentations, such as random rotations, brightness changes, and flips, the training data becomes more representative of real-world variability. After augmentation, the system's ability to correctly identify employees under various conditions improves, demonstrating enhanced performance and practical applicability.

Satellite Image Analysis for Land Cover Classification

Satellite imagery for land cover classification–distinguishing urban from rural areas, water bodies, forests, and so on–also benefits from augmentation. Images taken at different times of the day or year present variations in lighting and shadow. Initial models might confuse shadows with water bodies or misclassify urban areas obscured by clouds. By applying augmentations that mimic these conditions, such as random brightness and contrast adjustments or synthetic occlusions, the classification accuracy increases. For instance, after training with augmented data, a model will improve its classification accuracy of water bodies.

Augmentation Impact on CIFAR-10 Model Training

We can see the impact of augmentation on our training example from *Chapter 4: Venturing into Artificial Neural Networks*. We will use the following augmentations:

```
# Additional augmentations for CIFAR-10 training data
transform_augmented = transforms.Compose([
    transforms.RandomCrop(32, padding=4),
    transforms.RandomHorizontalFlip(),
    transforms.ColorJitter(brightness=0.1, contrast=0.1, saturation=0.1,
hue=0.1),
    transforms.ToTensor(),
    transforms.Normalize((0.5, 0.5, 0.5), (0.5, 0.5, 0.5)),
])

# Use the augmented transform for the training dataset
trainset_augmented = torchvision.datasets.CIFAR10(root='./data',
train=True,
                                                  download=True,
transform=transform_augmented)
trainloader_augmented = torch.utils.data.DataLoader(trainset_augmented,
batch_size=4,
                                                    shuffle=True)

# Rest of the training setup remains the same...
```

Here, we are not using augmentations like RandomErase; the images in CIFAR-10 datasets are very small (32x32). It is crucial to assess what augmentations will improve the performance and which augmentations modify the images to the extent that they lose valuable information required for accurate training.

Updated Code with Augmentations

```
# Updated code with new augmentations on the CIFAR-10 dataset
import torch
import torchvision
import torchvision.transforms as transforms

# Set up the transform to normalize the data
transform = transforms.Compose([
    transforms.RandomCrop(32, padding=4),
    transforms.RandomHorizontalFlip(),
    transforms.ColorJitter(brightness=0.1, contrast=0.1, saturation=0.1,
hue=0.1),
    transforms.ToTensor(),
    transforms.Normalize((0.5, 0.5, 0.5), (0.5, 0.5, 0.5)),
])

# Load the CIFAR-10 dataset
trainset = torchvision.datasets.CIFAR10(root='./data', train=True,
download=True, transform=transform)
trainloader = torch.utils.data.DataLoader(trainset, batch_size=4,
shuffle=True)

testset = torchvision.datasets.CIFAR10(root='./data', train=False,
download=True, transform=transform)
testloader = torch.utils.data.DataLoader(testset, batch_size=4,
shuffle=False)

classes = ('plane', 'car', 'bird', 'cat', 'deer', 'dog', 'frog',
'horse', 'ship', 'truck')

# Define the neural network
import torch.nn as nn
import torch.nn.functional as F

class SimpleCNN(nn.Module):
    def __init__(self):
        super(SimpleCNN, self).__init__()
        self.conv1 = nn.Conv2d(3, 6, 5)
        self.pool = nn.MaxPool2d(2, 2)
        self.conv2 = nn.Conv2d(6, 16, 5)
        self.fc1 = nn.Linear(16 * 5 * 5, 120)
        self.fc2 = nn.Linear(120, 84)
        self.fc3 = nn.Linear(84, 10)

    def forward(self, x):
```

```
        x = self.pool(F.relu(self.conv1(x)))
        x = self.pool(F.relu(self.conv2(x)))
        x = x.view(-1, 16 * 5 * 5)
        x = F.relu(self.fc1(x))
        x = F.relu(self.fc2(x))
        x = self.fc3(x)
        return x

net = SimpleCNN()

# Compile the model with torch.compile for PyTorch 2.0
compiled_net = torch.compile(net)

# Set up the loss function and optimizer
import torch.optim as optim

criterion = nn.CrossEntropyLoss()
optimizer = optim.SGD(compiled_net.parameters(), lr=0.001, momentum=0.9)

# Train the network
for epoch in range(5):  # Loop over the dataset multiple times
    running_loss = 0.0
    for i, data in enumerate(trainloader, 0):
        inputs, labels = data
        optimizer.zero_grad()
        outputs = compiled_net(inputs)
        loss = criterion(outputs, labels)
        loss.backward()
        optimizer.step()
        running_loss += loss.item()
        if i % 2000 == 1999:    # Print every 2000 mini-batches
            print('[%d, %5d] loss: %.3f' %
                  (epoch + 1, i + 1, running_loss / 2000))
            running_loss = 0.0

print('Finished Training')

# Test the network on the test data
correct = 0
total = 0
with torch.no_grad():
    for data in testloader:
        images, labels = data
        outputs = compiled_net(images)
        _, predicted = torch.max(outputs.data, 1)
        total += labels.size(0)
        correct += (predicted == labels).sum().item()
```

```
print('Accuracy of the network on the 10000 test images: %d %%' % (100 *
correct / total))
```

Figure 6.14: *Accuracy after training our SimpleCNN classifier on CIFAR-10 dataset with augmentations*

We got an improvement of 6% from our previous version. Although the images in CIFAR-10 dataset are smaller for impact with data augmentations, in the next chapter we will see cases where it is much more impactful and also look at some limitations and risks.

Best Practices for Data Augmentation and Preprocessing

Data augmentation is a powerful technique for improving the robustness and performance of machine learning models, particularly in the domain of computer vision. It involves generating new training samples from the existing ones by applying random jitters and perturbations, helping the model generalize better from limited training data. However, it's essential to know when and how to use augmentation effectively.

Scenarios and Use Cases

The following is the list of use cases and scenarios:

- **Insufficient Data:** When the dataset is too small, augmentations can artificially expand the diversity of the training set, helping to prevent overfitting and allowing the model to learn more general features.
- **Imbalanced Classes:** In scenarios where some classes are underrepresented, augmentation can help to balance the dataset by generating more examples of the minority class.
- **Model Generalization:** If a model performs well on the training data but poorly on the validation or test data, augmentation can introduce more variability, encouraging the model to learn more robust features.
- **Real-world Variability:** For tasks where the deployment environment will present data in various conditions (for example, different lighting or weather conditions in autonomous vehicle navigation), augmentation can simulate these conditions during training.
- **Domain-Specific Augmentations:** Certain tasks may benefit from custom augmentations that are specific to the domain. For instance, medical image

analysis may use augmentations that mimic common artifacts found in medical scans.

Incorporation Strategies

The incorporation strategies are listed as follows:

- **Incremental Complexity:** Start with simple augmentations, such as flips and rotations, and progressively introduce more complex ones based on the model's performance.
- **Pipeline Diversity**: Implement a diverse set of augmentations to cover a wide range of variations. However, ensure these augmentations are relevant to the problem at hand.
- **Consistency with Test Conditions**: Augmentations should reflect the types of variation expected during testing. Irrelevant augmentations might lead the model to learn features that are not useful.
- **Resource Constraints**: Consider the computational cost. More complex augmentations require additional processing power and time, which might not be justifiable in all scenarios.

Limitations and Risks

While data augmentation can significantly enhance model training, it's not without limitations and potential pitfalls. The following are the limitations and risks associated with data augmentation:

- **Risk of Misleading the Model:** If augmentations don't accurately reflect the real-world scenarios or if they're applied too aggressively, they can introduce noise and misleading information, which can confuse the model and degrade the performance.
- **Quality Degradation:** Excessive augmentation can degrade the quality of the data. For instance, too much zooming, cropping, or warping might result in the loss of critical features necessary for the model to make accurate predictions.
- **Computational Overhead:** Augmentations increase the computational burden. Each new augmentation adds to the time required for training, which can be significant for large-scale or real-time systems.
- **Class Distortion:** Certain augmentations might distort class-specific features. For example, while flipping images might be beneficial for general object recognition, it can harm performance in tasks like reading text, where direction matters.
- **Bias Introduction:** Augmentations can inadvertently introduce or reinforce bias in the dataset. If not carefully monitored, they can skew the model's understanding of the data, leading to biased predictions.

Best Practices for Avoiding Risks

The best practices for avoiding risks are as follows:

- **Validation:** Always validate the effect of augmentation on a separate validation set that has not been augmented.
- **Monitoring:** Keep track of augmentation parameters and performance metrics to understand their impact and avoid over-augmenting.
- **Balance:** Strive for a balance between the original and augmented data to ensure the model does not become biased towards the augmented data.
- **Pertinence:** Augmentations should be pertinent to the task. Avoid unnecessary augmentations that do not contribute to the model's ability to generalize.
- **Experimentation:** Experiment with augmentations incrementally. Monitor performance and adjust the strategy accordingly.

By adhering to these best practices, practitioners can effectively leverage data augmentation and preprocessing to enhance the performance of their computer vision models without falling into common traps that might otherwise lead to suboptimal results.

Conclusion

We have conducted a thorough investigation of the revolutionary effects that preprocessing and data augmentation have on the creation of machine learning models throughout this chapter. We have explored a wide range of augmentations, identified the situations that call for their use, and developed best practices to guarantee their successful execution. Our experience has shown that, even if these techniques are effective, they must be used carefully to improve performance without introducing bias or changing the underlying facts.

We are at the cusp of an amazing concept called transfer learning as we move from comprehending data augmentation to the next stage in our investigation of computer vision with PyTorch. With significantly less computational cost and time than training a model from scratch, this novel approach promises to usher in an era where the immense knowledge gained by pre-trained models on large datasets can be harnessed and adjusted to new, particular applications.

In the forthcoming chapter, "*Exploring Transfer Learning with PyTorch*," we will delve into the mechanics and philosophy of transfer learning. We will learn how this technique not only accelerates the development process but also opens the doors to state-of-the-art performance, even when data is scarce. This chapter will serve as a guide to the practical application of transfer learning within the PyTorch ecosystem, showcasing the ease with which one can adopt pre-trained models and adapt them to fit diverse and nuanced tasks.

The synergy between data augmentation and transfer learning cannot be overstated. While augmentation empowers us to expand and diversify our datasets, transfer learning allows us to stand on the shoulders of giants, taking what has already been learned and building upon it. As we step into the realm of transfer learning, we carry with us the insights and wisdom gained from understanding data augmentation, ready to witness the dramatic enhancements it can bring to model performance.

CHAPTER 7

Exploring Transfer Learning with PyTorch

Introduction

In this chapter, we delve into the realm of transfer learning, a technique that has become a cornerstone in the world of deep learning. This approach allows us to take a model trained on one task and repurpose it for another, leveraging previously learned features to achieve remarkable performance with less data and in less time. We will focus on harnessing the power of transfer learning within PyTorch, a framework that offers a rich ecosystem of tools and pre-trained models.

We'll start by uncovering the essentials of transfer learning, from its definition to the key concepts such as feature extraction and fine-tuning. Understanding these principles is crucial, as they form the basis of how transfer learning accelerates the training process and enhances model performance across diverse applications.

As we progress, practical examples will guide you through the process of applying transfer learning to a vision task. We'll demonstrate how to select the right pre-trained model, tailor it to new data, and refine the learning process. By implementing these steps in PyTorch, you will gain hands-on experience that solidifies your theoretical understanding.

The chapter will culminate in a critical evaluation of transfer learning's impact, comparing models fine-tuned with pre-trained weights against those trained from scratch. This A/B testing will not only highlight the quantitative benefits of transfer learning but also provide insights into its strategic advantages. By the end of this chapter, you'll be equipped with both the knowledge and practical skills to effectively apply transfer learning to your own projects in PyTorch.

Structure

In this chapter, the following topics will be covered:

- Definition and Overview
- Advantages of Transfer Learning
- Understanding Pre-trained Models
- Using Pre-trained Models in PyTorch
- Applying Transfer Learning to a Vision Task
- Impact of Transfer Learning on Model Performance
- Best Practices and Common Pitfalls

Definition and Overview

Imagine being an expert pianist, and you decide to learn the violin. While these are distinct instruments, your knowledge of music theory, rhythms, and coordination transfer over and can make the learning process quicker. This exemplifies the essence of transfer learning in the context of artificial intelligence (AI): leveraging knowledge from one domain to expedite learning in another.

In technical terms, transfer learning repurposes the layers of neural networks trained on vast amounts of data, typically on large-scale tasks like ImageNet, to benefit smaller or related problems. This not only saves time and computational resources but also allows for the development of models in domains where data is scarce.

Historical Context and Development

Transfer learning is not a new idea. Its roots can be traced back to the psychology of learning and the principle of learning transfer that has been discussed since the early 20th century. In AI, transfer learning became prevalent with the rise of deep learning and the availability of large datasets and pre-trained networks. It became a game-changer, allowing for state-of-the-art results in many domains with minimal data.

Key Concepts in Transfer Learning

- **Feature Extraction:** This process involves using the representations learned by a pre-trained network to extract meaningful features from new samples. The early layers of a network might capture universal features such as edges and textures, which can be beneficial for many tasks.
- **Fine-Tuning:** This goes a step beyond feature extraction. After initial feature extraction, the layers of the network are slightly adjusted or "fine-tuned" by

continuing the training process on a new dataset. This allows the network to adapt these features to the specifics of the new task.

Importance of Transfer Learning

- **Accelerated Learning:** Transfer learning significantly reduces the time to develop and train a model. Pre-trained models come with learned features from large datasets that could take weeks to train from scratch. Starting with these learned features, one can reach higher levels of performance much quicker.
- **Reduced Data Requirements:** One of the biggest challenges in machine learning is gathering enough data. Transfer learning mitigates this by using pre-trained networks that have already learned a lot about the world, reducing the amount of new data required to train a good model.
- **Broad Applicability:** From medical diagnosis to playing computer games, transfer learning has shown broad applicability. It has democratized the use of deep learning, enabling smaller organizations with limited resources to implement cutting-edge technology.

By tapping into the foundational principles of transfer learning, we offer a bridge from past knowledge to future innovation. This technique aligns with the ethos of modern AI development: more efficient, accessible, and versatile models that can adapt to a plethora of tasks with varying data landscapes. The next sections will delve deeper into how this pivotal approach is redefining the paradigms of machine learning and AI.

In the realm of AI, transfer learning is akin to standing on the shoulders of giants. It takes the monumental achievements of previous models, developed and honed over time on expansive and diverse datasets, and recontextualizes this knowledge for new, often more specialized applications.

The Efficacy of Transfer Learning

The efficacy of transfer learning lies in its flexibility and efficiency. A pre-trained model, such as those developed for large-scale image recognition tasks, contains a wealth of information about visual patterns. When such a model is applied to a new task, even if it's identifying medical images or classifying satellite imagery, the foundational understanding of visual features can be fine-tuned to suit these specialized requirements.

Cross-domain Applications

The true power of transfer learning shines through its cross-domain applications. Models trained on generic datasets have been successfully adapted for use in entirely different industries with surprisingly little need for customization. For instance, a model trained on everyday objects can assist in identifying defects in manufacturing processes or aid in agricultural monitoring systems.

Leveraging Pre-existing Models

Developers and researchers can access a variety of pre-trained models, thanks to the open-source community and institutions that share their work. These models are not just starting points; they encapsulate robust feature detectors and pattern recognizers that can be applied to countless tasks. This sharing of knowledge and resources is a testament to the collaborative spirit that drives progress in the field of AI.

Optimizing Model Performance

Through fine-tuning, transfer learning allows models to reach or even surpass the performance of models trained from scratch, especially in domains where data is not abundant. This process can involve unfreezing the last few layers of a pre-trained model and training them on a new dataset, thereby making the model more specialized without losing the general feature-detecting capabilities learned initially.

Implications for Industry and Research

The implications of transfer learning for industry and research are profound. Small startups can now develop sophisticated models without the need for extensive data or computational resources. Researchers in academia and medicine can utilize advanced AI without dedicating extensive time to model development, focusing instead on their areas of expertise.

A Catalyst for Innovation

In conclusion, transfer learning is not just a methodology; it's a catalyst for innovation. It allows the knowledge captured by AI to transcend its original confines, catalyzing progress across various domains and democratizing access to technology. It's a cornerstone in the evolution of AI, ensuring that the knowledge we gain from one task can illuminate the path to countless others.

As we segue into the next chapter, "*Exploring Transfer Learning with PyTorch*," we will journey through the practicalities of applying these principles. We will dissect how pre-trained models can be obtained, modified, and deployed to serve novel purposes. We will examine the tangible impacts of these techniques on model performance across various tasks. The reader will emerge with a toolkit not just of technical know-how but also of strategic insights into the application of transfer learning to achieve their goals in the field of computer vision.

Advantages of Transfer Learning

Transfer learning has become a transformative force in machine learning, particularly in fields where data is a premium commodity, and computational efficiency is of the essence. This section delves into the myriad benefits that transfer learning brings to the table, focusing on its efficiency in training, enhanced performance with small datasets, and versatile applicability across various domains.

Efficiency in Training

One of the most compelling advantages of transfer learning is the efficiency it introduces to the training process. Training a deep learning model from scratch requires considerable computational power and time, often necessitating weeks of fine-tuning and optimization on high-end GPUs. Transfer learning sidesteps this resource-intensive phase by leveraging the weights and features of a model already trained on a large benchmark dataset, such as ImageNet.

When employing transfer learning, a significant portion of the model–especially the initial layers that capture universal features like edges and textures–does not need extensive retraining. Instead, these layers are 'frozen,' and only the final layers are tweaked to adapt to the new dataset. This approach drastically reduces the time and computational cost, making powerful models accessible to researchers and practitioners without the need for exorbitant resources.

Improved Performance on Small Datasets

Another significant benefit is the performance boost that transfer learning provides, especially when dealing with small datasets. Conventionally, deep learning models thrive on large amounts of data–the more, the better–to fine-tune their parameters and avoid overfitting. However, in many specialized fields, such data is scarce or expensive to procure.

Transfer learning comes to the rescue by utilizing a pre-trained model's learned features, which are then applied to the new task with a much smaller dataset. By transferring the 'knowledge' gleaned from a related task with abundant data, the model requires only fewer examples to learn from and can often perform better than a model trained from scratch on a limited dataset.

Transfer Learning in Various Domains

The utility of transfer learning isn't confined to a single area; its benefits ripple across numerous domains. In healthcare, models trained on general images can be fine-tuned to detect anomalies in medical scans. In agriculture, models proficient in image classification can be adapted to monitor crop health. The versatility of transfer learning is particularly advantageous in specialized fields where data is rare and domain expertise is crucial.

The real-world applications of transfer learning are vast and growing. In autonomous vehicles, models trained on general driving scenarios are fine-tuned to understand specific weather conditions or geographies. In retail, models are adapted to enhance the shopping experience by recognizing products in various settings. In each case, transfer learning not only provides a head start but also shapes models to cater to niche requirements with surprising efficacy.

In essence, transfer learning is akin to learning a new language by drawing on the knowledge of a language one is already proficient in. Just as knowing Latin can make learning Spanish more efficient, having access to a model trained on a comprehensive dataset simplifies the process of training a model for a related, yet distinct task. This transfer of learning not only saves time and resources but also opens doors to high-quality performance in scenarios where traditional training methods might falter due to constraints on data and computation.

As we proceed in our exploration of PyTorch and its capabilities, the subsequent chapters will be built on these advantages, demonstrating through practical examples and case studies how transfer learning can be implemented to elevate model performance and accelerate the development cycle. Readers will be equipped not just with theoretical understanding but also with actionable knowledge, enabling them to harness the power of transfer learning in their projects.

Understanding Pre-trained Models

The era of deep learning has been markedly accelerated by the availability of pre-trained models, which are akin to sharing wisdom across various applications. These models are not just repositories of millions of parameter values but a condensed form of vast computational effort and knowledge. This section offers a comprehensive look into the intricacies of pre-trained models, exploring their architecture and the essence of their learned parameters and highlighting some of the most influential models that have made a mark in the field of computer vision and beyond.

The Anatomy of a Pre-trained Model

A pre-trained model in deep learning is essentially a network that has been previously trained on a large dataset. To understand a pre-trained model, one must first dissect its two foundational elements: the network architecture and the learned weights and biases.

Network Architecture

The architecture of a neural network refers to the structured arrangement of layers and neurons designed to capture patterns from data. Each architecture is like a unique scaffold, where the arrangement and connections of nodes are meticulously designed to optimize performance for specific tasks. For example, convolutional neural networks (CNNs) are structured specifically to handle image data.

Let's take a glance at a simple CNN architecture using PyTorch:

```
import torch
import torch.nn as nn

class SimpleCNN(nn.Module):
    def __init__(self):
        super(SimpleCNN, self).__init__()
        # Convolutional layer block 1
        self.conv1 = nn.Conv2d(in_channels=3, out_channels=32, kernel_
size=3, padding=1)
        self.relu1 = nn.ReLU()
        self.pool1 = nn.MaxPool2d(kernel_size=2)

        # Convolutional layer block 2
        self.conv2 = nn.Conv2d(in_channels=32, out_channels=64, kernel_
size=3, padding=1)
        self.relu2 = nn.ReLU()
        self.pool2 = nn.MaxPool2d(kernel_size=2)

        # Fully connected layers
        self.fc1 = nn.Linear(in_features=64 * 16 * 16, out_features=512)
        self.relu3 = nn.ReLU()
        self.fc2 = nn.Linear(in_features=512, out_features=10)

    def forward(self, x):
        # Block 1
        x = self.pool1(self.relu1(self.conv1(x)))
        # Block 2
        x = self.pool2(self.relu2(self.conv2(x)))
        # Flatten and pass through the fully connected layers
        x = x.view(x.size(0), -1)
        x = self.relu3(self.fc1(x))
        x = self.fc2(x)
        return x

# Instantiate the model
simple_cnn = SimpleCNN()
```

In this example, **SimpleCNN** is a rudimentary model, suitable for learning simple patterns in image data. However, pre-trained models like VGGNet or ResNet are far more complex and have been trained on extensive datasets like ImageNet.

But let us say that our **SimpleCNN** model was trained on a training set of medical images and achieved suitable accuracy. Now, if we want to train the **SimpleCNN** for another task, instead of training from scratch, we can use the weights we used in previous projects and use them here. If both tasks are similar, the time it takes for our model to converge will be a lot smaller. The model will preserve all the lower-level features that it learned in the first project.

This becomes very important when we are talking about models that contain millions of parameters or even billions with the new large language models.

Learned Weights and Biases

Weights and biases are the learnable parameters of a neural network. In a pre-trained model, these parameters are the result of extensive training on a large dataset. They capture the essence of the patterns that the model has learned to recognize, from the simple to the complex. When you load a pre-trained model, you inherit these learned patterns, which can then be fine-tuned or adapted to new but related tasks.

```
# Loading a pre-trained ResNet model
resnet = torchvision.models.resnet18(pretrained=True)
```

With the **pretrained=True** flag, the model **resnet** now contains weights that have been optimized on the ImageNet dataset, ready to be used or adapted further.

We will be able to leverage the power of models with weights that have been converged for complex tasks with millions of images and thousands of classes

Popular Pre-trained Models in Computer Vision

The domain of computer vision has been particularly enriched by a variety of pre-trained models. Each model comes with its unique strengths, tailored to different types and scales of image recognition tasks as listed here:

- **VGGNet:** It is known for its simplicity and depth, with several configurations leading up to 19 layers, it's an excellent model for understanding deep CNNs.
- **ResNet:** Featuring residual learning to ease the training of networks that are substantially deeper than those used previously; it uses shortcut connections to leap over some layers.
- **Inception (GoogleNet):** It uses a network-in-network architecture with parallel convolutions, capturing information at various scales.

- **FCN (Fully Convolutional Network):** For semantic segmentation, which involves classifying each pixel in an image, FCNs are pivotal. They can take input of any size and output a correspondingly-sized segmentation map. This architecture has been instrumental in tasks that require understanding the spatial layout of objects in an image, such as autonomous driving and medical image diagnostics.
- **Mask R-CNN:** An extension of the Faster R-CNN, Mask R-CNN adds a branch for predicting segmentation masks on each Region of Interest (RoI), effectively combining object detection with instance segmentation. This model has seen widespread adoption for tasks where pinpointing and delineating each object instance in an image is crucial.
- **YOLO (You Only Look Once):** For real-time object detection, YOLO models are renowned for their speed and efficiency. They divide the image into a grid, and each grid cell predicts objects and bounding boxes. It's particularly useful in scenarios where the speed of detection is critical, such as in surveillance systems or real-time traffic analysis.
- **U-Net:** With its unique U-shaped architecture, U-Net is tailored for biomedical image segmentation. The model is designed to work with fewer training samples and to yield more precise segmentations, which is essential in medical imaging where annotated images are scarce and the accuracy of segmentation is paramount.
- **RetinaNet:** RetinaNet solves the problem of class imbalance in object detection by introducing a novel loss function, the Focal Loss. It's particularly effective for detecting objects across a wide range of sizes within an image, making it suitable for detecting pedestrians and vehicles in autonomous vehicle systems.
- **DeepLab:** DeepLab architectures employ atrous convolutions for fine-grained segmentation tasks, utilizing numerous parallel filters with different sampling rates to capture multi-scale context. This is particularly helpful for detailed scene understanding in images where capturing the context at different scales is essential.

These models have become standards in the field, often serving as starting points for a range of computer vision tasks.

Using Pre-trained Models in PyTorch

Pre-trained models are one of the most significant enablers of progress in deep learning, especially in the field of computer vision. PyTorch, being a leading deep learning framework, offers a comprehensive model zoo with a wide array of models that have been pre-trained on various datasets. In this section, we will explore how to access, understand, and modify these models to suit specific needs.

PyTorch Model Zoo: A Catalogue of Pre-trained Models

The PyTorch model zoo, accessible through the torchvision module, is akin to a treasure trove for machine learning practitioners. It includes a wide variety of models, such as AlexNet, VGG, ResNet, Inception, and more, which have been trained on massive datasets like ImageNet. These models can be employed for tasks, such as image classification, object detection, segmentation, and more.

We saw examples of VGG and ResNet in *Chapter 5: Diving Deep into Convolutional Neural Networks* (CNNs), where we can load the architecture with pre-trained weights directly using torchvision.

Loading Pre-trained Models in PyTorch

To use a pre-trained model in PyTorch, you must import the necessary modules and load the model. PyTorch makes this process straightforward:

```
# Import torchvision models
import torchvision.models as models

# Load the pre-trained ResNet-18 model
resnet18 = models.resnet18(pretrained=True)
```

The **`pretrained=True`** flag automatically downloads the model's parameters that have been trained on ImageNet.

Step-by-Step Code Examples

Let's go through a step-by-step example of using a pre-trained VGG-16 model for image classification:

Classification with ResNet-50

```
import torch
import torchvision.transforms as transforms
from PIL import Image
import torchvision.models as models

# Load the pre-trained ResNet-50 model
model_classification = models.resnet50(pretrained=True)
model_classification.eval()

# Define the transform
transform_classification = transforms.Compose([
    transforms.Resize(256),
```

```
    transforms.CenterCrop(224),
    transforms.ToTensor(),
    transforms.Normalize(mean=[0.485, 0.456, 0.406], std=[0.229, 0.224,
0.225]),
])

# Load and preprocess the image
image = Image.open('test.png').convert('RGB')
input_tensor = transform_classification(image).unsqueeze(0)  # Create a
mini-batch as expected by the model

# Inference
with torch.no_grad():
    output_classification = model_classification(input_tensor)

# Get the predicted class
_, predicted_class = torch.max(output_classification, 1)
print(f'Predicted class (Classification): {predicted_class.item()}')
```

In this example, we used the ResNet model, renowned for its deep architecture and residual connections that facilitate the training of networks with a large number of layers. The code snippet demonstrated how to load a pre-trained ResNet model from PyTorch's model zoo, preprocess an input image, and perform classification. It encapsulates the essence of transfer learning by utilizing a model trained on a vast dataset (ImageNet) and applying it to classify a new image, showcasing the efficiency of using pre-trained models for quick deployment.

After processing an image through the ResNet model, the output is a tensor that contains the prediction scores for each class in the dataset on which the model was trained (such as ImageNet's 1,000 classes). The scores represent the model's confidence levels for each class. To interpret the results, we typically apply a softmax function to convert these scores into probabilities. The class with the highest probability is taken as the model's final prediction. It is also common to retrieve the top-five predictions to see a set of probable labels the model considers relevant to the image.

In the following output, you can see the input image and the predicted output:

Figure 7.1: *Input image and output from pre-trained ResNet-50 model*

Segmentation with DeepLabV3

```
import torch
import torchvision.transforms as transforms
from PIL import Image
import torchvision.models.segmentation as segmentation_models

# Load the pre-trained DeepLabV3 model
model_segmentation = segmentation_models.deeplabv3_resnet101(pre-
trained=True)
model_segmentation.eval()

# Define the transform
transform_segmentation = transforms.Compose([
    transforms.Resize(256),
    transforms.ToTensor(),
    transforms.Normalize(mean=[0.485, 0.456, 0.406], std=[0.229, 0.224,
0.225]),
])

# Preprocess the image and add a batch dimension
image = Image.open('test.png').convert('RGB')
input_tensor = transform_segmentation(image).unsqueeze(0)

# Inference
with torch.no_grad():
    output_segmentation = model_segmentation(input_tensor)['out'][0]
segmentation = output_segmentation.argmax(0)

# Convert the segmentation tensor to a PIL image
to_pil = transforms.ToPILImage()
```

```
segmentation_pil = to_pil(segmentation.byte())

# Save the segmentation mask
segmentation_pil.save('segmentation_output.png')
print('Segmentation mask saved as segmentation_output.png')
```

The DeepLabV3 model, equipped with an atrous convolution and spatial pyramid pooling, is adept at understanding the context and delineating object boundaries in an image. The provided code illustrates the process of loading DeepLabV3 with a pre-trained backbone from PyTorch, running it on an input image, and generating a segmented output. This exemplifies how pre-trained models can be leveraged for complex tasks like semantic segmentation, which is pivotal for applications such as autonomous driving and medical image analysis.

For semantic segmentation, the DeepLabV3 model produces a different kind of output. Each pixel in the input image is assigned a class from the set of classes that the model is trained to recognize. The output is a matrix with the same width and height as the input image, where each element corresponds to a class index. These class indices are often visualized as a color map overlaid on the original image, where each color corresponds to a different class, allowing us to see exactly which parts of the image have been classified into which categories. In the following output, you can see the input image and the predicted output.

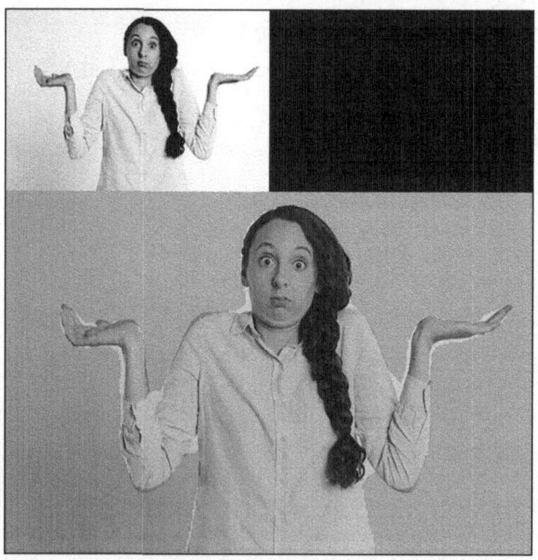

Figure 7.2: *Input image, output segmentation mask, and mask overlaid on input image*

Object Detection with Faster R-CNN

```
import torch
import torchvision.transforms as transforms
from PIL import Image, ImageDraw
import torchvision.models.detection as detection_models
```

```
# Load the pre-trained Faster R-CNN model
model_detection = detection_models.fasterrcnn_resnet50_fpn(pre-
trained=True)
model_detection.eval()

# Load and preprocess the image
image = Image.open('test.png')
transform_detection = transforms.Compose([transforms.ToTensor()])
input_tensor = transform_detection(image).unsqueeze(0)

# Inference
with torch.no_grad():
    predictions = model_detection(input_tensor)

# Draw the bounding boxes and labels on the image
draw = ImageDraw.Draw(image)
for element in range(len(predictions[0]['boxes'])):
    boxes = predictions[0]['boxes'][element].cpu().numpy()
    score = predictions[0]['scores'][element].cpu().numpy()
    label = predictions[0]['labels'][element].cpu().numpy()

    # Draw the box with a threshold for scores to filter weak detections
    if score > 0.5:
        draw.rectangle([(boxes[0], boxes[1]), (boxes[2], boxes[3])],
outline="red", width=3)
        draw.text((boxes[0], boxes[1]), f'Label: {label}', fill="red")

# Save the image with detections
image.save('detection_output.png')
print('Detection output saved as detection_output.png')
```

Faster R-CNN, an object detection model, uses a Region Proposal Network to detect object boundaries. The code showed how to load a pre-trained Faster R-CNN model, perform object detection on an image, and then save the results with drawn bounding boxes and labels. This segment of the code serves as an example of applying transfer learning to object detection tasks, illustrating the model's capability to identify multiple objects and their locations within an image, which is vital for surveillance, inventory management, and many more applications.

In object detection with Faster R-CNN, the model outputs several pieces of information for each detected object: the bounding box coordinates, a class label, and a confidence score. The bounding box specifies the location of the object in the image, and the class label tells us what the object is. The confidence score indicates how certain the model is about the object's presence and classification. This information allows us to not only know what objects are in the image but also where they are located and how confident the model is in its prediction.

In the following output, you can see the input image and the predicted output:

Figure 7.3: *Input image and output image with objects detected drawn on the input input*

Keypoint Detection with Keypoint R-CNN

```
import torch
from PIL import Image, ImageDraw
import torchvision.transforms as transforms
import torchvision.models.detection as detection_models

# Load the pre-trained Keypoint R-CNN model
model_keypoint = detection_models.keypointrcnn_resnet50_fpn
(pretrained=True)
model_keypoint.eval()

# Preprocess the image
image = Image.open('test.png')
transform_keypoint = transforms.Compose([transforms.ToTensor()])
input_tensor = transform_keypoint(image).unsqueeze(0)

# Inference
with torch.no_grad():
    prediction_keypoint = model_keypoint(input_tensor)

# Draw keypoints
draw = ImageDraw.Draw(image)
for person in prediction_keypoint[0]['keypoints']:
    keypoints = person.cpu().numpy()
    scores = person[:, 2]
    for kp, s in zip(keypoints, scores):
        if s > 2:  # The model outputs a score of 0, 1, or 2 for
visibility
            draw.ellipse([(kp[0] - 3, kp[1] - 3), (kp[0] + 3, kp[1] +
3)], fill="blue")
```

```
# Save the image with keypoints
image.save('keypoint_output.png')
print('Keypoint output saved as keypoint_output.png')
```

Keypoint R-CNN extends Faster R-CNN by adding a keypoint detection head to the network. The code described the process of loading this model, executing it on an image to detect human poses by identifying keypoints, and then saving the visualized keypoints on the image. This reflects the adaptability of pre-trained models to tasks beyond simple classification, highlighting their potential in human-computer interaction, animation, sports analytics, and other areas where understanding human poses is crucial.

Keypoint R-CNN produces a complex output that includes both object detections (as in Faster R-CNN) and keypoint predictions. For each detected person in the image, the model provides a set of keypoints, which typically correspond to parts of the human body, such as elbows, knees, eyes, and so on. Along with the keypoints, the model outputs a visibility score, indicating the confidence that a keypoint is correctly placed and visible. The coordinates of these keypoints allow us to map a human pose onto the image. This output is essential for understanding human gestures or movements and is widely used in motion analysis and augmented reality.

In the following output, you can see the input image and the predicted output.:

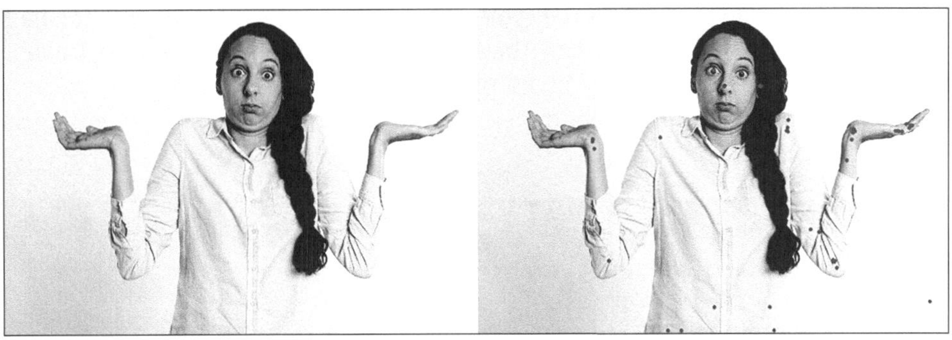

Figure 7.4: *Input image and output image with keypoints detected drawn on the input input*

Replacing the Top Layer

Sometimes, we need to adapt these models for tasks slightly different from what they were originally trained for. This often involves replacing the top layer and fine-tuning the model.

Here's how you can replace the top layer of a pre-trained model:

```
import torch.nn as nn

# Replace the top layer for fine-tuning
num_features = vgg16.classifier[6].in_features
```

```
vgg16.classifier[6] = nn.Linear(num_features, number_of_classes)
# 'number_of_classes' is the number of your new classes
```

In the upcoming sections, we will take a look at how this can be achieved to change the number of classes and use transfer learning to adapt pre-trained weights for a different task.

Applying Transfer Learning to a Vision Task

When embarking on a new vision task, the selection of the appropriate pre-trained model is crucial. A good starting point is to consider the similarity between your task and the tasks the models were originally trained for. Models trained on a diverse set of images, such as those from ImageNet, can be a good general-purpose choice. For instance, ResNet-50, with its deep architecture, is a versatile model that provides a strong backbone for many vision tasks due to its balance between complexity and performance.

Preprocessing Data for Transfer Learning

Before utilizing a pre-trained model, your data must be formatted and normalized to match the input specifications of the model. For a model trained on ImageNet, inputs are typically resized to 224x224 pixels and normalized using the mean and standard deviation of the ImageNet dataset. Here's an example of preprocessing steps in PyTorch:

```
from torchvision import transforms

# Define the standard ImageNet transformation
preprocess = transforms.Compose([
    transforms.Resize(256),
    transforms.CenterCrop(224),
    transforms.ToTensor(),
    transforms.Normalize(mean=[0.485, 0.456, 0.406], std=[0.229, 0.224,
0.225]),
])
```

This transformation should be applied to both training and validation datasets to maintain consistency.

Feature Extraction: Using a Model as a Fixed Feature Extractor

To use a pre-trained model as a fixed feature extractor, you can freeze the weights of all the layers except for the final classification layer. This can be done by setting **`requires_grad`** to **`False`** for all parameters, except for those in the last layer. Here's how you can modify ResNet-50 for CIFAR-10:

```
from torchvision.models import resnet50
from torch import nn

# Load a pre-trained ResNet-50 model
model = resnet50(pretrained=True)

# Freeze all the layers
for param in model.parameters():
    param.requires_grad = False

# Replace the last layer to match CIFAR-10's classes (10 classes)
num_features = model.fc.in_features
model.fc = nn.Linear(num_features, 10)
```

This model can now be used to extract features from CIFAR-10 images, which can be used to train a simple classifier.

Fine-Tuning: Adapting Pre-trained Models with New Data

Fine-tuning involves not only replacing the final layer but also retraining some of the earlier layers with your dataset, which allows the model to adapt to new features. This is particularly useful when your dataset is sufficiently large and different from the dataset the model was originally trained on. In PyTorch, fine-tuning is straightforward:

```
# Assume 'model' is already defined as above

# Unfreeze some of the last layers
for param in list(model.layer4.parameters()) + list(model.fc.
parameters()):
    param.requires_grad = True

# Proceed with the training loop
# Define loss function and optimizer
criterion = nn.CrossEntropyLoss()
optimizer = torch.optim.SGD(model.parameters(), lr=0.001, momentum=0.9)

# Define your training loop
for epoch in range(num_epochs):
    # Training and update steps here...
    pass
```

In this code, we unfreeze the last block of the ResNet (layer4) along with the fully connected layer, allowing them to be updated during training. We will look into more details further in the chapter on how to fine-tune end-to-end.

Strategies for Effective Fine-Tuning

Effective fine-tuning requires careful consideration of several factors including:

- **Learning Rate:** Use a smaller learning rate to avoid large updates that can destroy the pre-trained features.
- **Layer Selection:** Unfreeze layers selectively, typically the higher-level ones, since they contain more task-specific features.
- **Data Augmentation:** Augment the training data to provide a richer set of features for the model to learn from.
- **Regularization:** Apply regularization techniques like dropout or weight decay to prevent overfitting on the new dataset.

Hands-on Code Example: Fine-tuning ResNet-50 on CIFAR-10

Here is a complete code snippet that illustrates how to fine-tune ResNet-50 on CIFAR-10 using PyTorch.

In this example, we will load the pre-trained weights of ResNet-50 from the PyTorch model zoo. Then, we will change the last layer so that it can work on the CIFAR-10 dataset.

Lastly, we will compare the accuracy of running it for 10 epochs to see how it is compared to our custom SimpleCNN and how it is compared to a model trained from scratch for the same number of epochs.

```
import torch
import torchvision
import torchvision.transforms as transforms
from torchvision.models import resnet50
from torch import nn

# Data preparation
transform = transforms.Compose([
    transforms.Resize(224),
    transforms.ToTensor(),
    transforms.Normalize((0.5, 0.5, 0.5), (0.5, 0.5, 0.5))
])

trainset = torchvision.datasets.CIFAR10(root='./data', train=True,
download=True, transform=transform)
```

```
trainloader = torch.utils.data.DataLoader(trainset, batch_size=32,
shuffle=True, num_workers=2)

testset = torchvision.datasets.CIFAR10(root='./data', train=False,
download=True, transform=transform)
testloader = torch.utils.data.DataLoader(testset, batch_size=32,
shuffle=False, num_workers=2)

# Load the pre-trained model and modify it for CIFAR-10
model = resnet50(weights="IMAGENET1K_V2")
# Freeze all layers first
for param in model.parameters():
    param.requires_grad = False
# Unfreeze some layers
for param in list(model.layer4.parameters()) + list(model.fc.
parameters()):
    param.requires_grad = True
# Modify the last layer
model.fc = nn.Linear(model.fc.in_features, 10)

# Move the model to GPU if available
device = torch.device("cuda:0" if torch.cuda.is_available() else "cpu")
model.to(device)

# Define loss function and optimizer
criterion = nn.CrossEntropyLoss()
optimizer = torch.optim.SGD(filter(lambda p: p.requires_grad, model.
parameters()), lr=0.001, momentum=0.9)

# Training loop
num_epochs = 10
for epoch in range(num_epochs):
    model.train()
    running_loss = 0.0
    for i, data in enumerate(trainloader, 0):
        inputs, labels = data
        inputs, labels = inputs.to(device), labels.to(device)

        optimizer.zero_grad()

        outputs = model(inputs)
        loss = criterion(outputs, labels)
        loss.backward()
        optimizer.step()

        running_loss += loss.item()
```

```
    print(f'Epoch {epoch + 1}, Loss: {running_loss / len(trainloader)}')

# Save the trained model
torch.save(model.state_dict(), 'finetuned_resnet50_cifar10.pth')

# Function to calculate accuracy
def calculate_accuracy(loader, model):
    correct = 0
    total = 0
    model.eval()  # Set the model to evaluation mode

    with torch.no_grad():  # No need to track the gradients
        for data in loader:
            images, labels = data
            images, labels = images.to(device), labels.to(device)
            outputs = model(images)

            _, predicted = torch.max(outputs.data, 1)
            total += labels.size(0)
            correct += (predicted == labels).sum().item()

    accuracy = 100 * correct / total
    return accuracy

# Calculate accuracy on the validation set
val_accuracy = calculate_accuracy(testloader, model)
print(f'Accuracy of the network on the test images: {val_accuracy:.2f}%')
```

```
Epoch 1, Loss: 0.7701484623745856
Epoch 2, Loss: 0.40084931716770983
Epoch 3, Loss: 0.2991041644373271
Epoch 4, Loss: 0.22613211420155532
Epoch 5, Loss: 0.1708905622464386
Accuracy of the network on the test images: 89.34%
```

Figure 7.5: *Loss on training pre-trained model for 5 epochs and accuracy output from the preceding script*

Hands-on Code Example: Training ResNet-50 on CIFAR-10 from scratch

Now, we will modify the previous example to train the ResNet-50 model from scratch on the CIFAR-10 dataset without using pre-trained weights. This script includes the setup of the dataset, model initialization, training loop, and evaluation of the test set.

```
import torch
import torchvision
import torchvision.transforms as transforms
import torch.nn as nn
import torch.optim as optim
from torchvision import models

# Set up the transforms for the CIFAR-10 dataset
transform = transforms.Compose([
    transforms.Resize((224, 224)), # Resize images to the size that
ResNet expects
    transforms.ToTensor(),
    transforms.Normalize((0.5, 0.5, 0.5), (0.5, 0.5, 0.5))
])

# Load the CIFAR-10 training dataset
trainset = torchvision.datasets.CIFAR10(root='./data', train=True,
                                        download=True, transform=
transform)
trainloader = torch.utils.data.DataLoader(trainset, batch_size=4,
                                          shuffle=True, num_workers=2)

# Load the CIFAR-10 test dataset
testset = torchvision.datasets.CIFAR10(root='./data', train=False,
                                       download=True, transform=
transform)
testloader = torch.utils.data.DataLoader(testset, batch_size=4,
                                         shuffle=False, num_workers=2)

# Define the classes
classes = ('plane', 'car', 'bird', 'cat', 'deer', 'dog', 'frog',
'horse', 'ship', 'truck')

# Initialize the ResNet-50 model
model = models.resnet50(pretrained=False) # No pretrained weights
num_ftrs = model.fc.in_features
model.fc = nn.Linear(num_ftrs, len(classes)) # Replace the last layer

# Use a GPU if available
device = torch.device("cuda:0" if torch.cuda.is_available() else "cpu")
model.to(device)

# Set up the loss function and optimizer
criterion = nn.CrossEntropyLoss()
optimizer = optim.SGD(model.parameters(), lr=0.001, momentum=0.9)
```

```
# Training loop
for epoch in range(10):  # Loop over the dataset multiple times
    running_loss = 0.0
    for i, data in enumerate(trainloader, 0):
        # Get the inputs; data is a list of [inputs, labels]
        inputs, labels = data
        inputs, labels = inputs.to(device), labels.to(device)

        # Zero the parameter gradients
        optimizer.zero_grad()

        # Forward pass
        outputs = model(inputs)
        loss = criterion(outputs, labels)

        # Backward pass and optimize
        loss.backward()
        optimizer.step()

        # Print statistics
        running_loss += loss.item()
        if i % 2000 == 1999:    # Print every 2000 mini-batches
            print(f'[{epoch + 1}, {i + 1:5d}] loss: {running_loss / 
2000:.3f}')
            running_loss = 0.0

print('Finished Training')

# Save the trained model
PATH = './cifar_resnet50.pth'
torch.save(model.state_dict(), PATH)

# Load the model for evaluation
model = models.resnet50(pretrained=False)
model.fc = nn.Linear(num_ftrs, len(classes))
model.load_state_dict(torch.load(PATH))
model.to(device)

# Function to calculate accuracy
def calculate_accuracy(loader, model):
    correct = 0
    total = 0
    model.eval()  # Set the model to evaluation mode

    with torch.no_grad():  # No need to track the gradients
```

```
        for data in loader:
            images, labels = data
            images, labels = images.to(device), labels.to(device)
            outputs = model(images)
            _, predicted = torch.max(outputs.data, 1)
            total += labels.size(0)
            correct += (predicted == labels).sum().item()

    accuracy = 100 * correct / total
    return accuracy

# Calculate accuracy on the test set
test_accuracy = calculate_accuracy(testloader, model)
print(f'Accuracy of the network on the test images: {test_accuracy
:.2f}%')
```

```
Epoch 1, Loss: 1.9914705469942093
Epoch 2, Loss: 1.437778747844696
Epoch 3, Loss: 1.162368810274303
Epoch 4, Loss: 0.9345788255292177
Epoch 5, Loss: 0.7733281003485247
Finished Training
Accuracy of the network on the test images: 69.63%
```

Figure 7.6: *Loss on training scratch model for 5 epochs and accuracy output from the preceding script*

Model Performance Metrics

We can get the models' metrics, such as ROC-Curve, accuracy, precision, recall, and F1 score. This gives an insight into how our trained model performed. We can leverage a script very similar to what we used in the previous chapter to achieve this.

```
import torch
import torchvision.transforms as transforms
import torchvision
from sklearn.metrics import precision_score, recall_score, f1_score,
roc_curve, auc, confusion_matrix, accuracy_score
import numpy as np
import matplotlib.pyplot as plt
from itertools import product
from torchvision import models
from torch.utils.data import DataLoader

# Device configuration
device = torch.device('cuda' if torch.cuda.is_available() else 'cpu')
```

```
# Load the trained ResNet-50 model
model_path = 'resnet50_cifar10.pth'
model = models.resnet50(pretrained=False)
num_ftrs = model.fc.in_features
model.fc = torch.nn.Linear(num_ftrs, 10)  # CIFAR-10 has 10 classes
model = model.to(device)
model.load_state_dict(torch.load(model_path))
model.eval()

# CIFAR-10 validation dataset
transform = transforms.Compose([
    transforms.Resize(256),
    transforms.CenterCrop(224),
    transforms.ToTensor(),
    transforms.Normalize(mean=[0.485, 0.456, 0.406], std=[0.229, 0.224,
0.225]),
])

validation_set = torchvision.datasets.CIFAR10(root='./data',
train=False, download=True, transform=transform)
validation_loader = DataLoader(validation_set, batch_size=64,
shuffle=False)

# Function to get predictions and targets
def get_predictions_and_targets(loader, model):
    all_preds = []
    all_targets = []
    with torch.no_grad():
        for images, targets in loader:
            images, targets = images.to(device), targets.to(device)
            outputs = model(images)
            _, preds = torch.max(outputs, 1)
            all_preds.extend(preds.cpu().numpy())
            all_targets.extend(targets.cpu().numpy())
    return all_preds, all_targets

# Get predictions and targets from the model
predictions, targets = get_predictions_and_targets(validation_loader,
model)

# Calculate metrics
accuracy = accuracy_score(targets, predictions)
precision = precision_score(targets, predictions, average='macro')
recall = recall_score(targets, predictions, average='macro')
f1 = f1_score(targets, predictions, average='macro')
```

```
# Output the metrics
print(f'Accuracy: {accuracy}\nPrecision: {precision}\nRecall: {recall}\
nF1 Score: {f1}')

# ROC Curve and AUC
# For ROC and AUC, we need to get the probability scores of classes
probabilities = []
with torch.no_grad():
    for images, _ in validation_loader:
        images = images.to(device)
        outputs = model(images)
        probabilities.extend(torch.softmax(outputs, dim=1).cpu().
numpy())

probabilities = np.array(probabilities)
# Calculate ROC curve and ROC area for each class
fpr = dict()
tpr = dict()
roc_auc = dict()
for i in range(10):
    fpr[i], tpr[i], _ = roc_curve(targets, probabilities[:, i], pos_
label=i)
    roc_auc[i] = auc(fpr[i], tpr[i])

# Plot all ROC curves
plt.figure()
colors = iter(plt.cm.rainbow(np.linspace(0, 1, 10)))
for i, color in zip(range(10), colors):
    plt.plot(fpr[i], tpr[i], color=color, lw=2,
             label='ROC curve of class {0} (area = {1:0.2f})'.format(i,
roc_auc[i]))

plt.plot([0, 1], [0, 1], 'k--', lw=2)
plt.xlim([0.0, 1.0])
plt.ylim([0.0, 1.05])
plt.xlabel('False Positive Rate')
plt.ylabel('True Positive Rate')
plt.title('Receiver Operating Characteristic for CIFAR-10 classes')
plt.legend(loc="lower right")
plt.show()

# Confusion Matrix
conf_matrix = confusion_matrix(targets, predictions)
# Plot the confusion matrix as an image
fig, ax = plt.subplots(figsize=(10,10))
cax = ax.matshow(conf_matrix, cmap=plt.cm.Blues)
```

```
fig.colorbar(cax)
plt.xlabel('Predicted')
plt.ylabel('True')
plt.title('Confusion Matrix for CIFAR-10 Classification')
# Print the confusion matrix
tick_marks = np.arange(len(validation_set.classes))
plt.xticks(tick_marks, validation_set.classes, rotation=45)
plt.yticks(tick_marks, validation_set.classes)
plt.imshow(conf_matrix, interpolation='nearest', cmap=plt.cm.Blues)
thresh = conf_matrix.max() / 2.
for i, j in product(range(conf_matrix.shape[0]), range(conf_matrix.
shape[1])):
    plt.text(j, i, format(conf_matrix[i, j], 'd'),
             horizontalalignment="center",
             color="white" if conf_matrix[i, j] > thresh else "black")

plt.tight_layout()
plt.savefig('confusion_matrix.png')  # Save the confusion matrix as an
image
plt.show()
```

```
Accuracy: 0.6623
Precision: 0.7163997712224904
Recall: 0.6622999999999999
F1 Score: 0.6669511945689012
```

Figure 7.7: *Accuracy, Precision, Recall, and F1 score of the model trained with pre-trained weights*

```
Accuracy: 0.3382
Precision: 0.4500842943985474
Recall: 0.3382
F1 Score: 0.3277026444789191
```

Figure 7.8: *Accuracy, Precision, Recall, and F1 score of the model trained from scratch*

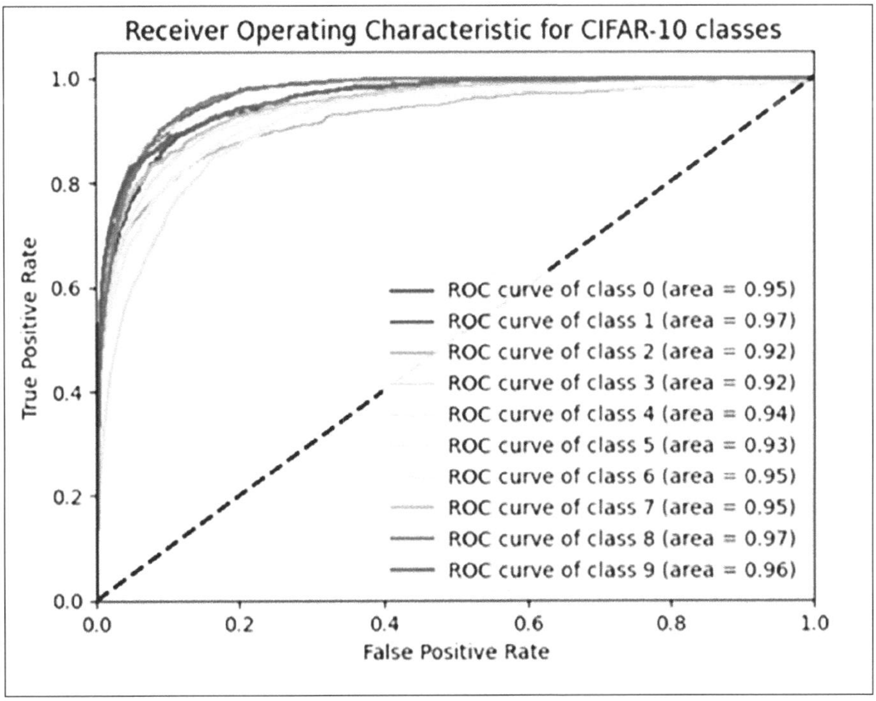

Figure 7.9: *ROC- Curve of the model trained with pre-trained weights*

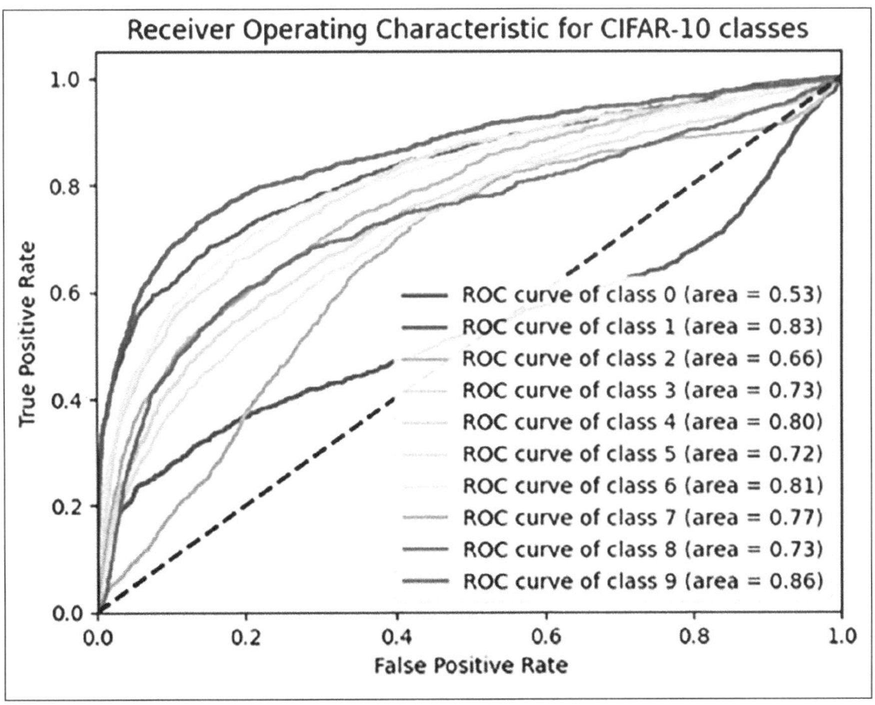

Figure 7.10: *ROC- Curve of the model trained from scratch*

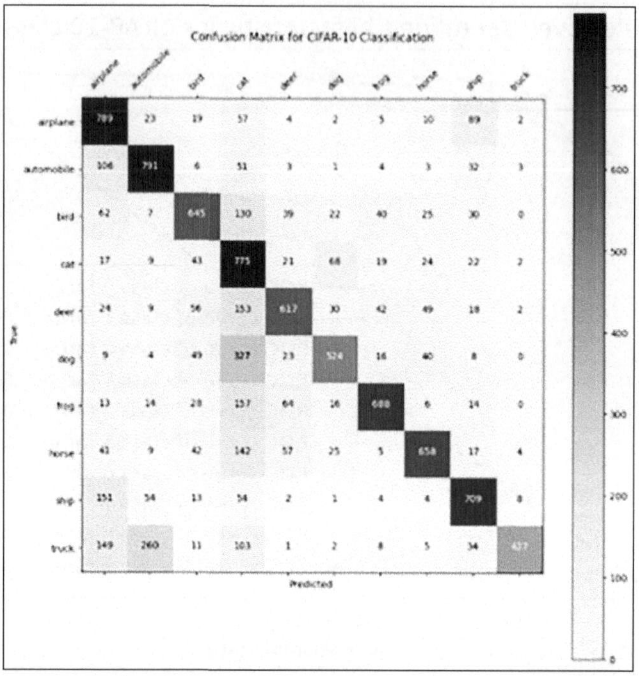

Figure 7.11: *Confusion Matrix of the model trained with pre-trained weights*

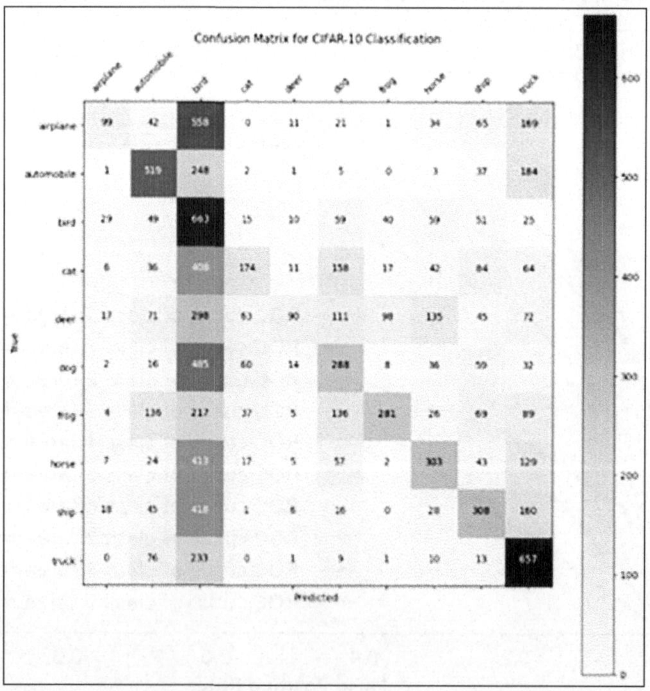

Figure 7.12: *Confusion Matrix of the model trained from scratch*

Comparison Pre-trained vs. Scratch

If we look at the output of the training, we can see that in the first epoch itself, the difference in loss is very high, 0.77 for the model started from pre-trained weights and 1.99 for the model started from scratch. Since the pre-trained model is already trained on the ImageNet dataset, it has learned all the low-level features and does not need to train for that. While in the case of training from scratch, the weights are initialized randomly so, the amount of training required is a lot higher.

Also, when we look at the accuracy, in 5 epochs, the pre-trained version was able to achieve 89% accuracy, while the model from scratch could only reach 69.63%. Another thing to note here is that compared to our SimpleCNN, these perform a lot better since they are very complex architectures proven to perform well on such image tasks.

We will look at the other metrics to compare the two models in the next section on A/B testing for choosing one model over another.

Impact of Transfer Learning on Model Performance

Transfer learning has revolutionized the field of machine learning, particularly within the domain of computer vision. By leveraging pre-trained models, practitioners can jump-start the training process, often leading to better model performance on a variety of metrics, including accuracy, precision, and recall.

Quantitative Benefits: Accuracy, Precision, and Recall

When discussing the quantitative benefits of transfer learning, we primarily refer to enhancements in model performance metrics. Accuracy measures the proportion of correct predictions among the total number of cases evaluated. Precision assesses the model's ability to return only relevant instances, while recall measures the model's ability to find all relevant instances within a dataset.

Consider the example of fine-tuning a ResNet model pre-trained on ImageNet for a new task, such as classifying images in the CIFAR-10 dataset. The rich feature representations learned from ImageNet provide a starting point that often leads to higher accuracy, as the model can generalize from a broad range of visual concepts.

Here's a code snippet to demonstrate the impact on accuracy, precision, and recall using a pre-trained model:

```
# Assuming that 'model_ft' is the fine-tuned model and 'model' is trained
from scratch
from sklearn.metrics import precision_score, recall_score, accuracy_
score

# Load the datasets and model
# ... (omitted for brevity)

# Function to get predictions
def get_predictions(loader, model):
    all_predictions = []
    all_targets = []
    model.eval()
    with torch.no_grad():
        for inputs, targets in loader:
            inputs, targets = inputs.to(device), targets.to(device)
            outputs = model(inputs)
            _, predictions = torch.max(outputs, 1)
            all_predictions.extend(predictions.cpu().numpy())
            all_targets.extend(targets.cpu().numpy())
    return all_predictions, all_targets

# Get predictions
predictions_ft, targets_ft = get_predictions(testloader, model_ft)
predictions, targets = get_predictions(testloader, model)

# Calculate metrics
accuracy_ft = accuracy_score(targets_ft, predictions_ft)
precision_ft = precision_score(targets_ft, predictions_ft, average='
macro')
recall_ft = recall_score(targets_ft, predictions_ft, average='macro')

accuracy = accuracy_score(targets, predictions)
precision = precision_score(targets, predictions, average='macro')
recall = recall_score(targets, predictions, average='macro')

# Output the metrics
print(f"Fine-tuned Model: Accuracy: {accuracy_ft}, Precision:
{precision_ft}, Recall: {recall_ft}")
print(f"From Scratch Model: Accuracy: {accuracy}, Precision:
{precision}, Recall: {recall}")
```

We have a similar snippet in our training code to get accuracy, but this snippet takes it further to get precision and recall as well.

Addressing Overfitting with Transfer Learning

Overfitting is a common problem in machine learning, where a model learns the training data too well, including its noise and outliers, which hampers its performance on unseen data. Transfer learning can mitigate this issue. Pre-trained models have been exposed to a wide variety of data, helping them to generalize better. When fine-tuning a model, only the final layers may need to be trained on the new dataset, reducing the risk of overfitting on that smaller dataset.

A/B Testing - Fine-Tuned versus Scratch Model

In the pursuit of understanding the real-world impact of transfer learning, we perform an A/B test between two models: one fine-tuned with ImageNet pre-trained weights and another trained from scratch. This comparative analysis illuminates the quantitative advantages that transfer learning confers upon model performance.

We first set up the CIFAR-10 validation dataset and load our two contestants, ensuring they are evaluated under identical conditions. By invoking the get_predictions function for each model, we gather predictions over the entire validation dataset.

Subsequently, we calculate accuracy, precision, recall, and F1 score for both models. These metrics serve as our performance indicators, providing insight into how each model fares in classifying unseen data. Not only do they offer a holistic view of model performance, but they also pinpoint areas where transfer learning may have conferred the most benefit.

Finally, by comparing these metrics, we observe the differences in performance, which may manifest as higher accuracy and better generalization for the fine-tuned model. This A/B test not only validates the effectiveness of transfer learning but also offers a template for readers to conduct their own comparative studies.

By incorporating this A/B testing methodology into your workflow, you can make data-driven decisions about the deployment of models and gain a deeper understanding of transfer learning's practical benefits. This approach serves as a bridge between theoretical knowledge and practical application.

```
import torch
import torchvision
import torchvision.transforms as transforms
from sklearn.metrics import accuracy_score, precision_score, recall_
score, f1_score
from torch.utils.data import DataLoader
from torchvision import models
```

```
# Assuming 'resnet50_cifar10_finetuned.pth' is the fine-tuned model and
'resnet50_cifar10_scratch.pth' is the from-scratch model
fine_tuned_model_path = 'resnet50_cifar10_finetuned.pth'
scratch_model_path = 'resnet50_cifar10_scratch.pth'

# Device configuration
device = torch.device('cuda' if torch.cuda.is_available() else 'cpu')

# Load models
def load_model(model_path):
    model = models.resnet50(pretrained=False)
    num_ftrs = model.fc.in_features
    model.fc = torch.nn.Linear(num_ftrs, 10)  # CIFAR-10 has 10 classes
    model.load_state_dict(torch.load(model_path))
    model = model.to(device)
    model.eval()
    return model

# Load both models
fine_tuned_model = load_model(fine_tuned_model_path)
scratch_model = load_model(scratch_model_path)

# CIFAR-10 validation dataset
transform = transforms.Compose([
    transforms.Resize(256),
    transforms.CenterCrop(224),
    transforms.ToTensor(),
    transforms.Normalize(mean=[0.485, 0.456, 0.406], std=[0.229, 0.224,
0.225]),
])

validation_set = torchvision.datasets.CIFAR10(root='./data',
train=False, download=True, transform=transform)
validation_loader = DataLoader(validation_set, batch_size=64,
shuffle=False)

# Get predictions
def get_predictions(loader, model):
    all_preds = []
    with torch.no_grad():
        for images, _ in loader:
            images = images.to(device)
            outputs = model(images)
            _, preds = torch.max(outputs, 1)
            all_preds.extend(preds.cpu().numpy())
    return all_preds
```

```
# Get predictions for both models
fine_tuned_predictions = get_predictions(validation_loader, fine_tuned_
model)
scratch_predictions = get_predictions(validation_loader, scratch_model)

# Get actual targets
targets = [target.cpu().numpy() for _, target in validation_set]

# Calculate metrics for both models
def calculate_metrics(targets, predictions):
    accuracy = accuracy_score(targets, predictions)
    precision = precision_score(targets, predictions, average='macro')
    recall = recall_score(targets, predictions, average='macro')
    f1 = f1_score(targets, predictions, average='macro')
    return accuracy, precision, recall, f1

fine_tuned_metrics = calculate_metrics(targets, fine_tuned_predictions)
scratch_metrics = calculate_metrics(targets, scratch_predictions)

# Print A/B Testing Results
print("Fine-Tuned Model Metrics: Accuracy: {:.2f}, Precision: {:.2f},
Recall: {:.2f}, F1 Score: {:.2f}".format(*fine_tuned_metrics))
print("Scratch Model Metrics: Accuracy: {:.2f}, Precision: {:.2f},
Recall: {:.2f}, F1 Score: {:.2f}".format(*scratch_metrics))

# Evaluate the difference
differences = [ft - sc for ft, sc in zip(fine_tuned_metrics, scratch_
metrics)]
print("\nDifferences (Fine-Tuned - Scratch): Accuracy: {:.2f}, Precision:
{:.2f}, Recall: {:.2f}, F1 Score: {:.2f}".format(*differences))
```

From the previous section, we can compare the different metrics and get a quantitative measure when comparing two models. From the different metrics, it is quite evident that the model started from pre-trained weights surpasses the model trained from scratch by a very big margin.

Impact of Transfer Learning

Transfer learning is most effective when the source and target domains have some overlap in feature space but can vary significantly in the labels or tasks. Tasks that have limited labeled data can see the most substantial benefits from transfer learning, as the pre-trained model brings in the knowledge that the algorithm would otherwise need to learn from scratch.

For instance, models trained on large-scale image datasets such as ImageNet have learned to identify edges, textures, and patterns that are universally applicable across various image recognition tasks. When such a model is fine-tuned for a specific task like medical image diagnosis, where annotated data may be scarce, the gains in performance can be significant.

In conclusion, transfer learning can substantially improve model performance, particularly when training data for the task at hand is limited. It enhances generalization, reduces overfitting, and leads to better accuracy, precision, and recall. The empirical benefits of transfer learning can be readily evaluated through careful experimentation and comparison, as evidenced in practice and by the previously mentioned code examples.

Best Practices and Common Pitfalls in Transfer Learning

In this section, we summarize the accumulated wisdom on applying transfer learning effectively, along with the common pitfalls that practitioners may encounter. This guidance is designed to serve as a navigational aid in the pursuit of successful machine-learning projects, reflecting the principles and examples we've explored throughout this book.

Do's When Applying Transfer Learning

- **Start with a pre-trained model:** Whenever possible, begin your project with a model pre-trained on a large and comprehensive dataset like ImageNet. This gives you a robust starting point, as seen with our ResNet-50 model applied to CIFAR-10.
- **Fine-tune carefully:** Monitor the training, as we demonstrated in the fine-tuning of our ResNet model, to avoid catastrophic forgetting of useful features.
- **Use appropriate data augmentation:** This can vastly increase the diversity of your training dataset, helping the model generalize better to new data.
- **Regularize strategically:** Apply techniques like dropout and weight decay judiciously to prevent overfitting, a principle we highlighted in earlier chapters.

Don'ts When Applying Transfer Learning

- **Overwrite pre-trained weights recklessly:** When loading a pre-trained model, ensure that you don't inadvertently reset weights, which can nullify the advantage of transfer learning.
- **Ignore the data distribution:** Transfer learning works best when the new task's data distribution is similar to the original training data. Ignoring this can lead to poor performance.

- **Neglect model complexity:** A model that's too complex for your task can lead to overfitting, while one that's too simple may not learn the necessary features.

Troubleshooting Common Issues

- **Model not improving:** If the performance plateaus, consider adjusting the learning rate or the point at which you begin fine-tuning layers in the network.
- **Overfitting:** Incorporate more data augmentation, add dropout layers, or collect more varied training data.
- **Underfitting:** Decrease regularization or unfreeze more layers of the network to allow for more feature adaptation.

Making the Most of Transfer Learning: A Checklist for Practitioners

1. **Evaluate task similarity:** Determine how close your target task is to the task the model was originally trained on. As we saw with our ResNet model, transferring to CIFAR-10 was effective due to the visual nature of both tasks.
2. **Start with feature extraction:** Use the pre-trained network as a fixed feature extractor before trying to fine-tune the entire model.
3. **Gradually increase complexity:** Begin by training just the final classification layer, then progressively unfreeze earlier layers as needed.
4. **Monitor validation performance:** Regularly check performance on a validation set to diagnose issues like overfitting or underfitting early.
5. **Keep learning rates low:** When fine-tuning, use low learning rates to avoid catastrophic changes to the learned features.
6. **Leverage domain-specific pre-trained models:** If available, use a model pre-trained on a dataset that is closer to your domain to capture more relevant features.

By adhering to these best practices and staying aware of potential pitfalls, practitioners can leverage the powerful capabilities of transfer learning more effectively. Throughout this book, we've seen the dramatic impact that judicious use of pre-trained models can have, from improving performance on small datasets to accelerating the training process.

When applying the principles and examples provided, such as those involving the PyTorch Model Zoo or the adaptation of the ResNet-50 model for CIFAR-10, practitioners should always aim for a thoughtful balance between leveraging learned features and adapting to new tasks. This balance is crucial, as it allows for the efficient application of transfer learning while avoiding common traps like overfitting or catastrophic forgetting.

Through careful planning, methodical execution, and continuous evaluation, transfer learning can be a transformative tool in the arsenal of both budding and seasoned machine learning practitioners.

Conclusion

As we close this chapter on transfer learning with PyTorch, we reflect on the potent combination of pre-trained models and fine-tuning strategies that can catapult image classification tasks to new heights of accuracy and efficiency. We have journeyed through the fundamentals, examined the nuances of applying pre-trained models to novel tasks, and dissected the intricacies of fine-tuning. Our hands-on examples have not only demonstrated the practical application of these concepts but also laid a solid foundation for understanding more complex image classification challenges.

Transfer learning serves as a bridge between the rudimentary use of deep learning models and the mastery of more advanced techniques. We've seen how a model like ResNet, pre-trained on ImageNet, can be repurposed and fine-tuned to excel on a dataset as diverse as CIFAR-10. This adaptability is what makes transfer learning an invaluable skill in the machine learning toolbox.

As we segue into the next chapter, *Advanced Image Classification Models*, we carry forward the principles and practices that have served us well. The upcoming chapter promises a deep dive into the architectures that are reshaping the landscape of computer vision. We'll peel back the layers of complexity that define models, such as ResNet, VGG, and Inception, and explore their unique contributions to the field.

Chapter 8
Advanced Image Classification Models

Introduction

As we navigate through the landscape of machine learning, image classification stands as a pivotal domain where significant strides have been made. The evolution of image classification models tells a story of relentless pursuit, from the simple perceptrons to the deep and complex networks of today. This journey reflects a constant theme in machine learning: the quest for models that not only perform well on the datasets they were trained on but also generalize effectively to new and unseen data.

The early days saw models that relied on hand-crafted features and linear classifiers. However, the advent of Convolutional Neural Networks (CNNs) marked a paradigm shift. LeCun's LeNet-5 was one of the first CNNs to be successfully applied to digit recognition, sowing the seeds for what would become deep learning. The real momentum, however, was gained with the AlexNet architecture, which triumphed at the ImageNet competition, firmly establishing deep learning as the method of choice for image classification tasks.

This chapter builds upon that foundation and delves into the sophisticated architectures that define modern image classification models. Here, we will dissect the inner workings of well-known architectures, such as ResNet, VGG, and Inception. Each of these models has contributed uniquely to the field, addressing specific challenges and setting new benchmarks for performance. As we unravel the complexity of these models, the chapter will maintain a balance between depth and accessibility, catering to both newcomers eager to learn the ropes and seasoned practitioners looking to deepen their expertise.

In the pages that follow, we will provide an Overview of Advanced Image Classification Models, charting their development and the theoretical underpinnings that guide their design. A detailed Deep Dive into ResNet, VGG, and Inception Architectures will offer a granular view of these models, shedding light on their groundbreaking features such as skip connections and depth-wise separable convolutions.

We will then transition into the practical side by Implementing Advanced Models in PyTorch 2.0. Step-by-step guides will lead you through the process of creating these models from scratch and adapting them to new tasks, with best practices highlighted to ensure smooth development and deployment.

The chapter will round out with Training and Evaluating Advanced Models, where we will discuss strategies for effectively training these deep networks and the metrics that should be used to evaluate their performance. Finally, a comparison of these models will be drawn in Comparing Model Performance, providing a clear perspective on when and where each model excels.

Prepare to embark on an insightful journey through the advanced frontiers of image classification. By the end of this chapter, you will not only grasp the theoretical aspects of these models but also gain the practical skills to implement and leverage them in PyTorch, pushing the boundaries of what you can achieve in the exciting field of computer vision.

Structure

In this chapter, the following topics will be covered:

- Deepening Foundations: A Quick Refresher
- Understanding Advanced Image Classification Models
- Deep Dive into VGG
- Deep Dive into ResNet
- Deep Dive into Inception
- Comparing Model Performance

Deepening Foundations: A Quick Refresher

Before we delve into the architectural marvels of advanced image classification models, let's revisit the core concepts that paved the way for their inception. This refresher will help align our understanding and appreciation for the solutions these advanced architectures provide.

Convolutional Neural Networks (CNNs)

At the heart of modern image classification lie Convolutional Neural Networks (CNNs), a class of deep neural networks that have achieved immense success in visual understanding. CNNs are specialized for processing data with a grid-like topology, such as images, by taking advantage of the inherent features of the visual world, such as the spatial hierarchy of shapes and textures.

A standard CNN comprises several layers:

- **Convolutional layers:** They apply a set of learnable filters to the input image, capturing features, such as edges and textures. The convolution operation preserves the spatial relationship between pixels by learning image features using small squares of input data.
- **Activation functions:** Non-linearities, such as the Rectified Linear Unit (ReLU), introduce non-linear properties to the system, enabling the network to learn a vast range of mappings from input to output.
- **Pooling layers:** These layers perform down-sampling operations to reduce the spatial size of the representation, diminishing the number of parameters and computation in the network, and hence helping to control overfitting.
- **Fully connected layers:** After several convolutional and pooling layers, the high-level reasoning in the neural network is done through fully connected layers. In a fully connected layer, every input is connected to every output by a learnable weight.

Backpropagation and Learning

Learning in CNNs is achieved through a process called backpropagation. This algorithm, in its essence, computes gradients of the loss function with respect to network weights by applying the chain rule of calculus iteratively backward through the network layers. These gradients are then used to update the weights of the network, typically using a gradient descent optimization algorithm.

Feature Maps

When a filter scans the input image, it creates a feature map that gives us information about the presence of specific features in the input. The depth of the feature map corresponds to the number of filters used. This design enables CNNs to automatically and adaptively learn spatial hierarchies of features from data.

Challenges and Advanced Solutions

Despite the groundbreaking impact of CNNs, as dataset complexity and network depth increased, new challenges arose:

- **Vanishing Gradients:** In very deep networks, gradients can become vanishingly small during backpropagation, making it difficult to train models, as the weights in the early layers receive very small updates. This could result in the network being unable to learn effectively.

- **Exploding Gradients**: Conversely, gradients can grow exponentially through layers, leading to very large updates and causing the model to diverge during training.
- **Computational Efficiency**: Deep networks require significant computational power and memory. Optimizing these networks to train and run efficiently on available hardware is a perennial challenge.

Advanced architectures such as VGG, ResNet, and Inception addressed these challenges in innovative ways:

- **VGG** solved computational challenges by using very small (3x3) convolution filters throughout the network, allowing deeper architectures.
- **ResNet** introduced the concept of skip connections or residual connections, where the input to a layer is added to the output, mitigating the issue of vanishing gradients as it allows for direct paths for the gradient to flow.
- **Inception** brought forth the idea of performing convolutions of different sizes in parallel to capture information at various scales, while also optimizing computational efficiency through dimensionality reduction.

A Foundation for Complex Architectures

Understanding the aforementioned concepts is vital in our exploration of advanced models. When you appreciate the solutions brought by VGG, ResNet, and Inception, you can comprehend the leap in performance with each successive architecture. These models have set new benchmarks and continue to inspire ongoing research and development in computer vision.

As we transition through this chapter, we will not only delve deeper into these architectures but will also see how they mitigate the challenges traditional CNNs face. Each of these advanced models carries forward the legacy and learnings from its predecessors, combining them with novel ideas to push the envelope of what's possible in image classification.

These advancements demonstrate the beauty of innovation in the field of neural networks: how the community builds upon established concepts to overcome obstacles and set new frontiers. This knowledge serves as your key to unlocking the full potential of computer vision tasks.

With this refresher in mind, let's embark on a deep-dive exploration into advanced image classification models, where robustness is intertwined with architectural ingenuity, giving rise to systems capable of perceiving the visual world with remarkable precision and speed. And as we journey through each advanced model, remember that these are not merely complex networks, but stepping stones to achieving new heights in the world of computer vision.

Now that we have reiterated the bedrock on which advanced image classification models stand, the stage is set for us to embrace the rich architectural tapestries that these models present. Through detailed examinations and hands-on coding sessions, you will not only build a working knowledge of their structures but also gain the expertise to tailor them to meet the nuanced demands of various visual tasks. Let us proceed with an eager mindset, as a solid understanding of these pioneering models equips us with the tools to ride the wave of innovation, unlocking yet unseen capabilities in the realm of computer vision with PyTorch 2.0.

Understanding Advanced Image Classification Models

As we go beyond the basic functionalities of Convolutional Neural Networks (CNNs), we encounter advanced image classification models that have redefined what computers can perceive and interpret from visual inputs. While the basic principles of neural networks still apply, these advanced models incorporate structural innovations that address specific challenges and maximize performance. Within this section, we will explore the key characteristics that distinguish models, such as VGG, ResNet, and Inception, unpack the reasoning behind their successful architectures, and delve into their popular use cases.

Key Characteristics of Advanced Models

- **Increased Depth and Complexity**: Advanced models often feature increased depth, with more layers added to enable the extraction of higher-level features from raw inputs. However, beyond merely stacking more layers, these models optimize network depth to enhance learning capabilities without falling prey to diminishing returns or training difficulties.
- **Specialized Layer Structures**: Offering a departure from the standard convolution-pooling structure, these models present innovative layer arrangements and connections. For instance, Inception models use parallel convolutions of different sizes, while ResNet introduces skip connections, allowing layers to learn from both their immediate predecessors and earlier activations at the same time.
- **Optimized Performance**: Advanced models are engineered for high performance, both in terms of generalization on unseen data and computational efficiency in training and inference. Techniques such as batch normalization and depth-wise separable convolutions are often employed to speed up learning and reduce the number of parameters.
- **Enhanced Regularization Techniques**: These models incorporate advanced regularization techniques to prevent overfitting despite their large capacity.

This could include methods, such as dropout, data augmentation, and stochastic depth, all meant to ensure the models generalize well to new data.

- **Modular Design**: Some advanced models adopt a modular approach, building the network out of repeatable building blocks or modules. This not only simplifies the architecture conceptually but also allows for greater flexibility in designing networks of varying depths and capacities.

Reasoning Behind Architectural Success

VGG (Visual Geometry Group)

The VGG architecture is celebrated for its simplicity, uniformity, and depth. The consistent use of small (3x3) convolutional filters throughout the network is a key to its success. This choice allows for capturing the spatial hierarchy of features with a reduced number of parameters, as several stacked small filters can emulate the receptive field of larger filters but with finer control over feature extraction. VGG networks are easy to implement, train, and adapt, making them a favorite starting point for many computer vision tasks.

ResNet (Residual Networks)

ResNet's breakthrough was in addressing the vanishing gradients problem, a significant hindrance in training deep networks. Its residual blocks, each with a skip connection that adds the input of the block to its output, allow gradients to flow directly through the network without diminishing across layers. This innovation enables the training of very deep networks by effectively bypassing layers during backpropagation if they are not needed for a particular task, a concept aptly named "identity shortcut connections." ResNet architectures have proven to be versatile and robust, achieving state-of-the-art results in various computer vision benchmarks.

Inception

The Inception architecture, with the keyword "multiply and conquer," emphasizes width over depth. Inception modules perform several different convolutions in parallel and concatenate their outputs. By aggregating diverse feature maps, the network can analyze the input with a rich variety of filters without an explosion in computational cost. Furthermore, it utilizes dimensionality reduction techniques to manage the channel sizes, preserving computational efficiency. The various versions of Inception have evolved to refine and balance the network's width and depth, ensuring efficient computation and strong representational power.

Popular Use Cases

- **Image Classification**: This is the quintessential use case for these models.

With their capacity to learn nuanced features and patterns, they lead the performance charts in popular benchmarks such as ImageNet.

- **Object Detection and Localization**: Beyond classification, these networks can be repurposed as feature extractors in systems designed for object detection and localization. By interpreting the rich feature maps they produce, models like Faster R-CNN and YOLO integrate these architectures to determine not only what objects are present in an image but also where they are.
- **Content-Based Image Retrieval**: In applications where the similarity between images needs to be determined (for example, finding images that are visually similar), the embeddings produced by these advanced models provide a powerful summary of an image's content which can be compared against a database of known images.
- **Style Transfer and Image Generation**: Advanced models can decipher and manipulate the stylistic elements of images, informing algorithms that can transfer artistic styles or generate new images that comply with learned visual patterns.
- **Medical Imaging**: Due to their fine-grained feature detection, these models are increasingly employed in medical imaging tasks such as identifying tumors in MRI scans or detecting anomalies in X-rays.

Innovative architectures such as VGG, ResNet, and Inception exemplify how creative design can lead to significant improvements in what computer vision algorithms can achieve. These models encapsulate the ongoing quest to replicate and exceed human visual capabilities with machines by learning to interpret complex visual data in a scalable, efficient, and accurate manner. As we progress through this chapter, we will dissect these architectures piece by piece, revealing the inner mechanics that drive their success. Through understanding and implementation, you will learn not just to use these models, but also to thoughtfully adapt them to your purposes, continuing the cycle of innovation that drives forward the field of computer vision.

Diving Deep into VGG

When discussing breakthroughs in the panorama of deep learning image classification, the architecture known as VGG, developed by the Visual Geometry Group at the University of Oxford, stands out for its conceptual straightforwardness and remarkable depth. VGG's design philosophy set a new standard for deep neural networks. It's renowned for its sequential arrangement of convolution layers, which are remarkable for their uniformity. There are several variations of this model—primarily distinguished by their depth—VGG16 and VGG19 being the most well-known.

Model Architecture and Variants

At its core, VGG's architecture comprises an assembly of consecutive convolutional layers with small 3x3 receptive fields, followed by max-pooling operations. This simplicity in the convolutional architecture forms the primary motif for VGG, repeated throughout with increasing depth. Layers are arranged in blocks, with each max-pooling step essentially compressing the spatial dimension of the feature maps, while the depth increases.

VGG16 consists of 16 layers, including 13 convolutional layers and 3 fully connected layers. It interlaces convolutional layers with a stride of one and padding to preserve spatial resolution, with pooling layers that halve the dimensions of the feature map to condense information. Similarly, **VGG19** includes 19 layers with 16 convolutional and 3 fully connected, extending the depth further.

Simplicity and Depth

The VGG models illustrate the power of simplicity aligned with depth in architectural design. Despite the sophistication of deeper and more conditional architectures, VGG's uniform utilization of 3x3 filters throughout every convolutional layer harnesses powerful feature extraction capabilities.

This simplicity engenders a formative strength, providing a homogeneous and reiterative structure that can capture increasingly complex features at various levels of abstraction. Each consecutive pooling layer contributes to the learning of features at multiple scales, which is particularly effective in visual recognition tasks.

The VGG Architecture Explained

VGG's architectural contribution lies in its use of multiple stacked 3x3 convolutional layers, which, with a stride of one and padding to maintain spatial resolution, effectively provide a larger receptive field similar to that of a larger filter while enhancing the learning of features with additional non-linearities. This stack, separated by max-pooling layers, conveys a hierarchy of learned features from the simple to the abstract.

Following the convolutional layers, three fully-connected layers suffice, including one as a final output layer tuned to the number of classes for a given task. VGG's structure is synonymous with depth, proving in practice that deeper networks can lead to better feature hierarchies.

Implementing VGG in PyTorch

PyTorch's object-oriented nature facilitates the clean definition of a VGG architecture. We will now step through a PyTorch implementation of VGG16; due to space and resource constraints, we'll focus on VGG16, but expanding this to VGG19 follows similarly by increasing the number of convolutional layers.

```
import torch.nn as nn
import torch

class VGG16(nn.Module):
    def __init__(self, num_classes=1000):  # VGG16 has 1000 classes by
default
        super(VGG16, self).__init__()
        self.features = self._create_features()
        self.classifier = self._create_classifier(num_classes)

    def _create_features(self):
        layers = [
            # Block 1
            nn.Conv2d(3, 64, kernel_size=3, padding=1),
            nn.ReLU(inplace=True),
            nn.Conv2d(64, 64, kernel_size=3, padding=1),
            nn.ReLU(inplace=True),
            nn.MaxPool2d(kernel_size=2, stride=2),
            # Block 2
            nn.Conv2d(64, 128, kernel_size=3, padding=1),
            nn.ReLU(inplace=True),
            nn.Conv2d(128, 128, kernel_size=3, padding=1),
            nn.ReLU(inplace=True),
            nn.MaxPool2d(kernel_size=2, stride=2),
            # Block 3
            nn.Conv2d(128, 256, kernel_size=3, padding=1),
            nn.ReLU(inplace=True),
            nn.Conv2d(256, 256, kernel_size=3, padding=1),
            nn.ReLU(inplace=True),
            nn.Conv2d(256, 256, kernel_size=3, padding=1),
            nn.ReLU(inplace=True),
            nn.MaxPool2d(kernel_size=2, stride=2),
            # Block 4
            nn.Conv2d(256, 512, kernel_size=3, padding=1),
            nn.ReLU(inplace=True),
            nn.Conv2d(512, 512, kernel_size=3, padding=1),
            nn.ReLU(inplace=True),
            nn.Conv2d(512, 512, kernel_size=3, padding=1),
            nn.ReLU(inplace=True),
            nn.MaxPool2d(kernel_size=2, stride=2),
            # Block 5
            nn.Conv2d(512, 512, kernel_size=3, padding=1),
            nn.ReLU(inplace=True),
            nn.Conv2d(512, 512, kernel_size=3, padding=1),
```

```
            nn.ReLU(inplace=True),
            nn.Conv2d(512, 512, kernel_size=3, padding=1),
            nn.ReLU(inplace=True),
            nn.MaxPool2d(kernel_size=2, stride=2)
        ]
        return nn.Sequential(*layers)

    def _create_classifier(self, num_classes):
        layers = [
            nn.Linear(512 * 7 * 7, 4096), nn.ReLU(inplace=True),
            nn.Dropout(),
            nn.Linear(4096, 4096), nn.ReLU(inplace=True),
            nn.Dropout(),
            nn.Linear(4096, num_classes)
        ]
        return nn.Sequential(*layers)

    def forward(self, x):
        x = self.features(x)
        x = torch.flatten(x, start_dim=1)  # Flatten the tensor for clas-
sifier intake
        x = self.classifier(x)
        return x
```

The layers inside **_create_features()** denote the convolution and max-pooling layers, while **_create_classifier()** encapsulates the dense layers that conclude the architecture.

Sequential Layout

The network is implemented as a sequence of convolutional layers, where the number of filters doubles after each max pooling layer, starting from 64 and going up to 512. This property makes it easy to define the model in a modular way.

Here's an example of how to define the VGG16 architecture in PyTorch:

import **torch.nn** as **nn**

```
# Defining each block of the VGG16 architecture
def make_layers(cfg):
    layers = []
    in_channels = 3
    for v in cfg:
        if v == 'M':
            layers += [nn.MaxPool2d(kernel_size=2, stride=2)]
        else:
```

```
            layers += [nn.Conv2d(in_channels, v, kernel_size=3, 
padding=1),
                       nn.BatchNorm2d(v),
                       nn.ReLU(inplace=True)]
            in_channels = v
    return nn.Sequential(*layers)

# Configuration for VGG16
cfg = [64, 64, 'M', 128, 128, 'M', 256, 256, 256, 'M', 512, 512, 512, 
'M', 512, 512, 512, 'M']

class VGG16(nn.Module):
    def __init__(self, num_classes=1000):
        super(VGG16, self).__init__()
        # Feature extraction part
        self.features = make_layers(cfg)

        # Classifier part
        self.classifier = nn.Sequential(
            nn.Linear(512 * 7 * 7, 4096),
            nn.ReLU(True),
            nn.Dropout(),
            nn.Linear(4096, 4096),
            nn.ReLU(True),
            nn.Dropout(),
            nn.Linear(4096, num_classes),
        )

    # The VGG16 forward pass
    def forward(self, x):
        x = self.features(x)
        x = x.view(x.size(0), -1)  # Flatten the tensor for the 
classifier
        x = self.classifier(x)
        return x
```

VGG16 implementation in PyTorch exemplifies how traditional and powerful convolutional neural network architectures can be applied to modern machine learning problems. Its uniform architecture, combined with the capability of being easily modified and extended, has established VGG16 as a workhorse of deep learning for computer vision. With a predefined architecture and pretrained weights, PyTorch streamlines the process of creating, adapting, and deploying these models for a myriad of tasks.

Importing VGG from PyTorch's Model Zoo

PyTorch's model zoo grants access to pretrained network architectures, allowing for easy instantiation and integration into projects:

```
from torchvision import models

vgg16_pretrained = models.vgg16(weights=None)
```

Leveraging Pretrained Weights

Leveraging pretrained weights is straightforward with PyTorch's models:

```
import torchvision

vgg16_pretrained = torchvision.models.vgg16(weights=torchvision.models.
VGG16_Weights.DEFAULT)
vgg16_pretrained.classifier[6] = nn.Linear(4096, 100)  # Change the last
layer to fit CIFAR100
```

This single line alters the final dense layer to accommodate 100 classes, typical of CIFAR100, while benefiting from ImageNet's pretrained weights.

Training and Evaluating VGG on CIFAR100

The CIFAR100 dataset presents a multi-class image classification problem with 100 categories. Each category contains 600 images, and the small size of each image (32x32 pixels) makes it both a manageable and challenging dataset.

Data Pre-processing and Augmentation Steps

For data pre-processing, normalization is necessary so that each color channel has mean zero and unit variance. This facilitates model training by providing numerically stable inputs:

```
from torchvision.transforms import transforms
transform = transforms.Compose([
    transforms.RandomCrop(32, padding=4),
    transforms.RandomHorizontalFlip(),
    transforms.ToTensor(),
    transforms.Normalize((0.5071, 0.4867, 0.4408), (0.2009, 0.1984,
0.2023)),
])
```

Data augmentation implements random horizontal flips and random crops, simulating variations that the model should be invariant to.

Training Code

The training loop in PyTorch iterates through the CIFAR100 data loader, applying backpropagation to update weights:

```
# Define device for training
device = torch.device("cuda:0" if torch.cuda.is_available() else "cpu")

# Map to device
vgg16_pretrained = vgg16_pretrained.to(device)

optimizer = torch.optim.SGD(vgg16_pretrained.parameters(), lr=0.01,
momentum=0.9)
criterion = nn.CrossEntropyLoss()

# Create data loaders
train_dataset = torchvision.datasets.CIFAR100(root='./data', train=True,
download=True, transform=transform)
test_dataset = torchvision.datasets.CIFAR100(root='./data', train=False,
download=True, transform=transform)

train_loader = torch.utils.data.DataLoader(train_dataset, batch_size=64,
shuffle=True)
test_loader = torch.utils.data.DataLoader(test_dataset, batch_size=64,
shuffle=False)

# Set number of epochs to train
number_of_epochs = 5

# Loop for each epoch
for epoch in range(number_of_epochs):
    running_loss = 0.0
    for i, data in enumerate(train_loader, 0):
        inputs, labels = data[0].to(device), data[1].to(device)
        optimizer.zero_grad()
        outputs = vgg16_pretrained(inputs)
        loss = criterion(outputs, labels)
        loss.backward()
        optimizer.step()
        running_loss += loss.item()
    print(f'Epoch {epoch + 1}: Loss: {running_loss / len(train_loader)}')

# Save the model's state dictionary
torch.save(vgg16_pretrained.state_dict(), 'vgg16_cifar100.pth')
```

```
Epoch 1: Loss: 1.630416536346421
Epoch 2: Loss: 1.5624679418476037
Epoch 3: Loss: 1.5073729947095027
Epoch 4: Loss: 1.4377963458333174
Epoch 5: Loss: 1.4102273747286833
Epoch 6: Loss: 1.3745591128268815
Epoch 7: Loss: 1.3385358903261706
Epoch 8: Loss: 1.305282829743822
Epoch 9: Loss: 1.2908474900533475
Epoch 10: Loss: 1.2709745466709137
```

Figure 8.1: *Output of training the VGG-16 model on the CIFAR100 dataset for 100 epochs*

Evaluation Code

After training, it's essential to evaluate the model's performance on a validation or test set to gauge generalization:

```
correct, total = 0, 0
with torch.no_grad():
    for data in test_loader:
        images, labels = data[0].to(device), data[1].to(device)
        outputs = vgg16_pretrained(images)
        _, predicted = torch.max(outputs.data, 1)
        total += labels.size(0)
        correct += (predicted == labels).sum().item()
print(f'Accuracy on test images: {100 * correct // total}%')
```

```
Accuracy on test images: 55%
```

Figure 8.2: *Accuracy on the test set after training the model for 10 epochs*

Strengths and Limitations

The strengths of VGG lie in its depth, leading to rich feature representation and its uniform architecture, which simplifies learning. It is an excellent model for transfer learning and feature extraction tasks. However, limitations include its substantial computational cost and inefficiencies compared to modern architectures such as ResNets or DenseNets that utilize shortcut connections or feature reuse for better performance.

In summary, VGG's introduction sparked a depth-oriented trend in CNN architecture design, revealing the power of deep and rich feature hierarchies. Through hands-on PyTorch implementation, observation via TensorBoard, and integration with training and evaluation loops, we find VGG to be a pivotal architecture that propels us further into unlocking the mysteries of computer vision.

Diving Deep into ResNet

ResNet, short for Residual Network, radically changed the course of deep learning architectures upon its inception. Designed by Kaiming He and colleagues, ResNet addressed the degradation problem, enabling the training of very deep neural networks by using shortcut connections to jump over some layers.

Model Architecture and Variants

Unlike architectures that stack layers directly, ResNet introduces the concept of the residual block where layers learn residual functions with reference to the layer inputs. The network variants are often denoted by their depth, such as **ResNet-18**, **ResNet-34**, **ResNet-50**, **ResNet-101**, and **ResNet-152**.

In ResNet, convolutional blocks are followed by batch normalization and a ReLU activation function. The crucial element, however, is the addition of a shortcut connection before the activation function, allowing the network to learn an identity function. This ensures that the higher layers can perform at least as good as the lower layers, and not worse.

The Elegance of Residual Blocks

Residual blocks tackle the diminishing gradients problem by introducing direct paths for backpropagation. This design ensures that the gradients can flow through the network without significant degradation, allowing for previously unattainable deep networks.

Implementing ResNet in PyTorch

Let's step through a PyTorch implementation of ResNet. We will focus on ResNet-50 as a compromise between depth and computational efficiency:

```
import torch
import torch.nn as nn
from torchvision import models

class BasicBlock(nn.Module):
    expansion = 1
```

```
    def __init__(self, in_channels, out_channels, stride=1, downsample=-
None):
        super(BasicBlock, self).__init__()
        # 1x1 convolutions are used as bottlenecks for reducing and then
increasing dimensions,
        # without changing width/height size
        self.conv1 = nn.Conv2d(in_channels, out_channels, kernel_size=1,
stride=1, bias=False)
        self.bn1 = nn.BatchNorm2d(out_channels)
        # A 3x3 convolution is used in the middle
        self.conv2 = nn.Conv2d(out_channels, out_channels, kernel_
size=3, stride=stride, padding=1, bias=False)
        self.bn2 = nn.BatchNorm2d(out_channels)
        # Another 1x1 convolution with the expansion factor applied
        self.conv3 = nn.Conv2d(out_channels, out_channels * self.
expansion, kernel_size=1, stride=1, bias=False)
        self.bn3 = nn.BatchNorm2d(out_channels * self.expansion)
        self.relu = nn.ReLU(inplace=True)
        self.downsample = downsample

    def forward(self, x):
        identity = x if self.downsample is None else self.downsample(x)
        out = self.relu(self.bn1(self.conv1(x)))
        out = self.relu(self.bn2(self.conv2(out)))
        out = self.bn3(self.conv3(out))
        out += identity
        out = self.relu(out)
        return out

class ResNet(nn.Module):
    def __init__(self, block, layers, num_classes=1000):
        super(ResNet, self).__init__()
        self.in_channels = 64
        self.conv1 = nn.Conv2d(3, self.in_channels, kernel_size=7,
stride=2, padding=3, bias=False)
        self.bn1 = nn.BatchNorm2d(self.in_channels)
        self.relu = nn.ReLU(inplace=True)
        self.maxpool = nn.MaxPool2d(kernel_size=3, stride=2, padding=1)

        # Each _make_layer() creates one stage of blocks in ResNet
        self.layer1 = self._make_layer(block, 64, layers[0])
        self.layer2 = self._make_layer(block, 128, layers[1], stride=2)
        self.layer3 = self._make_layer(block, 256, layers[2], stride=2)
        self.layer4 = self._make_layer(block, 512, layers[3], stride=2)

        self.avgpool = nn.AdaptiveAvgPool2d((1, 1))  # Adaptive pooling
```

```
to fit the final layer
        self.fc = nn.Linear(512 * block.expansion, num_classes)

    def _make_layer(self, block, out_channels, blocks, stride=1):
        downsample = None
        if stride != 1 or self.in_channels != out_channels * block.
expansion:
            downsample = nn.Sequential(
                nn.Conv2d(self.in_channels, out_channels * block.
expansion, kernel_size=1, stride=stride, bias=False),
                nn.BatchNorm2d(out_channels * block.expansion),
            )
        layers = []
        layers.append(block(self.in_channels, out_channels, stride,
downsample))
        self.in_channels = out_channels * block.expansion
        for _ in range(1, blocks):
            layers.append(block(self.in_channels, out_channels))

        return nn.Sequential(*layers)

    def forward(self, x):
        x = self.relu(self.bn1(self.conv1(x)))
        x = self.maxpool(x)
        # ResNet layers
        x = self.layer1(x)
        x = self.layer2(x)
        x = self.layer3(x)
        x = self.layer4(x)

        x = self.avgpool(x)
        x = torch.flatten(x, 1)
        x = self.fc(x)
        return x

def resnet50(num_classes=1000):
    # Constructs a ResNet-50 model
    return ResNet(BasicBlock, [3, 4, 6, 3], num_classes)

# Instantiate a ResNet-50 model
model = resnet50(num_classes=1000)
```

This model can then be adjusted for tasks like CIFAR100 by changing the final fully connected layer to output 100 classes instead of 1000.

Basic Building Blocks

ResNet's architecture is composed of several stages of residual blocks that form the backbone of the network. Each block comprises batch normalization, activation layers, and trademark skip connections that give the architecture its name.

Here's a simplified implementation of a basic residual block, BasicBlock, which is a part of larger ResNet configurations such as ResNet-18 and ResNet-34:

```
class BasicBlock(nn.Module):
    expansion = 1
    def __init__(self, in_channels, out_channels, stride=1, downsample=-
None):
        super(BasicBlock, self).__init__()

        # First convolutional layer
        self.conv1 = nn.Conv2d(in_channels, out_channels, kernel_size=3,
stride=stride, padding=1, bias=False)
        self.bn1 = nn.BatchNorm2d(out_channels)
        self.relu = nn.ReLU(inplace=True)

        # Second convolutional layer
        self.conv2 = nn.Conv2d(out_channels, out_channels * BasicBlock.
expansion,
                               kernel_size=3, stride=1, padding=1,
bias=False)
        self.bn2 = nn.BatchNorm2d(out_channels * BasicBlock.expansion)

        # Optional downsampling
        self.downsample = downsample
        self.stride = stride

    def forward(self, x):
        residual = x

        # Passing input through conv1->bn1->relu stack
        out = self.conv1(x)
        out = self.bn1(out)
        out = self.relu(out)

        # Passing input through conv2->bn2 stack
        out = self.conv2(out)
        out = self.bn2(out)

        # Applying downsampling if needed
        if self.downsample is not None:
            residual = self.downsample(x)
```

```
        # Adding the input (identity or downsampled) to the output of
the residual block
        out += residual
        out = self.relu(out)

        return out
```

ResNet Model

We then use these foundational blocks to build the actual ResNet model. Here's a snippet showing the instantiation of a ResNet-50 which uses bottleneck blocks, which we will cover later, for efficiency:

```
class ResNet(nn.Module):

    def __init__(self, block, layers, num_classes=1000):
        super(ResNet, self).__init__()
        self.in_channels = 64

        # Initial convolutional layer with max-pooling
        self.conv1 = nn.Conv2d(3, self.in_channels, kernel_size=7,
stride=2, padding=3, bias=False)
        self.bn1 = nn.BatchNorm2d(self.in_channels)
        self.relu = nn.ReLU(inplace=True)
        self.maxpool = nn.MaxPool2d(kernel_size=3, stride=2, padding=1)

        # Residual layers
        self.layer1 = self._make_layer(block, 64, layers[0])
        self.layer2 = self._make_layer(block, 128, layers[1], stride=2)
        self.layer3 = self._make_layer(block, 256, layers[2], stride=2)
        self.layer4 = self._make_layer(block, 512, layers[3], stride=2)

        # Adaptive average pooling and the final fully connected layer
        self.avgpool = nn.AdaptiveAvgPool2d((1, 1))
        self.fc = nn.Linear(512 * block.expansion, num_classes)

        # Weight initialization
        for m in self.modules():
            if isinstance(m, nn.Conv2d):
                nn.init.kaiming_normal_(m.weight, mode='fan_out',
nonlinearity='relu')
            elif isinstance(m, nn.BatchNorm2d):
                nn.init.constant_(m.weight, 1)
                nn.init.constant_(m.bias, 0)

    # Helper function to create each ResNet layer
```

```
    def _make_layer(self, block, out_channels, blocks, stride=1):
        downsample = None
        if stride != 1 or self.in_channels != out_channels * block.
expansion:
            downsample = nn.Sequential(
                nn.Conv2d(self.in_channels, out_channels * block.
expansion,
                              kernel_size=1, stride=stride, bias=False),
                nn.BatchNorm2d(out_channels * block.expansion),
            )

        # The first block in the layer
        layers = [block(self.in_channels, out_channels, stride, down
sample)]
        self.in_channels = out_channels * block.expansion
        # Remaining blocks in the layer
        for _ in range(1, blocks):
            layers.append(block(self.in_channels, out_channels))

        return nn.Sequential(*layers)

    # The forward pass
    def forward(self, x):
        x = self.conv1(x)
        x = self.bn1(x)
        x = self.relu(x)
        x = self.maxpool(x)

        # Passing input through the layers
        x = self.layer1(x)
        x = self.layer2(x)
        x = self.layer3(x)
        x = self.layer4(x)

        # Pooling and classification
        x = self.avgpool(x)
        x = torch.flatten(x, 1)
        x = self.fc(x)

        return x
```

In ResNet-50, `block` would be a `Bottleneck` block as defined later, where each Bottleneck block has a `conv->bn->relu` pattern with the convolutions using a kernel size of 1 to reduce dimensions, 3 to apply the convolutional operation, and again 1 to restore dimensions, making efficient use of parameters.

ResNet-50: Bottleneck Blocks

ResNet-50 uses Bottleneck blocks, which consist of three layers. These blocks include an initial dimensionality reduction step using 1x1 convolutions, followed by the main 3x3 convolution, and then another 1x1 convolution to restore dimensionality. Here's an example Bottleneck block:

```
class Bottleneck(nn.Module):
    expansion = 4

    def __init__(self, in_channels, out_channels, stride=1, downsample=-
None):
        super(Bottleneck, self).__init__()

        # First 1x1 convolution
        self.conv1 = nn.Conv2d(in_channels, out_channels, kernel_size=1,
bias=False)
        self.bn1 = nn.BatchNorm2d(out_channels)

        # Second 3x3 convolution
        self.conv2 = nn.Conv2d(out_channels, out_channels, kernel_
size=3, stride=stride,
                               padding=1, bias=False)
        self.bn2 = nn.BatchNorm2d(out_channels)

        # Third 1x1 convolution with expansion
        self.conv3 = nn.Conv2d(out_channels, out_channels * self.
expansion, kernel_size=1, bias=False)
        self.bn3 = nn.BatchNorm2d(out_channels * self.expansion)

        self.relu = nn.ReLU(inplace=True)
        self.downsample = downsample
        self.stride = stride

        # Forward function remains the same as BasicBlock

# Instantiating ResNet-50 would involve using the Bottleneck block:
resnet50_model = ResNet(Bottleneck, [3, 4, 6, 3], num_classes=1000)
```

Bringing it All Together

Instantiate the ResNet model with the following:

```
def resnet50(num_classes=1000):
    # Constructs a ResNet-50 model
    return ResNet(Bottleneck, [3, 4, 6, 3], num_classes)
```

```
# Initialize a ResNet-50 model
resnet50_custom = resnet50(num_classes=1000)
```

In summary, implementing ResNet in PyTorch involves constructing the sequential blocks that define its architecture. Each block adds residual connections, allowing learning to occur even as the network depths grow. By instantiating these layers and defining the forward pass, a ResNet model can be created, trained, and used to solve complex image recognition challenges.

Importing ResNet from PyTorch's Model Zoo

Similar to the VGG model, PyTorch's Model Zoo provides pretrained ResNet models:

```
from torchvision import models
resnet50_pretrained = models.resnet50(weights=None)
```

Leveraging Pretrained Weights

Leveraging pretrained weights is straightforward with PyTorch's models:

```
import torchvision
resnet50_pretrained = torchvision.models.resnet50(weights=torchvision.
models.ResNet50_Weights.IMAGENET1K_V1)
resnet50_pretrained.fc = nn.Linear(resnet50_pretrained.fc.in_features,
100)  # Change the last layer to fit CIFAR100
```

This single line alters the final dense layer to accommodate 100 classes, typical of CIFAR100, while benefiting from ImageNet's pretrained weights.

Training and Evaluating ResNet on CIFAR100

The training and evaluation process for ResNet parallels those of other deep learning models, with adjustments required for the deeper network structure. Note that residual blocks may significantly increase training time, but they also provide marked improvements in learning efficiency.

Data Pre-processing and Augmentation Steps

Before feeding data to a convolutional neural network like ResNet, it's essential to perform pre-processing and data augmentation to standardize inputs and increase generalizability.

```
from torchvision.transforms import transforms

transform = transforms.Compose([
    transforms.RandomResizedCrop(224),  # ResNet typically requires
input images of size 224x224
```

```
    transforms.RandomHorizontalFlip(),
    transforms.ToTensor(),
    transforms.Normalize(mean=[0.485, 0.456, 0.406], std=[0.229, 0.224,
0.225]),  # Normalization parameters for ImageNet
])
```

Pre-processing normalizes the dataset with mean and standard deviation, matching those of the ImageNet dataset since the pretrained ResNet is commonly trained on ImageNet. Data augmentation techniques include random resizing and cropping, as well as horizontal flipping to introduce more variability and robustness to the model.

Training Code

Training involves iterating over our training dataset, feeding inputs to the ResNet model and performing backpropagation to adjust the weights. Here is the training loop in PyTorch:

```
import torch
import torch.nn as nn
from torchvision import models

# send model to GPU
device = torch.device("cuda:0" if torch.cuda.is_available() else "cpu")
resnet50_pretrained.to(device)

# Assuming we have a model named 'resnet50_pretrained' and dataloaders
'train_loader' defined
optimizer = torch.optim.SGD(resnet50_pretrained.parameters(), lr=0.001,
momentum=0.9)
criterion = nn.CrossEntropyLoss()

# Create data loaders
train_dataset = torchvision.datasets.CIFAR100(root='./data', train=True,
download=True, transform=transform)
test_dataset = torchvision.datasets.CIFAR100(root='./data', train=False,
download=True, transform=transform)

train_loader = torch.utils.data.DataLoader(train_dataset, batch_size=64,
shuffle=True)
test_loader = torch.utils.data.DataLoader(test_dataset, batch_size=64,
shuffle=False)

# Set number of epochs to train
number_of_epochs = 10
```

```
# Loop over the dataset multiple times
for epoch in range(number_of_epochs):
    resnet50_pretrained.train()  # Set model to training mode
    running_loss = 0.0
    for i, data in enumerate(train_loader, 0):
        # get the inputs; data is a list of [inputs, labels]
        inputs, labels = data[0].to(device), data[1].to(device)

        # zero the parameter gradients
        optimizer.zero_grad()


        # forward + backward + optimize
        outputs = resnet50_pretrained(inputs)
        loss = criterion(outputs, labels)
        loss.backward()
        optimizer.step()


        running_loss += loss.item()

    print(f'Epoch {epoch + 1}: Loss: {running_loss / len(train_
loader)}')

# Save the model's state dictionary
torch.save(resnet50_pretrained.state_dict(), 'resnet50_cifar100.pth')
```

Within the loop, the optimizer's gradients are first reset using **`optimizer.zero_grad()`**, and after the loss is calculated, **`loss.backward()`** is used for backpropagation, while **`optimizer.step()`** updates the model parameters.

```
Epoch 1: Loss: 3.119440778137168
Epoch 2: Loss: 1.7574083358430497
Epoch 3: Loss: 1.4686614196471242
Epoch 4: Loss: 1.3218359941106927
Epoch 5: Loss: 1.238509480224546
Epoch 6: Loss: 1.1689277666304119
Epoch 7: Loss: 1.1101623693543017
Epoch 8: Loss: 1.065161960204239
Epoch 9: Loss: 1.0353370446073429
Epoch 10: Loss: 0.9977153868169126
```

Figure 8.3: *Output of training the RerNet-50 model on the CIFAR100 dataset for 100 epochs*

Evaluation Code

After training, evaluating the model on a validation or test dataset is key to assessing its generalization capability.

```
resnet50_pretrained.eval()  # Set model to evaluation mode
correct = 0
total = 0
with torch.no_grad():
    for data in test_loader:
        images, labels = data[0].to(device), data[1].to(device)
        outputs = resnet50_pretrained(images)
        _, predicted = torch.max(outputs.data, 1)
        total += labels.size(0)
        correct += (predicted == labels).sum().item()

accuracy = correct / total
print(f'Accuracy of the network on test images: {100 * accuracy}%')
```

```
Accuracy of the network on test images: 68.19%
```

Figure 8.4: *Accuracy on the test set after training the model for 10 epochs*

During evaluation, gradients are not tracked, and the **`torch.no_grad()`** context manager tells PyTorch to ignore gradients for efficiency. The model's accuracy is then calculated based on its performance on the test dataset.

Strengths and Limitations

ResNet's main strength is its ability to train very deep neural networks, which was not feasible before its development. It's widely used as a starting architecture for many variants and tasks. One limitation is the increased model complexity, leading to higher computational costs. Also, while ResNets may prevent vanishing gradients, they can still suffer from other issues such as overfitting when not regularized appropriately.

Just like VGG revolutionized depth and architectural simplicity, ResNet has similarly instigated a profound change in how deep convolutional networks are understood and optimized. It has opened the door to building extremely deep architectures confidently, harnessing deep feature hierarchies. Through a practical PyTorch implementation, we can discover the robustness of ResNet and its substantial impact on modern computer vision challenges.

Diving Deep into Inception Networks

Inccption nctworks, originating from the Google Brain team, are a series of convolutional neural networks that introduced a novel concept of network-in-network architecture.

Among these, InceptionV3 has been a significant milestone that achieved state-of-the-art performance in classification and detection tasks. InceptionV3 incorporates several optimizations over its predecessors, such as factorized convolutions and expanded the inception module, to not only improve performance but also efficiency.

Model Architecture and Variants

The Inception model architecture is unique due to its inception modules. These modules perform multiple convolutions with different filter sizes in parallel and concatenate the results. The original Inception (GoogLeNet) had a 22-layer deep architecture, while InceptionV3 evolved into a 48-layer deep network with more sophisticated modules.

In InceptionV3, the inception modules were expanded to include factorized 7x7 convolutions, which were split into sequences of 1x7 and 7x1 convolutions to reduce the number of parameters. Moreover, InceptionV3 employed batch normalization for all its convolutional operations, as well as RMSProp optimizer and label smoothing, for stabilizing the training process.

The Elegance of Inception Modules

Inception modules allow the network to look at the same data through different perspectives using filters of various sizes, and then the multiple resultant feature maps are merged. This multi-level feature extraction makes the Inception networks extremely versatile for capturing patterns within images.

Implementing InceptionV3 in PyTorch

The actual implementation of InceptionV3 involves stacking different kinds of inception modules and auxiliary classifiers. The following snippet is a simplified version of the InceptionV3 class in PyTorch, capturing the essence of its architecture.

```
import torch.nn as nn
import torch.nn.functional as F

# Defining a basic inception module
class BasicInceptionModule(nn.Module):
    # Initialization for the inception module
    def __init__(self):
        super(BasicInceptionModule, self).__init__()
        # Defining branches with different filter types for the same input
        # ...

    # Forward pass that applies the branches and concatenates results
    def forward(self, x):
```

```
        # Apply convolutions on the same input and concatenate
        # ...
        return torch.cat([branch1x1, branch3x3, branch5x5, branch_pool],
1)

class InceptionV3(nn.Module):
    def __init__(self, num_classes=1000, aux_logits=True):
        super(InceptionV3, self).__init__()

        # Defining the initial convolution and pooling layers
        self.Conv2d_1a_3x3 = nn.Conv2d(3, 32, kernel_size=3, stride=2)
        # ... (Other layers not shown for brevity)

        # Stacking inception modules
        self.Mixed_5b = BasicInceptionModule()  # An example inception
module
        # ... (Other inception modules not shown for brevity)

        # Auxiliary classifier used in training
        if aux_logits:
            self.AuxLogits = InceptionAux(768, num_classes)

        # Final classifier replacing the fully connected layer in other
architectures
        self.fc = nn.Linear(2048, num_classes)

    def forward(self, x):
        # Forward pass through each layer up to a certain point
        # ...

        # In training mode, InceptionV3 uses an auxiliary output for the
middle of
        # the network to combat the vanishing gradient problem
        if self.training and self.AuxLogits is not None:
            aux = self.AuxLogits(x)

        # Final forward pass through later inception modules
        # ...

        # Adaptive average pooling and classifier
        x = F.adaptive_avg_pool2d(x, (1, 1))
        x = F.dropout(x, training=self.training)
        x = x.view(x.size(0), -1)
        x = self.fc(x)

        # If auxiliary classifier is used, return both main and auxiliary
outputs
```

```
        if self.training and self.AuxLogits is not None:
            return x, aux
        return x

# Helper function similar to ResNet's, for InceptionV3
def inception_v3(pretrained=False, **kwargs):
    if pretrained:
        # Load pretrained model
        # ...
    return InceptionV3(**kwargs)
```

This model can then be adjusted for tasks like CIFAR100 by changing the final fully connected layer to output 100 classes instead of 1000.

Basic Building Blocks

InceptionV3's network architecture differs notably from sequential models like VGG or even the modularly-sequential ResNet, due to its complex inception modules. Each inception block in InceptionV3 consists of several parallel paths with a combination of convolutional, pooling, and concatenation operations that work on the same input level. This structure increases the width of the network and allows it to capture information at different scales.

```
class BasicInceptionModule(nn.Module):
    # Initialization for the inception module
    def __init__(self):
        super(BasicInceptionModule, self).__init__()
        # Defining branches with different filter types for the same input
        # ...


    # Forward pass that applies the branches and concatenates results
    def forward(self, x):
        # Apply convolutions on the same input and concatenate
        # ...
        return torch.cat([branch1x1, branch3x3, branch5x5, branch_pool],
1)
```

Advanced Architectural Components

The full InceptionV3 network includes several of these inception modules stacked together, starting with simpler ones and progressing to more complex arrangements.

```
class InceptionV3(nn.Module):
    def __init__(self, num_classes=1000, aux_logits=True):
        # ...
        # This constructor sets up the initial convolutional layers,
```

```
which serve to process
        # the input image into a suitable form for the subsequent incep-
tion modules.
        # ...
```

Auxiliary Classifiers

Auxiliary classifiers are introduced in the middle of the network to combat the vanishing gradients problem by providing extra gradient signals.

```
        if aux_logits:
            self.AuxLogits = InceptionAux(768, num_classes)
        # ...
```

The gradient signals from the auxiliary classifiers are meant to help with the convergence of deeper layers during the training process.

Forward Pass Logic

The forward pass implements the series of inception modules, taking into account the presence of auxiliary classifiers.

```
    def forward(self, x):
        # ...
        # Here, the data flows through the network passing through the
convolutional base,
        # the inception modules, and finally reaching the auxiliary
classifier if present.
        # ...
```

Bringing it All Together

The **inception_v3** function is a factory method for creating and loading a pretrained InceptionV3 model if desired.

```
def inception_v3(pretrained=False, **kwargs):
    # ...
    # This function takes a pretrained parameter that determines whether
to load
    # pretrained weights, and constructs an InceptionV3 model with
optional keyword arguments.
```

The model can be customized for different datasets by adapting the final fully connected layer, which is responsible for producing predictions corresponding to the number of classes.

In summary, the PyTorch implementation of InceptionV3 demonstrates the network's intricacies and design ethos. This explanation addresses the key parts of the code to provide clear insight into how the model is structured and operates, leading to its successful application in various computer vision tasks. The detailed comments and structured code offer a narrative understanding of InceptionV3 for educators, practitioners, and enthusiasts looking to master or utilize this powerful architecture.

Importing InceptionV3 from PyTorch's Model Zoo

InceptionV3 comes with the advantage of being available as a pretrained model within PyTorch's model zoo. This means that it has already been trained on the large ImageNet dataset and can be fine-tuned or used directly for inference on a wide array of tasks.

```
import torchvision
inceptionv3_pretrained = torchvision.models.inception_v3(weights=None)
```

Leveraging Pretrained Weights

Like other models, InceptionV3's pretrained weights can be easily leveraged in PyTorch for new datasets, providing a strong starting point for further training.

```
import torchvision
import torch.nn as nn

inceptionv3_pretrained = torchvision.models.inception_v3(weights=torch-
vision.models.Inception_V3_Weights.IMAGENET1K_V1)
inceptionv3_pretrained.fc = nn.Linear(2048, 100)  # Change the last
layer to fit CIFAR100
```

This adjustment allows the use of ImageNet's pretrained weights as a feature extractor for the CIFAR100 dataset.

Training and Evaluating ResNet on CIFAR100

The training and evaluation process for InceptionV3 would be similar to other models discussed, accounting for the greater complexity and potential longer time due to its depth and intricate structure.

Data Pre-processing and Augmentation Steps

Proper data pre-processing and augmentation are critical steps when training neural networks. For InceptionV3, which was originally trained on ImageNet, common pre-processing steps include resizing the image to 299x299 pixels (the default input size for InceptionV3), normalizing the pixel values, and applying various data augmentation techniques to improve generalization.

```
from torchvision.transforms import transforms

# Data preprocessing and augmentation for InceptionV3
transform = transforms.Compose([
    transforms.Resize(299),  # Resize images to 299x299
    transforms.RandomHorizontalFlip(),  # Randomly flip images
horizontally
    transforms.RandomVerticalFlip(),  # Randomly flip images vertically
    transforms.ToTensor(),  # Convert images to tensors
    transforms.Normalize(mean=[0.485, 0.456, 0.406],  # Normalize to
match ImageNet's distribution
                         std=[0.229, 0.224, 0.225]),
])
```

This ensures that the input fed into the model during both the training and testing phases will mimic the characteristics of the data the model was originally trained on, allowing the pretrained network to perform better.

Training Code

The training setup for InceptionV3 will closely resemble the process used with other models. However, it is crucial to accommodate the specifics of the Inception architecture such as the auxiliary outputs that can be included during training.

```
import torch
import torch.nn as nn
from torchvision import models

# Move the model to GPU if available
device = torch.device("cuda:0" if torch.cuda.is_available() else "cpu")
inceptionv3_pretrained.to(device)


# Assuming we have a model 'inceptionv3_pretrained' and a dataloader
'train_loader'
optimizer = torch.optim.SGD(inceptionv3_pretrained.parameters(),
lr=0.001, momentum=0.9)
criterion = nn.CrossEntropyLoss()


# Create data loaders
train_dataset = torchvision.datasets.CIFAR100(root='./data', train=True,
download=True, transform=transform)
test_dataset = torchvision.datasets.CIFAR100(root='./data', train=False,
download=True, transform=transform)
```

```
train_loader = torch.utils.data.DataLoader(train_dataset, batch_size=32,
shuffle=True)
test_loader = torch.utils.data.DataLoader(test_dataset, batch_size=32,
shuffle=False)

# Set number of epochs to train
number_of_epochs = 10


# Train the model
for epoch in range(number_of_epochs):
    inceptionv3_pretrained.train()  # Set the model to training mode
    running_loss = 0.0
    for i, (inputs, labels) in enumerate(train_loader):
        inputs, labels = inputs.to(device), labels.to(device)
        optimizer.zero_grad()  # Zero the parameter gradients


        # Forward pass
        outputs, aux_outputs = inceptionv3_pretrained(inputs)
        loss1 = criterion(outputs, labels)
        loss2 = criterion(aux_outputs, labels)
        loss = loss1 + 0.4 * loss2  # Combine losses from the main and
auxiliary outputs
        loss.backward()  # Backpropagate the losses
        optimizer.step()  # Update weights


        running_loss += loss.item()


    print(f'Epoch {epoch + 1}: Loss: {running_loss / len(train_loader)}')

# Save the model's state dictionary
torch.save(inceptionv3_pretrained.state_dict(), 'inceptionv3_cifar100.
pth')
```

When using InceptionV3's architecture, note that during the training loop, the model's output consists of the final output as well as an auxiliary output. The loss is computed for both outputs with the auxiliary loss typically being weighted to have less impact.

```
Epoch 1: Loss: 4.352704811888888
Epoch 2: Loss: 1.5783041149301602
Epoch 3: Loss: 1.0175445510450836
Epoch 4: Loss: 0.7405642401379393
Epoch 5: Loss: 0.5667243113793681
Epoch 6: Loss: 0.44321320430778177
Epoch 7: Loss: 0.3450072900489773
Epoch 8: Loss: 0.2725202218174477
Epoch 9: Loss: 0.218437113982561
Epoch 10: Loss: 0.17106323043727661
```

Figure 8.5: *Output of training the Inception-v3 model on the CIFAR100 dataset for 10 epochs*

Evaluation Code

After the model has been trained, it's essential to evaluate its performance on a separate validation or test set to ensure it generalizes well to unseen data.

```
inceptionv3_pretrained.eval()  # Set the model to evaluation mode
correct = 0
total = 0
with torch.no_grad():
    for images, labels in test_loader:
        images, labels = images.to(device), labels.to(device)
        outputs, _ = inceptionv3_pretrained(images)  # Ignore auxiliary
outputs during inference
        _, predicted = torch.max(outputs.data, 1)
        total += labels.size(0)
        correct += (predicted == labels).sum().item()

accuracy = correct / total
print(f'Accuracy on the test set: {100 * accuracy}%')
```

```
Accuracy on the test set: 83.92%
```

Figure 8.6: *Accuracy on the test set after training the model for 10 epochs*

During evaluation, only the main output is used to compute accuracy, and gradient tracking is disabled to increase efficiency.

Strengths and Limitations

The Inception model's strengths lie in its depth and ability to capture complex representations with relatively few parameters, thanks to the inception modules.

However, architectures like Inception deal with increased complexity in their structure, making them more challenging to modify and potentially requiring more computational resources.

In sum, InceptionV3 is a model that reflects the innovative spirit of deep learning progress, combining elegant architectural choices with rigorous empirical validation. Through PyTorch's capabilities, the power of InceptionV3 can be harnessed efficiently, taking advantage of its modular design and the advanced techniques it employs to push forward the frontiers of computer vision.

Comparing Model Performance

When it comes to image classification tasks using convolutional neural networks (CNNs), VGG16, ResNet, and InceptionV3 stand out as prominent architectures, each with its unique approach to learning representations. Evaluating these models on the CIFAR100 dataset provides valuable insight into their performance and behavior in a multi-class classification scenario.

Performance Metrics

Accuracies attained by each model on the CIFAR-100 dataset:

- VGG16: 55%
- ResNet-50: 68.2%
- InceptionV3: 83.92%

Note, in all models, the training loss did not converge, so we could train them longer to get better accuracy with more epochs.

Architectural Strengths and Contributions

Let us recap the strengths and contributions of each model:

VGG16

The architecture is characterized by its simplicity and depth, utilizing repeated blocks of convolutional and pooling layers. VGG16's design paved the way for understanding how depth in a neural network influences learning. However, its uniformity may result in a less sophisticated feature extraction, lacking the representational power needed for more complex datasets.

ResNet

With the introduction of skip connections, ResNet allowed the training of much deeper networks by mitigating the vanishing gradient problem. The enhanced depth generally leads to a better hierarchical representation of data, as observed in its accuracy jump over VGG16. The balance between depth and learnability makes ResNet a solid performer across many tasks.

InceptionV3

InceptionV3 represents a departure from traditional layered architectures, focusing on parallelism and width within layers. Its inception modules incorporate multi-scale processing, which enables the model to extract features at various levels of abstraction effectively. The refinement employed in its design is likely the reason for its top performance in our evaluation.

Computational Efficiency

When it comes to computational resource requirements:

- **VGG16** is computationally heavy due to its deep architecture and large number of parameters.
- **ResNet-50** strikes a balance, managing depth with its efficient residual blocks.
- **InceptionV3**, despite its complexity, is optimized for computation through factorized convolutions.

Handling Overfitting

Overfitting is commonly combated in these models using dropout, weight decay, and data augmentation. The architectures inherently approach overfitting differently:

- **VGG16**, with its simpler structure, might require more aggressive regularization or data augmentation.
- **ResNet** employs batch normalization extensively, which has a regularizing effect.
- **InceptionV3's** structure, combining multiple filter sizes, provides robustness against overfitting by design.

Generalization to New Tasks

In terms of transfer learning capabilities:

- **VGG16** serves as a strong feature extractor and is frequently used as a base for other applications, given its simplicity and effectiveness.
- **ResNet** is known for its powerful performance when fine-tuned for different tasks.

- **InceptionV3's** ability to capture mixed-level features makes it versatile as a pretrained model for various vision applications.

Visualization of Model Performance

Graphical representation of the accuracy of each model shows the trend of performance over epochs. In this visualization, InceptionV3 would depict a smoother and steeper convergence, while ResNet would show resilience against the degradation problem. VGG16 might exhibit a more extended plateau, suggesting a potential need for more epochs or data augmentation to achieve higher accuracy.

Conclusion

Having built a solid foundation in image classification, we now turn the page to another exciting domain in computer vision–object detection. Unlike classification, which assigns a single label to an image, object detection is about identifying and localizing multiple objects within an image. This task combines classification with the challenge of pinpointing the position of each object using bounding boxes.

In the next chapter, we will delve into object detection models that have revolutionized how machines perceive and interpret the visual world around us. We will begin with Fast R-CNN, a model that introduced a breakthrough approach to object detection by incorporating region proposals with convolutional networks. Fast R-CNN set the stage for a family of models that operate swiftly and accurately, significantly improving over their predecessors.

We will also explore Single Shot Multibox Detector (SSD), renowned for its speed and efficiency. SSD extends the object detection frontier by eliminating the proposal generation step and enabling the detection of objects across various scales in one single forward pass of the network.

As we embark on this journey through the object detection landscape, expect to encounter concepts, such as bounding box regression, non-maximum suppression, and anchor boxes, tools that enable these models to achieve high precision and recall.

So, gear up as we continue to unravel the exciting advancements in computer vision with our next dive into the world of object detection, fully utilizing the robust framework of PyTorch 2.0 to develop models that can see and understand their surroundings with incredible acuity.

Chapter 9
Object Detection Models

Introduction

Object detection stands as a cornerstone of advancements in computer vision, imbued with the power to not only identify the contents of an image but also delineate the precise locations of individual objects. This dual capacity is transformative across various arenas, bearing profound implications for both everyday convenience and industry-specific applications.

In the retail sector, object detection facilitates inventory management through automated product recognition, significantly streamlining operations and diminishing prospects for human error. The technological leap reverberates in the healthcare industry, where it enhances diagnostic processes, supporting radiologists in pinpointing anomalies within medical imagery. The realm of security is another beneficiary, with real-time object detection bolstering monitoring efforts and enabling the rapid identification of potentially perilous activities.

The journey from image classification to object detection is akin to a maturation process in machine perception, advancing from the simpler task of assigning a label to an entire image, to the nuanced endeavor of localizing and classifying multiple entities within a single frame. This progression is reflected within this chapter as we transition from the image classification focus of *Chapter 8, Advanced Image Classification Models*, to the intricate task of object detection, underscoring the importance of spatiotemporal understanding.

En route to grasping the complexities of object detection models, it is crucial to anchor our knowledge in the foundational concepts central to the technology's application. Bounding boxes, the primary mechanism for object localization, are rectangular perimeters within an image that encapsulate actionable data–object vertices marking presence and position. These boxes are coupled with annotations–manual or automated labels–delineating object categories, entwined with coordinates to offer a comprehensive dataset upon which models can be trained.

The evaluation of object detection systems hinges on the precision of these localizations, gauged through established metrics such as the intersection over union (IoU) and the mean average precision (mAP). These performance indicators are invaluable in the optimization of object detection models, informing iterative enhancements and contributing to the refinement of algorithms capable of discerning subtleties within visual data.

Like any rapidly progressing field, object detection is not without its challenges. Variance in object scales, occlusions, and class imbalances are but a few of the hurdles to overcome. These complexities demand ingenious solutions, fostering technological advances that have catapulted the science of object detection from its rudimentary inception to the sophisticated models we will explore throughout this chapter—namely, YOLO (You Only Look Once), Faster R-CNN (Region-based Convolutional Neural Network), and SSD (Single Shot Multibox Detector).

The evolution of object detection models testifies to a narrative of relentless aspiration, tracing back to seminal frameworks like the Viola-Jones and HOG (Histogram of Oriented Gradients) detectors. These initial strides spearheaded the quest for innovation, eventually making way for the deep learning revolution that redefined potentialities. The shift to neural network-based architectures commenced with the pioneering R-CNN series, cultivating a lineage of progressively optimized frameworks that heralded new benchmarks in detection speed and accuracy.

As real-time detection became an industry clarion call, models such as YOLO and SSD emerged as poster children for an era prioritizing not only meticulous precision but also agile responsiveness. These cutting-edge models are a testament to visionaries seeking an equilibrium between rapid interpretation of visual data and meticulous accuracy—a balancing act that continues to ripple through contemporary object detection methodologies.

Structure

In this chapter, the following topics will be covered:

- Deepening Foundations
- Understanding Advanced Image Classification Models
- Diving deep into VGG
- Diving deep into ResNet
- Diving deep into Inception
- Comparing Model Performance

Deepening Foundations

As we dive deeper into the subject of object detection, this section extends upon the brief overture previously offered. Here, you will find an in-depth analysis of various subtopics that serve as building blocks for understanding the complex landscape of object detection. This section is meticulously partitioned into subsections that walk you through the nuanced relationship object detection has with image classification, introduce you to the technical terms and metrics that are central to the domain, outline the obstacles encountered, and provide a chronological commentary on the historical advancements of object detection models. The subsections will include:

- **From Classification to Detection:** Dissecting the evolution from image classification to the multifaceted dimensions of object detection.
- **Defining the Tools:** Diving into the terminologies, such as bounding boxes, annotations, and the technical specifics of prominent detection metrics.
- **Challenges on the Path:** Unpacking the complexities and inherent challenges that researchers and practitioners face.

Let's initiate our examination with the first subsection to comprehend the crucial transition from the world of image classification to the more intricate realm of object detection.

From Classification to Detection

Review of Image Classification: The previous chapter served as a detailed introduction to image classification, where models ascertain the predominant subject of a photograph and assign a category label accordingly. The foundation was laid using well-regarded architectures such as VGG, ResNet, and Inception models, emphasizing their proficiency in navigating the high-dimensional space of image pixels to detect patterns that coalesce into recognizable forms.

Yet, the canvas of computer vision is far more elaborate, extending beyond recognizing 'what' exists within an image to pinpoint 'where' it exists. As we advance into object detection models, we build upon the core principles of image classification but venture into the spatial aspect of analysis, translating the capability to recognize into the prowess to localize.

Expansion to Spatial Recognition: Object detection arises as an extension of image classification, augmenting it with an additional layer of intricacy by incorporating the concept of localization. While classification models yield a singular outcome that encapsulates the essence of an image, detection models dissect the visual data, identifying multiple objects, their boundaries, and their spatial interrelations within the same image.

For instance, a classification model would be adept at identifying a photograph as a beach scene, but an object detection model will delineate the umbrella, the surfboard, and the beach ball, providing precise bounding box coordinates for each item. This heightened perception is akin to how an artist not only paints a scene but also sketches individual subjects, enhancing the depth and detail of the visual narrative.

Bridging the Conceptual Gap

The Multidimensional Shift: The transition from image classification to object detection can be visualized as a shift from viewing images as a canvas with a singular focus subject to seeing them as a three-dimensional space bustling with numerous points of interest. This multidimensional shift requires models to develop a granular understanding of images, learning to categorize and isolate particular sections–essentially moving from a global view to an array of localized interpretations.

Importance for Machine Perception: Imbuing machines with the ability to detect objects mirrors the cognitive processes inherent to human visual perception. Our eyes and brains work in harmony to acknowledge our surroundings, identify items, and comprehend their relative locations–not merely recognizing a tree but understanding its presence in relation to the sidewalk, the street, and the skyline. In the digital world, this ability translates into algorithms that symbolize the spatial awareness critical to tasks, such as autonomous navigation, content moderation, and interactive robotics.

The challenge for object detection models lies in emulating this complex mechanism of perception and cognition within the constraints of algorithmic frameworks. The subsequent subsections will delve further into the technicalities that enable this while exploring the hurdles to overcome and frontiers yet to be conquered.

Defining the Tools

Within the realm of object detection lies a set of indispensable concepts that form the bedrock of the field. Proficiency in these ideas is paramount for any practitioner looking to harness the full potential of object-detection models. This subsection dives into the essentials of bounding boxes and localization, evaluates common metrics used to refine and evaluate detector performance, and highlights the perennial challenges faced in this sphere of computer vision.

Bounding Boxes and Localization:

- **Anatomy of a Bounding Box:** Bounding boxes are the most ubiquitous element in object detection, fundamental to the model's understanding of location. Each bounding box is defined by a set of coordinates and dimensions–typically the x and y positions of the top-left corner, coupled with the width and height. These parameters are critical in not only differentiating between objects but also in gauging their sizes and spatial relationships within the image. The precision with which these boxes can be calculated and drawn around objects underscores the reliability of an object detection model. A visual example further illustrates this by highlighting how bounding boxes encapsulate objects of interest within the clutter of a real-world scenario.

- **Labeling Techniques:** The reliability of any object detection system is entwined with the quality of its training data, where labeling plays a pivotal role. The process can be executed manually, calling upon human annotators to meticulously draw bounding boxes and label objects. However, the rise of automated tools and methodologies can expedite and scale this process. Automated techniques leverage machine learning algorithms to propose bounding box annotations, which are then verified by human annotators, ensuring high-quality data while maintaining efficiency. An overview of the most widely-used annotation tools provides insight into how datasets are prepared for training robust object detection systems.

Common Metrics and Evaluation Criteria:

- **Precision and Recall in Object Detection:** The twin metrics of Precision and Recall offer a dual lens through which the effectiveness of an object detector can be discerned. Precision indicates the accuracy of the positive predictions made by the model, whereas Recall measures the model's ability to find all the relevant instances in the dataset. For object detection, these metrics are calculated with respect to detected bounding boxes and their overlaps with ground truth annotations, representing the model's finesse and thoroughness.
- **Intersection over Union (IoU):** Intersection over Union is a fundamental metric in object detection that quantifies the overlap between the predicted bounding box and the ground truth box. An IoU score close to 1 suggests an excellent prediction, whereas a score nearer to 0 indicates little to no overlap. The intricacies of calculating IoU are demystified through iterative diagrams, showcasing how it serves as a definitive gauge for the precision of object localization.
- **Mean Average Precision (mAP):** The mAP metric provides an aggregate performance score across various classes and detection thresholds, reflecting the overall efficacy of the model. As one navigates through its calculation and nuances, it becomes apparent why mAP is favored in benchmarking object detectors and serves as the cornerstone for international challenge evaluations such as PASCAL VOC and COCO.

Challenges on the Path

- **Dealing with Variances:** Object detection models are frequently challenged by variances. These may arise from scale factors—where objects appear larger or smaller depending on their distance from the camera—deformation due to non-rigid movement, occlusion when objects are partially blocked, or background clutter that camouflages object presence. A deep dive into each of these facets reveals the resilience required from detection models to perceive reliably amidst the cacophony of real-life visual data.

- **Problems of Plenty and Scarcity:** Data is the lifeblood of machine learning, and object detection is no exception. But what happens when some objects are overrepresented in the training data (problems of plenty) while others barely make an appearance (problems of scarcity)? This class imbalance can skew a model's ability to generalize, tilting its predictions toward more commonly seen objects.

The development of object detection models has been a journey of steady advancements, where each breakthrough refined the process of teaching machines to 'see'. This progression, discussed from its early genesis to modern successes, has shaped a landscape where precision and quick decision-making are equally crucial. Just as we explored the various facets of image classification in the previous chapter, we have now extended that knowledge to the dynamics of object location and identification.

As we move from theory to practice, it's time to switch gears and start applying these concepts. The next section will introduce you to practical applications by building object detection models using PyTorch, the same powerful and versatile tool we've been mastering throughout this book.

Dataset Exploration: PASCAL VOC for Object Detection

In the realm of computer vision, the choice of dataset is crucial for training effective object detection models. One standout dataset that strikes a balance between complexity and manageability is the PASCAL Visual Object Classes (VOC) dataset. This section delves into the PASCAL VOC dataset, specifically focusing on its utilization within PyTorch through the *VOCDetection* class. We will cover the dataset's structure and the variety of classes it contains and provide code examples to illustrate how to load and interact with the data.

Understanding PASCAL VOC

The PASCAL VOC dataset is a benchmark in object detection, offering a diverse set of annotated images across 20 distinct object categories. These categories range from everyday items and animals to vehicles, encompassing a wide array of challenges for object detection models, such as varying scales, orientations, and occlusions.

Components of **VOCDetection**

The **VOCDetection** class in PyTorch's **torchvision.datasets** module simplifies accessing the PASCAL VOC dataset. Key components of this class include:

- **root**: The directory where the VOC datasets are stored or will be downloaded.
- **year**: Specifies the dataset year (for example, "**2007**" or "**2012**").
- **image_set**: Defines the subset to use ("**train**", "**val**", or "**trainval**").
- **download**: If set to True, the dataset will be downloaded if it's not already available locally.
- **transform**: A function/transform that takes in an image and returns a transformed version. Useful for pre-processing steps like normalization.

Classes in PASCAL VOC

The PASCAL VOC dataset contains 20 object classes, which are:

- **Person**: person
- **Animal**: bird, cat, cow, dog, horse, sheep
- **Vehicle**: airplane, bike, boat, bus, car, motorbikc, train
- **Indoor**: bottle, chair, dining table, potted plant, sofa, tv/monitor

Loading the Dataset with PyTorch

Here's how to load the PASCAL VOC dataset using the **VOCDetection** class in PyTorch:

```
from torchvision.datasets import VOCDetection
import torchvision.transforms as transforms

# Define transformations
transform = transforms.Compose([
    transforms.Resize((256, 256)),
    transforms.ToTensor(),
])

# Initialize the dataset
voc_dataset = VOCDetection(root='./voc_data',
                           year='2012',
                           image_set='train',
                           download=True,
                           transform=transform)

print(f"Number of images in the dataset: {len(voc_dataset)}")
```

```
Downloading http://host.robots.ox.ac.uk/pascal/VOC/voc2012/VOCtrainval_11-May-20
12.tar to ./voc_data/VOCtrainval_11-May-2012.tar
1999639552it [01:39, 20164585.59it/s]
Extracting ./voc_data/VOCtrainval_11-May-2012.tar to ./voc_data
Number of images in the dataset: 5717
```

Figure 9.1: *Output of script to test the VOCDetection class*

Displaying a Sample Image and Its Classes

To visualize an image and its corresponding annotations from the dataset, consider the following code snippet:

```
import matplotlib.pyplot as plt

# Load an image and its annotation
img, annotation = voc_dataset[10]  # Adjust index to explore other
images

# Display the image
plt.imshow(img.permute(1, 2, 0))
plt.axis('off')  # Hide axes
plt.show()

# Display classes of objects in the image
object_classes = [obj['name'] for obj in annotation['annotation']
['object']]
print("Classes in the image:", object_classes)
```

```
Classes in the image: ['dog']
```

Figure 9.2: *Label of the object in the image*

Figure 9.3: *Sample image from the VOCDetection dataset*

This code retrieves an image and its annotations, displays the image, and prints the classes of objects present. The annotations include details such as bounding box coordinates, but for simplicity, we're focusing on the object classes here.

Other Useful Functions of VOCDetection

The *VOCDetection* class also supports additional functionalities, such as:

- **`target_transform`:** Similar to transform but applied to the target/annotation. Useful for converting annotation formats.
- **transforms:** A function/transform that takes input and target and transforms them. Ideal for simultaneous transformations on the image and its annotations.

Difference between 2007 and 2012 datasets

The PASCAL Visual Object Classes (VOC) Challenge was an annual competition aimed at object detection and image classification tasks, which ran from 2005 to 2012. The datasets released for these challenges, particularly the ones from 2007 and 2012, have been widely used in computer vision research. The primary differences between the VOC 2007 and VOC 2012 datasets relate to the size of the datasets, the number of images, and the annotations they contain. Here's a breakdown of the key differences:

Size and Content:

- **VOC 2007:** Contains 9,963 images across 20 object categories, with annotations for object detection, including bounding boxes. The dataset is split into train, validation, and test sets.
- **VOC 2012:** Offers a larger collection with 22,531 images. Like the 2007 version, it includes annotations for object detection among the same 20 object categories. The increase in the number of images and annotations is aimed at providing a more challenging and varied dataset for training and evaluating models.

By leveraging the *VOCDetection* class, developers and researchers can easily access a rich dataset for training and evaluating object detection models. The variety of objects and challenges presented in PASCAL VOC make it an invaluable resource for understanding and improving object detection techniques.

Diving Deep into Fast R-CNN

Fast R-CNN, developed by Ross Girshick in 2015, is an evolution of the original R-CNN (Region-based Convolutional Neural Network) model. It was designed to address the inefficiencies of R-CNN and SPPnet, providing a faster, more efficient way to perform object detection. Fast R-CNN improves upon its predecessors by introducing a streamlined training process that updates the classifier and bounding box regressor simultaneously, and by utilizing a shared convolutional feature map for all objects in an image, significantly reducing computation time.

Importing Fast R-CNN in PyTorch 2.0

In PyTorch 2.0, Fast R-CNN can be accessed through the **torchvision** package, which includes a collection of pretrained models optimized for image classification and object detection tasks. While Fast R-CNN itself is a conceptual foundation for later models, for practical purposes, we often utilize Faster R-CNN, an improved version with an integrated Region Proposal Network (RPN) that directly works on feature maps to propose candidate object regions.

To import a pretrained Faster R-CNN model in PyTorch 2.0, use the following code:

```
import torchvision.models.detection as detection
from torchvision.models.detection import FasterRCNN_ResNet50_FPN_Weights

# Load a pretrained Faster R-CNN model
model = detection.fasterrcnn_resnet50_fpn(weights=FasterRCNN_ResNet50_
FPN_Weights.DEFAULT)
model.eval()  # Set the model to inference mode
```

Insights and Special Features of Fast R-CNN

Fast R-CNN introduced several key innovations:

- **ROI Pooling Layer:** This layer efficiently extracts a fixed-size feature vector from arbitrary-sized RoIs (Regions of Interest), allowing for a fully connected layer afterward.
- **Multi-task Loss:** Combines classification and bounding box regression into a single objective, streamlining the training process.
- **Efficiency:** By sharing computations across RoIs, Fast R-CNN is significantly faster than its predecessor.

Inference with PyTorch 2.0 and the PASCAL VOC Dataset

Performing inference on images from the PASCAL VOC dataset involves loading the dataset, pre-processing the images to match the input requirements of the model, and then running the model to detect objects.

Here is an example script for inference on a single image:

```
import torchvision.models.detection as detection
from torchvision.models.detection import FasterRCNN_ResNet50_FPN_Weights
from torchvision.transforms import functional as F
from PIL import Image
import matplotlib.pyplot as plt
```

```
from torchvision.datasets import VOCDetection
import torchvision.transforms as transforms
import torch

# Load a pretrained Faster R-CNN model
model = detection.fasterrcnn_resnet50_fpn(weights=FasterRCNN_ResNet50_
FPN_Weights.DEFAULT)
model.eval()  # Set the model to inference mode

# Initialize the dataset
voc_dataset = VOCDetection(root='./voc_data',
                           year='2012',
                           image_set='val',
                           download=False)


# Load an image and its annotation
image, annotation = voc_dataset[3]

# Load an image
image = image.convert("RGB")
image_tensor = F.to_tensor(image).unsqueeze(0)  # Transform and add
batch dimension

# Perform inference
with torch.no_grad():
    prediction = model(image_tensor)

# Visualizing the results
boxes = prediction[0]['boxes']
labels = prediction[0]['labels']
scores = prediction[0]['scores']

# For simplicity, let's show the first detected object
box = boxes[0].numpy()
label = labels[0].item()
score = scores[0].item()

# Draw the bounding box and label on the image
plt.imshow(image)
plt.gca().add_patch(plt.Rectangle((box[0], box[1]), box[2] - box[0],
box[3] - box[1], fill=False, color='red'))
plt.text(box[0], box[1], f'{label} {score:.2f}', color='white',
fontsize=12)
plt.axis('off')
plt.show()
```

Output:

***Figure 9.4:** Inference of the Fast-RCNN model on sample image from VOCDetection dataset*

Training Fast R-CNN and Evaluating Metrics

Training Fast R-CNN (or, more commonly, Faster R-CNN) on a dataset like PASCAL VOC requires setting up the dataset, defining the model, and specifying the loss functions for both the classifier and the bounding box regressor. PyTorch's **torchvision** library facilitates this process, we'll first outline the key components:

- **Dataset Preparation:** Load the PASCAL VOC dataset using **torchvision.datasets.VOCDetection** and apply the necessary transformations.
- **Model Configuration:** Instantiate the Faster R-CNN model with the desired backbones and parameters.
- **Training Loop:** Implement the training loop, including forward and backward passes, loss calculation, and optimizer steps.

Dataset Preparation

First, we need to prepare the PASCAL VOC dataset for training. This involves downloading the dataset, applying transformations to normalize the images, and preparing them in a format suitable for training the Faster R-CNN model.

```
import torchvision.transforms as transforms
from torchvision.datasets import VOCDetection
from torchvision.models.detection.faster_rcnn import FastRCNNPredictor
import torchvision
from torch.utils.data import DataLoader
import torch
```

```
def get_transform(train):
    transform_list = []
    # Converts the image, a PIL image, into a PyTorch Tensor
    transform_list.append(transforms.ToTensor())
    if train:
        # During training, randomly flip the training images
        # and ground-truth for data augmentation
        transform_list.append(transforms.RandomHorizontalFlip(0.5))
    return transforms.Compose(transform_list)

# Load the PASCAL VOC dataset
dataset = VOCDetection(root="./voc_data",
                       year="2012",
                       image_set="train",
                       download=False,
                       transform=get_transform(train=True))

# Update class_to_label mapping to include your classes
class_to_label = {
    'aeroplane': 1, 'bicycle': 2, 'bird': 3, 'boat': 4,
    'bottle': 5, 'bus': 6, 'car': 7, 'cat': 8,
    'chair': 9, 'cow': 10, 'diningtable': 11, 'dog': 12,
    'horse': 13, 'motorbike': 14, 'person': 15, 'pottedplant': 16,
    'sheep': 17, 'sofa': 18, 'train': 19, 'tvmonitor': 20
}

def preprocess_target(target):
    objects = target['annotation']['object']
    if not isinstance(objects, list):  # Handling the case when there's
a single object
        objects = [objects]
    boxes = []
    labels = []
    for obj in objects:
        bndbox = obj['bndbox']
        # Convert coordinates to float and arrange them in the format
[xmin, ymin, xmax, ymax]
        box = [
            float(bndbox['xmin']), float(bndbox['ymin']),
            float(bndbox['xmax']), float(bndbox['ymax'])
        ]
        boxes.append(box)

        # Convert class names to labels, adding 1 to each class label to
accommodate the background class
        label = class_to_label[obj['name']]
        labels.append(label)
```

```
# Convert lists to PyTorch tensors
    boxes_tensor = torch.tensor(boxes, dtype=torch.float32)
    labels_tensor = torch.tensor(labels, dtype=torch.int64)

    # Return the processed target
    return {'boxes': boxes_tensor, 'labels': labels_tensor}

transformed_dataset = [(img, preprocess_target(target)) for img, target
in dataset]

data_loader = DataLoader(transformed_dataset, batch_size=16, shuffle=True,
num_workers=1, collate_fn=lambda x: tuple(zip(*x)))
```

Model Configuration

Next, we configure the Faster R-CNN model. We'll use a pretrained model and replace the head with a new one, suited for the number of classes in the PASCAL VOC dataset (Please note: there are 20 object classes, plus one background class).

```
from torchvision.models.detection import FasterRCNN_ResNet50_FPN_Weights

def get_model(num_classes):
    # Load a pretrained model for classification and return
    # only the features
    model = torchvision.models.detection.fasterrcnn_resnet50_fpn
(weights=FasterRCNN_ResNet50_FPN_Weights.DEFAULT)
    # Get the number of input features for the classifier
    in_features = model.roi_heads.box_predictor.cls_score.in_features
    # Replace the pretrained head with a new one
    model.roi_heads.box_predictor = FastRCNNPredictor(in_features, num_
classes)

    return model

# Adjust num_classes to be 20 classes + 1 background = 21
model = get_model(num_classes=21)
```

Training Loop

For the training loop, we'll define the optimizer, move the model to the GPU if available, and iterate over the dataset for a given number of epochs. Due to the complexity and computational cost of training, we'll outline a simplified version for demonstration purposes.

```
# Parameters
num_epochs = 2
lr = 0.005
```

```
momentum = 0.9
weight_decay = 0.0005

# Optimizer
params = [p for p in model.parameters() if p.requires_grad]
optimizer = torch.optim.SGD(params, lr=lr, momentum=momentum, weight_
decay=weight_decay)


# Training loop
for epoch in range(num_epochs):
    model.train()
    for images, targets in data_loader:

        loss_dict = model(images, targets)

        losses = sum(loss for loss in loss_dict.values())

        # Backpropagation
        optimizer.zero_grad()
        losses.backward()
        optimizer.step()

    print(f"Epoch {epoch+1}, Loss: {losses.item()}")
```

Evaluation and Metrics Calculation

Calculating these metrics across the entire dataset involves iterating over the dataset, storing the model's predictions, and comparing these predictions against the ground truth annotations to compute the metrics.

```
import torch
import torchvision
from torchvision.datasets import VOCDetection
from torchvision.models.detection import fasterrcnn_resnet50_fpn
from torchvision.transforms import functional as F
from torch.utils.data import DataLoader
from torchvision.models.detection import FasterRCNN_ResNet50_FPN_Weights

# Ensure COCO tools are available for mAP calculation
# Install pycocotools if not already installed: pip install pycocotools
from pycocotools.cocoeval import COCOeval
from pycocotools.coco import COCO
import os
import numpy as np
import json
```

```
# Dataset Preparation
def get_transform(train):
    transforms = []
    transforms.append(torchvision.transforms.ToTensor())
    return torchvision.transforms.Compose(transforms)

def collate_fn(batch):
    return tuple(zip(*batch))

def create_dataset_val():
    dataset = VOCDetection(root="./voc_data",
                           year="2012",
                           image_set="val",
                           download=False,
                           transform=get_transform(train=False))
    return dataset

data_loader_val = DataLoader(create_dataset_val(), batch_size=1,
collate_fn=collate_fn, num_workers=4)

# Model Loading

model = fasterrcnn_resnet50_fpn(weights=FasterRCNN_ResNet50_FPN_Weights.
DEFAULT)
model.eval()

# Evaluation Function
def evaluate(model, data_loader):
    model.eval()
    coco = COCO()  # Placeholder for COCO format ground truths, you need
to replace this with the actual initialization
    coco_dt = []  # Placeholder for detections in COCO format

    # Manual image_id assignment
    image_id = 0  # Start with 0 or 1 depending on your preference

    for images, targets in data_loader:
        with torch.no_grad():
            outputs = model(images)

        for i, output in enumerate(outputs):
            # Convert predictions to COCO format
            pred_boxes = output['boxes'].cpu().numpy()
            pred_scores = output['scores'].cpu().numpy()
            pred_labels = output['labels'].cpu().numpy()

            for idx in range(len(pred_boxes)):
```

```
                detection = {
                    "image_id": image_id,  # Use manual image_id
                    "category_id": pred_labels[idx],
                    "bbox": [float(x) for x in pred_boxes[idx]],
                    "score": float(pred_scores[idx])
                }
                coco_dt.append(detection)

            # Increment the image_id for the next image
            image_id += 1

    with open("coco_dt.json", "w") as f:
        json.dump(coco_dt, f)

    cocoDt = coco.loadRes("coco_dt.json")
    cocoEval = COCOeval(coco, cocoDt, "bbox")
    cocoEval.evaluate()
    cocoEval.accumulate()
    cocoEval.summarize()

evaluate(model, data_loader_val)
```

Diving Deep into SSD: Single Shot MultiBox Detector

Single Shot MultiBox Detector (SSD), introduced by Wei Liu et al. in 2016, stands out as a pivotal model in the realm of object detection for its exceptional balance between speed and accuracy. Unlike its predecessors, which typically involve a two-step process (proposal generation followed by object detection), SSD simplifies this into a single step, directly predicting object classes and locations in one go. This innovation not only accelerates the detection process but also maintains competitive accuracy, making SSD ideal for real-time applications.

Incorporating SSD into PyTorch 2.0

PyTorch 2.0's **torchvision** package conveniently includes a pretrained SSD model, facilitating its integration into object detection tasks. This model is optimized for both efficiency and performance, making it a go-to choice for developers and researchers alike.

To leverage a pretrained SSD model in PyTorch 2.0, the following code snippet can be used:

```
import torchvision.models.detection as detection
import torchvision.models.detection.ssd as ssd
```

```
from torchvision.models.detection import SSD300_VGG16_Weights

# Load the pretrained SSD model
model = detection.ssd300_vgg16(weights=SSD300_VGG16_Weights.DEFAULT)
model.eval()  # Switch the model to inference mode
```

Key Features of SSD

SSD introduces several noteworthy features that contribute to its effectiveness:

- **Multi-Scale Feature Maps:** SSD processes the image through a series of convolutional layers of decreasing sizes, allowing it to detect objects at various scales.
- **Default Boxes and Aspect Ratios:** For each feature map location, SSD generates multiple default boxes of different aspect ratios, enabling it to match a variety of object shapes.
- **Joint Localization and Classification:** SSD simultaneously predicts the bounding box offsets and class probabilities for each default box, streamlining the detection process.

Object Detection with SSD on the PASCAL VOC Dataset

Applying SSD to detect objects in the PASCAL VOC dataset involves pre-processing the images to fit the model's input requirements and executing the model to obtain predictions.

Here's an example of using SSD for inference on the PASCAL VOC dataset:

```
import torchvision.models.detection as detection
import torchvision.models.detection.ssd as ssd
from torchvision.datasets import VOCDetection
import torchvision.transforms as transforms
from PIL import Image
import matplotlib.pyplot as plt
import torch
from torchvision.models.detection import SSD300_VGG16_Weights

# Load the pretrained SSD model
model = detection.ssd300_vgg16(weights=SSD300_VGG16_Weights.DEFAULT)
model.eval()  # Switch the model to inference mode

# Function to load and transform images
def transform_image(image):
    transform = transforms.Compose([
```

```
        transforms.Resize((300, 300)),
        transforms.ToTensor()
    ])
    return transform(image).unsqueeze(0)  # Add batch dimension

# Load an example image from the PASCAL VOC dataset
dataset = VOCDetection(root='./voc_data', year='2012', image_set='val',
download=False)
image, _ = dataset[3]  # Sample image
image = transform_image(image)

# Perform inference
with torch.no_grad():
    prediction = model(image)

# Visualization
det_boxes = prediction[0]['boxes']
det_labels = prediction[0]['labels']
det_scores = prediction[0]['scores']

# Display the image and the detected bounding boxes
fig, ax = plt.subplots(1)
ax.imshow(image.squeeze().permute(1, 2, 0))
for box in det_boxes:
    rect = plt.Rectangle((box[0], box[1]), box[2] - box[0], box[3] -
box[1], fill=False, color='red')
    ax.add_patch(rect)
    break
plt.show()
```

Figure 9.5: *Output of SSD model on sample image from PASCAL VOC 2012*

Training SSD on PASCAL VOC

Training SSD involves preparing the dataset, initializing the model with the appropriate number of object classes, and executing a training loop. The setup is very similar to what we created for Fast-RCNN.

Evaluation and Metrics Calculation

Evaluating SSD's performance on the PASCAL VOC dataset involves calculating metrics, such as precision, recall, IoU, and mAP. The process is akin to the evaluation steps outlined in the Fast R-CNN section, with adjustments for SSD's output format.

Due to space constraints, the detailed evaluation script is omitted. However, the procedure closely mirrors that of Fast R-CNN, requiring a dataset in COCO format for mAP calculation and utilizing pycocotools for the evaluation metrics.

Diving Deep into YOLOv5: The Apex of Speed and Accuracy in Object Detection

YOLOv5, the latest iteration in the "*You Only Look Once*" series, is a cutting-edge object detection model known for its exceptional speed and accuracy. Developed by Ultralytics, YOLOv5 has been fine-tuned for performance and efficiency, making it one of the most popular choices for real-time object detection tasks. Its lightweight architecture, combined with state-of-the-art detection capabilities, enables rapid deployment across various platforms, including edge devices.

Setting Up YOLOv5 with PyTorch

Unlike its predecessors, YOLOv5 is implemented in PyTorch, making it seamlessly integrate with PyTorch workflows. To get started with YOLOv5, you can clone the Ultralytics repository and use their pretrained models or train your own model on a custom dataset.

First, ensure you have the YOLOv5 repository cloned and all necessary dependencies installed:

```
git clone https://github.com/ultralytics/yolov5
cd yolov5
pip install -r requirements.txt
```

To load a pretrained YOLOv5 model:

```
import torch

# Load the pretrained YOLOv5 model
model = torch.hub.load('ultralytics/yolov5', 'yolov5s', pretrained=True)
```

YOLOv5's Architectural Highlights

YOLOv5 improves upon the YOLO architecture with several enhancements:

- **Automatic Anchor Optimization:** YOLOv5 automatically adjusts its anchor boxes to better fit the specific dataset it's trained on, improving detection accuracy.
- **Cross-Stage Partial Networks (CSPNet):** This feature reduces computational cost while maintaining detection performance.
- **Mosaic Data Augmentation:** An innovative data augmentation technique that combines four training images into one, enhancing the model's robustness to various object scales and orientations.

Object Detection with YOLOv5 on Custom Images

Detecting objects with YOLOv5 is straightforward, thanks to the Ultralytics framework. Here's how to run inference on custom images:

```
import torch
from torchvision.datasets import VOCDetection

# Load the pretrained YOLOv5 model
model = torch.hub.load('ultralytics/yolov5', 'yolov5s', pretrained=True)

# Load an example image from the PASCAL VOC dataset
dataset = VOCDetection(root='./voc_data', year='2012', image_set='val',
download=False)
image, _ = dataset[3]  # Sample image

# Perform inference
results = model(image)

# Results show
results.show()
```

Figure 9.6: *Output of YOLO v5 model on sample image from PASCAL VOC 2012*

The **`results.show()`** method conveniently displays the image with bounding boxes, class labels, and confidence scores.

Training and Evaluation YOLOv5 on the PASCAL VOC Dataset

Training YOLOv5 on a custom dataset like PASCAL VOC involves preparing your dataset in the appropriate format and configuring a training script. YOLOv5 expects the dataset to be in a specific directory structure and annotation format (YOLO format).

Prepare your dataset: Convert the PASCAL VOC annotations to YOLO format and organize your dataset directory as follows:

```
dataset/
    images/
        train/
        val/
    labels/
        train/
        val/
```

Train the model: Use the YOLOv5 training script. Adjust the batch size and epochs according to your setup.

```
python train.py --img 640 --batch 16 --epochs 50 --data VOC.yaml
--weights yolov5s.pt
```

Here, **`voc.yaml`** is a configuration file that specifies the dataset paths, class names, and number of classes. The YOLO v5 repository provides this YAML file with all the required configurations to start this training.

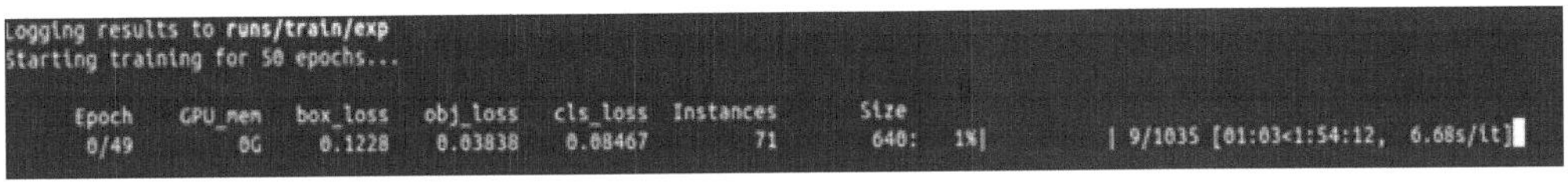

Figure 9.7: *Output of running YOLO v5 training on VOC.yaml*

Evaluating YOLOv5's Performance

YOLOv5's repository includes scripts for evaluation. To evaluate a trained model on the validation set, you can use the following command:

```
python val.py --weights yolov5s.pt --data VOC.yaml --img 640 --iou 0.65
--half
```

This script calculates precision, recall, mAP@.5, and mAP@.5:.95, among other metrics, providing a comprehensive overview of your model's performance. This can run only after you have fine-tuned the model on the VOC.yaml dataset. The pretrained weights contain 80 classes.

Conclusion

As we conclude our journey through the dynamic world of object detection with YOLOv5, it's clear that the evolution of deep learning models has significantly enhanced our ability to interpret and understand the visual world around us. YOLOv5, with its remarkable blend of speed, accuracy, and efficiency, stands as a testament to the ongoing innovations in the field of computer vision. This model, embodying the principle of "You Only Look Once," has not only simplified the detection process but also opened up new vistas for real-time applications, bringing the futuristic vision of AI closer to reality.

YOLOv5's prowess in handling complex object detection tasks across diverse environments showcases the remarkable strides we've made. By incorporating features such as automatic anchor optimization, CSPNet, and mosaic data augmentation, YOLOv5 adapts and thrives in varied detection scenarios, pushing the boundaries of what automated systems can perceive and understand. Moreover, its accessibility and ease of integration into PyTorch workflows democratize cutting-edge technology, allowing researchers and practitioners alike to leverage its capabilities for their unique needs.

The model's versatility extends beyond mere object detection; it serves as a foundation for more sophisticated analyses and applications, from tracking objects across video frames to aiding in automated surveillance and even enhancing customer experiences through real-time analysis. The adaptability and robustness of YOLOv5 underscore the transformative potential of deep learning in reshaping our interaction with digital content and the physical world.

However, the realm of computer vision extends beyond identifying and classifying objects within a frame. While we've discussed the various models and techniques for object detection, the next crucial step in the deep learning journey is understanding how to optimize model performance effectively. As we transition into our next chapter, *Tips and Tricks to Improve Model Performance*, we will dive deep into advanced techniques that can elevate the performance of your models. From understanding the challenges of overfitting and underfitting to applying regularization methods such as dropout and batch normalization, we will explore essential strategies to ensure efficient training. This chapter will also cover hyperparameter tuning, early stopping, and the power of ensemble models to boost overall model accuracy. By the end, you'll be equipped with the tools and methods to fine-tune and enhance the models you've built, ensuring they perform optimally across various tasks in computer vision.

CHAPTER 10
Tips and Tricks to Improve Model Performance

Introduction

Model performance is a crucial factor in determining the success of any machine learning project. While building and training models are foundational, optimizing them for real-world applications requires advanced techniques. Simply training a model on a dataset is often not enough, as factors such as overfitting, underfitting, inefficient training processes, and poorly tuned hyperparameters can all negatively affect performance. To address these challenges, it is essential to fine-tune models, ensuring they generalize well to unseen data while maintaining efficiency.

In this chapter, we explore a series of advanced methods to optimize model performance. These methods range from regularization techniques such as dropout and batch normalization to fine-tuning hyperparameters and applying ensemble learning strategies. The goal is to equip you with the tools necessary to identify potential issues in your models and implement solutions that boost their overall accuracy and robustness.

We begin by revisiting two fundamental concepts—overfitting and underfitting—which can undermine your model's ability to generalize. Drawing from the discussions in previous chapters, such as the training of Convolutional Neural Networks (CNNs) in *Chapter 5, Diving Deep into Convolutional Neural Networks* (CNNs) and object detection models like Faster R-CNN in *Chapter 9, Object Detection Models* we will demonstrate how these phenomena affect models in computer vision tasks. Understanding how to detect and mitigate overfitting and underfitting is the first step in optimizing performance.

Next, we dive into regularization techniques. Dropout, first introduced in *Chapter 5, Diving Deep into Convolutional Neural Networks* (CNNs) as a means of improving CNN performance, will be examined more closely. By randomly dropping neurons during training, dropout helps prevent models from relying too heavily on specific features, thereby improving their generalization capabilities. Batch normalization, another key technique, will also be discussed in detail, focusing on how it can stabilize and speed up training by normalizing the inputs to each layer.

The chapter will then move into hyperparameter tuning, an often overlooked but critical aspect of model optimization. Whether it's tuning the learning rate, adjusting batch sizes, or determining the optimal number of layers, hyperparameter tuning can have a significant impact on performance. We will discuss various tuning techniques, from manual experimentation to more systematic approaches, such as grid search and random search.

Finally, we will explore ensemble learning methods, such as bagging, boosting, and stacking, to combine the strengths of multiple models. These techniques allow you to leverage different models' abilities to correct each other's weaknesses, thereby improving overall performance.

By the end of this chapter, you will have a robust set of strategies to improve your models, ensuring they perform optimally across a wide range of computer vision tasks, from image classification to object detection.

Structure

In this chapter, the following topics will be covered:

- Understanding Overfitting and Underfitting
- Regularization Techniques: Dropout and Batch Normalization
- Hyperparameter Tuning Techniques
- Using Early Stopping for Efficient Training
- Ensemble Models for Improved Performance

Understanding Overfitting and Underfitting

In machine learning, overfitting and underfitting are two critical challenges that can significantly affect model performance. Both these issues stem from the model's ability, or lack thereof, to generalize from the training data to unseen data. Understanding how to detect and address these issues is essential for improving model accuracy and robustness.

Overfitting

Overfitting occurs when a model becomes too complex and learns the noise or random fluctuations in the training data rather than the underlying patterns. As a result, the model performs exceptionally well on the training data but struggles to generalize to new, unseen data. Overfitting is particularly common when working with large models, such as Convolutional Neural Networks (CNNs) or complex object detection architectures, such as YOLO and Faster R-CNN.

When a model overfits, it essentially "memorizes" the training data rather than learning the relationships within the data. This can be observed by a significant gap between the training and validation accuracies or losses, with training accuracy being high while validation accuracy remains much lower.

Indicators of Overfitting

- **Training Loss vs. Validation Loss:** A clear sign of overfitting is when the training loss continues to decrease while the validation loss begins to increase. This indicates that the model is performing well on the training data but is failing to generalize.
- **High Variance:** Overfitted models often have high variance, meaning their performance can fluctuate significantly with small changes in the training data. This variance is problematic for real-world applications, where the model is expected to perform consistently on new data.

Example of Overfitting in Faster R-CNN: Let's consider the Faster R-CNN object detection model, which was discussed in the previous chapter. If the model is trained for too long on a dataset such as PASCAL VOC without proper regularization, it may begin to overfit. The model would achieve high accuracy on the training set but struggle when evaluated on the validation set.

```
# Example: Training Faster R-CNN with overfitting symptoms
import torchvision.models.detection as detection

# Load pre-trained Faster R-CNN model
model = detection.fasterrcnn_resnet50_fpn(pretrained=True)
model.train()

# Example training loop
for epoch in range(50):  # Training for too many epochs
    train_loss = train_one_epoch(model)  # Hypothetical function
    val_loss = validate(model)  # Hypothetical function

    print(f'Epoch {epoch}, Train Loss: {train_loss}, Validation Loss:
{val_loss}')
```

```
    # Check for overfitting
    if train_loss < val_loss:
        print("Warning: Model may be overfitting.")
```

In this scenario, if you notice the training loss continues to decrease but the validation loss starts increasing, you can suspect overfitting is occurring. Without interventions such as early stopping or dropout (covered in later sections), this model might not perform well on real-world data.

Underfitting

Underfitting, on the other hand, occurs when a model is too simplistic and cannot capture the underlying patterns in the data. This happens when the model is not complex enough to learn the relationships between the input features and the output labels. As a result, it performs poorly on both the training and validation sets.

Underfitting typically occurs when the model's architecture is too simple, lacks sufficient parameters, or when trained for too few epochs. In these cases, the model fails to grasp the essential features of the dataset, leading to poor performance across the board. Unlike overfitting, underfitting is easier to detect since the model's performance is subpar from the outset.

Indicators of Underfitting

- **High Training Loss:** If the training loss is high and doesn't decrease significantly during training, the model might be underfitting.
- **Low Complexity:** Underfitting is often a result of a model being too simple for the task. For instance, using a small neural network for a complex computer vision task can lead to underfitting.
- **Inadequate Training:** If a model isn't trained for enough epochs or doesn't have enough data to learn from, it may underfit.

Example of Underfitting in YOLO: Let's consider the YOLO (You Only Look Once) model, another object detection model discussed in the previous chapter. YOLO is designed to work well with large datasets and complex object detection tasks. However, if the model is trained for too few epochs or with a very small network, it might underfit, leading to poor performance.

```
# Example: Training YOLO with underfitting symptoms
import torch
from torchvision import models

# Load a pre-trained YOLO model with a small architecture (hypothetical)
model = models.yolo_small(pretrained=True)
model.train()
```

```
# Example training loop for few epochs (leading to underfitting)
for epoch in range(3):  # Too few epochs
    train_loss = train_one_epoch(model)  # Hypothetical function
    val_loss = validate(model)  # Hypothetical function

    print(f'Epoch {epoch}, Train Loss: {train_loss}, Validation Loss:
{val_loss}')

    # Underfitting case
    if train_loss > val_loss:
        print("Warning: Model is underfitting.")
```

In this case, if you notice the training loss remains high even after a few epochs, the model may be underfitting. Increasing the number of training epochs, adding more layers, or using a larger architecture can help the model learn the patterns in the data more effectively.

Strategies to Address Overfitting and Underfitting

Reducing Overfitting:

- **Regularization Techniques:** Regularization methods such as dropout (covered in the next section) and L2 regularization can prevent the model from relying too much on specific neurons or weights.
- **Early Stopping:** Implementing early stopping allows the training process to halt when the validation performance starts to degrade, preventing overfitting (discussed in detail later in this chapter).
- **Cross-Validation:** Using cross-validation during training can help detect overfitting early and ensure that the model generalizes well across different subsets of the data.

Addressing Underfitting:

- **Increase Model Complexity:** One of the simplest ways to tackle underfitting is to increase the model complexity by adding more layers or neurons. For instance, moving from a shallow CNN to a deeper architecture such as ResNet can improve performance on complex tasks.
- **Train for More Epochs:** Underfitting often happens when the model hasn't been trained long enough to capture patterns in the data. Training the model for additional epochs can allow it to learn more complex relationships.
- **Use Pretrained Models:** Transfer learning, as introduced in *Chapter 7, Exploring Transfer Learning with PyTorch* can help address underfitting by leveraging models that have already learned meaningful representations from larger datasets.

Balancing Model Performance

The key to achieving optimal model performance lies in striking a balance between overfitting and underfitting. Too complex a model and you risk overfitting, too simple and you risk underfitting. Techniques such as hyperparameter tuning, regularization, and early stopping, covered in this chapter, are vital tools in achieving this balance.

Regularization Techniques: Dropout and Batch Normalization

Regularization techniques are essential for improving model generalization and preventing overfitting. In this section, we will explore two of the most widely used regularization methods: dropout and batch normalization. Both techniques have been instrumental in optimizing deep learning models, especially for complex tasks such as image classification and object detection, which we covered in previous chapters.

Dropout and batch normalization are especially beneficial in Convolutional Neural Networks (CNNs), as discussed earlier. These techniques can make a significant difference in CNNs, such as ResNet and Inception, which rely on deep layers and complex architectures. By introducing dropout and batch normalization, we can enhance the robustness of models and ensure they perform well on unseen data.

Dropout: An Effective Regularization Technique

Dropout is a popular regularization method introduced to prevent neural networks from overfitting by randomly "dropping out" (that is, setting to zero) a portion of neurons during the training process. This forces the network to learn more robust features and prevents it from relying too heavily on specific neurons. Dropout has been particularly effective in large models such as CNNs, where the depth of the network makes it more prone to overfitting.

In essence, dropout works by introducing noise into the network, making it harder for the model to rely on individual neurons. During each iteration of training, a randomly selected subset of neurons is ignored, meaning that their contributions are not considered in that iteration. This forces the model to spread the learning across multiple neurons, improving its ability to generalize to unseen data.

Working of Dropout

Dropout operates during training by randomly selecting neurons to be "dropped" with a probability p. For example, if p = 0.5, approximately 50% of the neurons will be dropped during each training iteration. After training, during the inference phase, all neurons are used, but their output is scaled down by the probability p. This scaling ensures that the network behaves consistently between the training and testing phases.

In the context of CNNs, dropout is commonly applied after fully connected layers, as these layers are more likely to overfit due to their high number of parameters. However, dropout can also be applied after convolutional layers, especially in very deep networks like those we discussed in *Chapter 5, Diving Deep into Convolutional Neural Networks* (CNNs), such as ResNet and Inception, where preventing overfitting becomes critical.

Implementing Dropout in PyTorch

PyTorch makes it easy to implement dropout by using the nn.Dropout layer. You can add dropout to your model by simply inserting it between layers. Here's an example of how to implement dropout in a CNN model:

```
import torch
import torch.nn as nn
import torch.optim as optim
import torch.nn.functional as F

class CNNWithDropout(nn.Module):
    def __init__(self):
        super(CNNWithDropout, self).__init__()
        # Define a simple CNN architecture
        self.conv1 = nn.Conv2d(3, 32, kernel_size=3)
        self.conv2 = nn.Conv2d(32, 64, kernel_size=3)
        self.dropout = nn.Dropout(0.5)  # Dropout with 50% probability
        self.fc1 = nn.Linear(64 * 6 * 6, 128)
        self.fc2 = nn.Linear(128, 10)

    def forward(self, x):
        x = F.relu(self.conv1(x))
        x = F.max_pool2d(F.relu(self.conv2(x)), 2)
        x = x.view(-1, 64 * 6 * 6)  # Flatten the feature map
        x = self.dropout(F.relu(self.fc1(x)))  # Apply dropout after
fully connected layer
        x = self.fc2(x)
        return x

# Instantiate the model
model = CNNWithDropout()

# Example optimizer and loss function
optimizer = optim.Adam(model.parameters(), lr=0.001)
criterion = nn.CrossEntropyLoss()
```

In this example, we apply dropout with a probability of 0.5 after the first fully connected layer (`fc1`). This ensures that 50% of the neurons are randomly ignored during each training iteration, forcing the model to learn more robust features.

Impact of Dropout on Model Performance

Dropout significantly reduces overfitting by making the network less reliant on individual neurons. In *Chapter 5, Diving Deep into Convolutional Neural Networks* (CNNs) we discussed how CNNs like ResNet, with their deep architectures, can benefit from dropout when trained on large image datasets such as CIFAR-10 or ImageNet. Without dropout, these models may overfit due to their high capacity and deep layers.

By applying dropout, you can achieve a balance between model complexity and generalization, allowing the model to perform better on unseen data. This is particularly useful in tasks such as image classification, where overfitting is a common problem due to the high dimensionality of image data.

Tuning the Dropout Probability

Choosing the right dropout probability is critical. Too low a value (for example, `p = 0.1`) may not effectively prevent overfitting, while too high a value (for example, `p = 0.9`) may prevent the model from learning useful features. In practice, a probability of `p = 0.5` is often used in fully connected layers, while smaller probabilities (for example,`p = 0.2`) are more commonly applied to convolutional layers.

Batch Normalization: Stabilizing the Training Process

Batch normalization is another powerful regularization technique that addresses a different aspect of training deep neural networks. It works by normalizing the output of each layer so that the distribution of inputs to the next layer remains consistent throughout training. This helps stabilize and accelerate the training process by reducing the internal covariate shift, a phenomenon where the distribution of inputs to a layer changes during training, making it harder for the model to converge.

Batch normalization was introduced earlier while discussing CNNs like ResNet and Inception. These deep architectures, which consist of many layers, can suffer from unstable training if the inputs to each layer vary too much. Batch normalization mitigates this by ensuring that the mean and variance of the activations remain constant across training batches.

Working of Batch Normalization

Batch normalization operates by normalizing the output of each layer to have a mean of 0 and a variance of 1, and then scaling the output using learned parameters. This normalization is applied to mini-batches of data during training, which ensures that the model doesn't experience large fluctuations in the activations, leading to faster and more stable convergence.

In addition to regularization, batch normalization also has the added benefit of allowing higher learning rates, which can significantly speed up training. This is because normalized inputs are less likely to cause exploding or vanishing gradients, two issues that can slow down or completely halt the training process in deep networks.

Implementing Batch Normalization in PyTorch

PyTorch provides the **`nn.BatchNorm2d`** layer for batch normalization in 2D convolutional layers and **`nn.BatchNorm1d`** for fully connected layers. Here's an example of how to implement batch normalization in a CNN model:

```
import torch
import torch.nn as nn
import torch.optim as optim
import torch.nn.functional as F

class CNNWithBatchNorm(nn.Module):
    def __init__(self):
        super(CNNWithBatchNorm, self).__init__()
        # Define a simple CNN architecture with Batch Normalization
        self.conv1 = nn.Conv2d(3, 32, kernel_size=3)
        self.bn1 = nn.BatchNorm2d(32)  # Batch normalization for first
convolutional layer
        self.conv2 = nn.Conv2d(32, 64, kernel_size=3)
        self.bn2 = nn.BatchNorm2d(64)  # Batch normalization for second
convolutional layer
        self.fc1 = nn.Linear(64 * 6 * 6, 128)
        self.fc2 = nn.Linear(128, 10)

    def forward(self, x):
        x = F.relu(self.bn1(self.conv1(x)))  # Apply batch normalization
after convolution
        x = F.max_pool2d(F.relu(self.bn2(self.conv2(x))), 2)
        x = x.view(-1, 64 * 6 * 6)
        x = F.relu(self.fc1(x))
        x = self.fc2(x)
        return x

# Instantiate the model
model = CNNWithBatchNorm()

# Example optimizer and loss function
optimizer = optim.Adam(model.parameters(), lr=0.001)
criterion = nn.CrossEntropyLoss()
```

In this example, we apply batch normalization after each convolutional layer (`conv1` and `conv2`). This ensures that the activations passed to subsequent layers are normalized, leading to more stable and efficient training.

Impact of Batch Normalization on Model Convergence

Batch normalization has a profound effect on model convergence, particularly in deep networks. Stabilizing the input distributions to each layer enables the use of higher learning rates, which in turn leads to faster convergence. In CNNs such as ResNet, batch normalization is a key factor in ensuring that the model can be trained efficiently on large datasets without suffering from unstable gradients.

In addition to improving convergence, batch normalization also acts as a form of regularization, reducing the need for techniques like dropout in some cases. This is because the normalization step inherently reduces the likelihood of overfitting by preventing neurons from becoming too sensitive to specific features in the training data.

Combining Dropout and Batch Normalization

While dropout and batch normalization are often used independently, they can also be combined in the same model to further improve performance. Dropout focuses on reducing overfitting by randomly ignoring neurons, while batch normalization stabilizes the training process and accelerates convergence. By using both techniques together, you can achieve a balance between preventing overfitting and ensuring stable training.

In *Chapter 5, Diving Deep into Convolutional Neural Networks* (CNNs) we explored how dropout was applied in models such as ResNet and Inception. Batch normalization was also an integral part of these models, ensuring that the deep layers could train efficiently. By combining both techniques, you can enhance the performance of these architectures, especially when working with complex datasets such as ImageNet or CIFAR-10.

Regularization is essential for ensuring that models generalize well to new data, and techniques like dropout and batch normalization are two of the most effective tools at your disposal. Dropout prevents overfitting by forcing the network to rely on multiple neurons, while batch normalization stabilizes training and accelerates convergence by normalizing activations. By implementing these techniques in PyTorch, you can significantly improve the performance of your deep learning models, particularly in tasks such as image classification and object detection.

As you continue to refine your models, keep in mind that both dropout and batch normalization can be adjusted to suit the specific needs of your architecture. Whether you're working with CNNs or more advanced models such as YOLO and Faster R-CNN, these regularization techniques will help ensure that your models perform optimally across various tasks.

Hyperparameter Tuning Techniques

Hyperparameter tuning is an essential part of optimizing a deep-learning model. Unlike model parameters, which are learned during training, hyperparameters are manually set by the user and can have a significant impact on model performance. Hyperparameters control various aspects of the training process, such as learning rate, batch size, and model complexity. In this section, we will explore different hyperparameter tuning techniques, including learning rate schedules, grid search, and random search. These methods help you find the optimal configuration for your model, improving both training efficiency and final performance.

Learning Rate Schedules

The learning rate is one of the most critical hyperparameters in deep learning. It controls the size of the steps that the optimizer takes during gradient descent. If the learning rate is too high, the model might overshoot the optimal solution, leading to instability. Conversely, if it is too low, the model may converge too slowly or get stuck in local minima.

A learning rate schedule adjusts the learning rate over time, helping to optimize the convergence process. A common practice is to start with a higher learning rate and gradually decrease it as training progresses. This allows the model to make larger updates early on when it is far from the optimal solution and finer updates as it gets closer.

Step Decay Learning Rate Schedule

One common learning rate schedule is step decay, where the learning rate is reduced by a factor at specific intervals. This approach allows for rapid learning in the early stages, followed by more refined updates later on.

Code Example: Implementing Step Decay in PyTorch

```
import torch.optim as optim

# Define the optimizer with an initial learning rate
optimizer = optim.SGD(model.parameters(), lr=0.1, momentum=0.9)

# Define a learning rate scheduler that decays the learning rate by a
factor of 0.1 every 10 epochs
scheduler = optim.lr_scheduler.StepLR(optimizer, step_size=10,
gamma=0.1)
```

```
# Training loop
for epoch in range(30):
    train_one_epoch(model, optimizer)  # Hypothetical function to train
model for one epoch
    scheduler.step()  # Update learning rate based on scheduler
    print(f'Epoch {epoch+1}, Learning Rate: {scheduler.get_last_lr()}')
```

In this example, the learning rate is reduced by a factor of 0.1 every 10 epochs, ensuring that the model makes larger updates in the initial stages of training and smaller updates later on.

Other Learning Rate Schedules

Other types of learning rate schedules include:

- **Exponential Decay:** The learning rate is reduced exponentially over time, which can be useful for models that require gradual fine-tuning.
- **Cosine Annealing:** The learning rate oscillates between a minimum and maximum value over the course of training, which can help escape local minima and improve convergence.

Grid Search

Grid search is one of the most straightforward techniques for hyperparameter tuning. It works by exhaustively searching through a specified set of hyperparameters, evaluating the model performance for each combination. While grid search is simple to implement, it can be computationally expensive, especially when working with large models and many hyperparameters. However, it is useful for small to medium-sized search spaces where every possible combination can be evaluated.

Working of Grid Search

In grid search, you define a set of possible values for each hyperparameter. The algorithm then trains the model on every possible combination of these values, using cross-validation to evaluate the performance of each configuration.

For example, if you're tuning the learning rate and batch size, you might specify a range of learning rates (for example, 0.001, 0.01, 0.1) and batch sizes (for example, 16, 32, 64). Grid search will train the model using each combination of these values and select the configuration that performs best on the validation set.

Code Example: Implementing Grid Search with Scikit-Learn

```
from sklearn.model_selection import GridSearchCV
from sklearn.ensemble import RandomForestClassifier
```

```
# Define the model and hyperparameter grid
model = RandomForestClassifier()
param_grid = {
    'n_estimators': [50, 100, 200],
    'max_depth': [10, 20, 30]
}

# Perform grid search with cross-validation
grid_search = GridSearchCV(model, param_grid, cv=5)
grid_search.fit(X_train, y_train)  # X_train and y_train are the training
data

print(f'Best Hyperparameters: {grid_search.best_params_}')
```

In this example, grid search is used to tune the number of estimators and the maximum depth of a Random Forest model. PyTorch users can also integrate grid search using libraries such as Ray Tune or Optuna, which simplify the hyperparameter tuning process.

Random Search

Random search is an alternative to grid search that samples random combinations of hyperparameters from the search space. While grid search evaluates every possible combination, random search randomly selects combinations to evaluate. This method is computationally more efficient than grid search and often yields similar results with fewer iterations.

Working of Random Search

In random search, you specify the range of values for each hyperparameter, and the algorithm randomly selects combinations to evaluate. Random search is particularly effective when the search space is large and when certain hyperparameters are more critical than others. For example, if only a few hyperparameters significantly impact model performance, the random search may find a good solution more quickly than the grid search.

Code Example: Implementing Random Search with Scikit-Learn

```
from sklearn.model_selection import RandomizedSearchCV
from sklearn.ensemble import RandomForestClassifier

# Define the model and hyperparameter distribution
model = RandomForestClassifier()
param_dist = {
    'n_estimators': [50, 100, 200],
```

```
    'max_depth': [10, 20, 30]
}

# Perform random search with cross-validation
random_search = RandomizedSearchCV(model, param_dist, n_iter=5, cv=5)
random_search.fit(X_train, y_train)

print(f'Best Hyperparameters: {random_search.best_params_}')
```

In this example, random search evaluates five random combinations of hyperparameters from the specified range. This method is often faster than grid search and works well when you don't need to test every possible combination.

Choosing the Right Technique

Choosing between grid search and random search depends on the size of your search space and the computational resources available. Grid search is useful for small search spaces where you want to evaluate every combination, while random search is more efficient for larger search spaces where evaluating every combination is impractical.

For large-scale projects or more complex models, advanced techniques such as **Bayesian optimization** or the use of tools such as **Ray Tune** can further improve the efficiency of hyperparameter tuning. These methods intelligently search the hyperparameter space, focusing on the most promising regions.

Hyperparameter tuning is a crucial step in optimizing deep learning models. Whether you're modifying the learning rate using schedules, performing grid search, or using random search, finding the right hyperparameters can significantly improve model performance. By applying these techniques, you can ensure that your models are not only accurate but also efficient and robust.

Using Early Stopping for Efficient Training

Training deep learning models often requires running multiple iterations (epochs) over the dataset to minimize the loss and optimize model performance. However, if training goes on for too long, the model can start to overfit, learning the noise in the training data instead of generalizing to new and unseen data. This is where **early stopping** comes into play. Early stopping is a technique that monitors model performance during training and halts the training process once the model stops improving on a validation set. It is particularly beneficial for preventing overfitting and optimizing training time.

In this section, we'll dive into how early stopping works, its key benefits, and how to implement it in PyTorch.

Working of Early Stopping

The idea behind early stopping is simple: instead of training a model for a fixed number of epochs, you monitor the performance of the model on a validation set after each epoch. When the validation performance,typically measured by the validation loss or validation accuracy, stops improving, training is stopped. This avoids overfitting and ensures that the model does not waste time continuing to train after reaching optimal performance.

Mechanism of Early Stopping

During training, early stopping evaluates the model's performance on a validation set at the end of each epoch. It maintains a "patience" parameter, which specifies how many epochs to wait after the last improvement before stopping the training. If the validation loss or another monitored metric has not improved after the defined number of "patience" epochs, the training process is stopped.

For example, if the patience is set to 5 and the model does not improve over the course of 5 epochs, training will halt. By stopping early, you can save computational resources and avoid overfitting to the training data.

Benefits of Early Stopping

Early stopping offers several important benefits for deep learning models:

- **Prevents Overfitting:** As we discussed in the earlier section on overfitting, models that train for too long can start to memorize the training data, reducing their ability to generalize. Early stopping prevents this by halting training when the model's performance on a validation set starts to degrade.
- **Reduces Training Time:** Early stopping helps reduce the overall training time. Instead of running a fixed number of epochs (some of which may be unnecessary), the training process is cut short when the model reaches optimal performance, saving computational resources.
- **Improves Model Generalization:** By stopping the training process at the point where the validation loss is minimized, early stopping ensures that the model is in its best state to generalize to unseen data. This results in better performance on real-world tasks.

Implementing Early Stopping in PyTorch

While PyTorch does not include early stopping by default, implementing it is straightforward. We can create an early stopping class that monitors the validation loss and stops training when the loss doesn't improve after a specified number of epochs.

Code Example: Early Stopping in PyTorch

Here's an implementation of early stopping in PyTorch, using a "patience" parameter to monitor validation loss:

```
import torch
import torch.nn as nn
import torch.optim as optim

class EarlyStopping:
    """Early stopping class to stop training when validation loss does
not improve."""
    def __init__(self, patience=5, delta=0):
        self.patience = patience
        self.delta = delta
        self.counter = 0
        self.best_loss = None
        self.early_stop = False

    def __call__(self, val_loss):
        if self.best_loss is None:
            self.best_loss = val_loss
        elif val_loss > self.best_loss - self.delta:
            self.counter += 1
            if self.counter >= self.patience:
                print("Early stopping triggered")
                self.early_stop = True
        else:
            self.best_loss = val_loss
            self.counter = 0

# Example training loop with early stopping
def train_model(model, train_loader, val_loader, criterion, optimizer,
patience=5):
    early_stopping = EarlyStopping(patience=patience)

    for epoch in range(100):  # Train for up to 100 epochs
        # Training phase
        model.train()
        for inputs, labels in train_loader:
            optimizer.zero_grad()
            outputs = model(inputs)
            loss = criterion(outputs, labels)
            loss.backward()
            optimizer.step()

        # Validation phase
```

```
        model.eval()
        val_loss = 0.0
        with torch.no_grad():
            for inputs, labels in val_loader:
                outputs = model(inputs)
                loss = criterion(outputs, labels)
                val_loss += loss.item()

        val_loss /= len(val_loader)
        print(f"Epoch {epoch+1}, Validation Loss: {val_loss:.4f}")

        # Check for early stopping
        early_stopping(val_loss)
        if early_stopping.early_stop:
            print(f"Training stopped at epoch {epoch+1}")
            break

# Example usage
model = nn.Linear(10, 1)  # Simple model for demonstration
optimizer = optim.Adam(model.parameters(), lr=0.001)
criterion = nn.MSELoss()

train_loader = [...]  # Your training data loader
val_loader = [...]  # Your validation data loader

# Train the model with early stopping
train_model(model, train_loader, val_loader, criterion, optimizer,
patience=5)
```

In this example, the **EarlyStopping** class monitors the validation loss at the end of each epoch. If the validation loss doesn't improve for a specified number of epochs (in this case, 5), then the training process is stopped. This prevents the model from continuing to train once it has reached its best performance on the validation set.

Key Parameters of Early Stopping

- **Patience:** The number of epochs to wait after the last improvement before stopping. A typical value might be between 5 and 10, depending on the complexity of the model and the dataset.
- **Delta:** This parameter allows you to define a minimum change in the validation loss that qualifies as an improvement. If the change in loss is smaller than the delta, it is not considered an improvement.

Understanding When to Use Early Stopping

Early stopping is particularly beneficial for large models and datasets where training can take a long time. For example, deep CNNs trained on complex datasets such as ImageNet can benefit from early stopping to avoid long and unnecessary training runs. Early stopping can also be useful when experimenting with different architectures and hyperparameters, allowing you to stop unpromising models early and move on to more promising configurations.

Early stopping is an invaluable tool for efficiently training deep learning models. By halting training when validation performance stops improving, early stopping not only prevents overfitting but also reduces training time. Implementing early stopping in PyTorch is simple and can significantly improve model performance, ensuring that your models are well-suited for real-world applications.

Ensemble Models for Improved Performance

Ensemble learning is a powerful technique that combines the predictions of multiple models to achieve better performance than any individual model could achieve alone. By aggregating the strengths of several models, ensemble methods help to reduce variance, bias, and overfitting, leading to improved generalization and robustness. In this section, we will explore three popular ensemble techniques–**bagging**, **boosting**, and **stacking**–and discuss how they can be applied to deep learning models, particularly object detection models, such as Faster R-CNN and YOLO.

Bagging (Bootstrap Aggregating)

Bagging is an ensemble technique that involves training multiple instances of the same model on different random subsets of the training data, often using bootstrapping (sampling with replacement). Each model is trained independently, and their predictions are combined (for example, by averaging or majority voting) to produce the final result. Bagging helps reduce the variance of the model, making it less prone to overfitting.

One well-known bagging algorithm is **Random Forest**, which trains multiple decision trees and aggregates their predictions. In deep learning, bagging can be applied to models such as CNNs or object detection models by training multiple versions of the model on different subsets of the data or with different initial weights.

Example: Bagging in PyTorch

```
import torch
import torch.nn as nn

# Example of averaging predictions from multiple models
def ensemble_predictions(models, inputs):
```

```
    predictions = [model(inputs) for model in models]
    avg_predictions = torch.mean(torch.stack(predictions), dim=0)
    return avg_predictions

# Assume we have three pre-trained models
models = [FasterRCNN(), YOLO(), YOLO()]

# Predict using the ensemble
inputs = [...]  # Input data
ensemble_output = ensemble_predictions(models, inputs)
```

In this example, we combine the predictions of multiple object detection models such as Faster R-CNN and YOLO to generate a more accurate and robust final prediction.

Boosting

Boosting is an iterative ensemble technique that trains models sequentially, with each new model focusing on correcting the errors made by the previous models. In contrast to bagging, boosting reduces bias by giving more weight to difficult-to-predict examples. The most popular boosting algorithm is AdaBoost, which assigns higher weights to misclassified samples and adjusts the models accordingly.

Boosting can be applied in deep learning by combining the predictions of weak learners (for example, shallow neural networks) to create a more powerful model. While boosting is more commonly associated with decision trees, it can also be used to boost CNNs and other deep models.

Example: Boosting with Gradient Boosting Frameworks: Boosting is often implemented using frameworks like **XGBoost** or **LightGBM**, which focus on improving decision trees. In deep learning, boosting can be combined with CNNs for classification tasks, though it's less common for object detection.

Stacking

Stacking is a more sophisticated ensemble technique that involves training multiple models and then combining their predictions using a "meta-model" or "meta-learner." The meta-model learns how to combine the outputs of the base models better, leading to improved performance. Unlike bagging and boosting, which combine model outputs directly, stacking allows the meta-model to learn more complex relationships between the base models' predictions.

In object detection, stacking can be used to combine the predictions of models such as Faster R-CNN and YOLO. For example, you could train Faster R-CNN and YOLO separately and then feed their outputs (for example, bounding box coordinates and class predictions) into a meta-model that combines the strengths of both.

Example: Stacking in Object Detection

```
import torch

# Example of stacking model outputs in object detection
def meta_model(faster_rcnn_output, yolo_output):
    # Combine outputs (e.g., averaging bounding boxes, class
probabilities)
    combined_output = (faster_rcnn_output + yolo_output) / 2
    return combined_output

# Assume outputs from two models
faster_rcnn_output = torch.tensor([...])
yolo_output = torch.tensor([...])

# Meta-model combines the outputs
stacked_output = meta_model(faster_rcnn_output, yolo_output)
```

In this example, the outputs of Faster R-CNN and YOLO are combined using a simple meta-model. In practice, a more sophisticated meta-model could be trained to intelligently weigh the outputs based on their strengths.

Ensemble Applications in Object Detection

Ensembling object detection models such as Faster R-CNN and YOLO can significantly improve performance by leveraging the strengths of each model. For example, Faster R-CNN excels at the accurate localization of objects, while YOLO is faster and better suited for real-time applications. By combining these models, you can achieve both high accuracy and speed, making the ensemble well-suited for tasks such as autonomous driving or surveillance.

Ensemble techniques such as bagging, boosting, and stacking can significantly enhance the performance of deep learning models by reducing bias, variance, and overfitting. In object detection, combining models such as Faster R-CNN and YOLO can lead to more accurate and robust results, making ensembling a valuable tool for improving model performance across a range of applications.

Conclusion

In this chapter, we explored several advanced techniques for improving model performance, each designed to enhance the accuracy, robustness, and efficiency of deep learning models. We began by examining the common pitfalls of overfitting and underfitting and discussed how regularization techniques such as dropout and batch normalization can help mitigate these issues. By applying these strategies, particularly in models such as CNNs and object detection architectures discussed in earlier chapters, you can achieve better generalization and more reliable performance on unseen data.

We also delved into hyperparameter tuning techniques, focusing on learning rate schedules, grid search, and random search. These methods allow you to fine-tune the various parameters that control model training, ensuring that your models achieve their best possible performance. The importance of optimizing these parameters cannot be overstated, as even small adjustments can significantly impact the accuracy and convergence of your models.

The chapter then covered early stopping, a critical tool for preventing overfitting and conserving computational resources by halting training when the model's performance on a validation set no longer improves. Finally, we explored ensemble methods, such as bagging, boosting, and stacking, which combine the strengths of multiple models to produce more accurate and robust predictions. These techniques are particularly powerful in tasks such as object detection, where combining models such as Faster R-CNN and YOLO can yield both high accuracy and speed.

As we continue on this journey into deep learning with PyTorch, the next chapter, will introduce you to a powerful framework designed to simplify and accelerate the training process. In this upcoming chapter, you'll learn how PyTorch Lightning can streamline complex training loops, handle distributed computing, and enable more efficient model optimization, allowing you to focus on scaling and fine-tuning your models with greater ease.

CHAPTER 11

Efficient Training with PyTorch Lightning

Introduction

In deep learning, the process of training models often involves writing a significant amount of boilerplate code, especially when handling tasks like optimization, checkpointing, and device management. This can make the training process cumbersome and harder to manage, particularly as models and datasets grow larger. **PyTorch Lightning** is a lightweight framework that builds on top of PyTorch, designed to streamline the training process while maintaining flexibility. By abstracting away many of the repetitive tasks involved in training models, PyTorch Lightning allows developers and researchers to focus on the core logic of their models.

The main goal of PyTorch Lightning is to make PyTorch code more **modular, scalable, and cleaner**, ensuring that researchers can scale their models across multiple GPUs or even distributed environments with minimal effort. Let's explore the three main benefits that PyTorch Lightning brings to the table.

Structure

In this chapter, the following topics will be covered:

- Key Benefits of Pytorch Lightning
- Converting PyTorch Code to PyTorch Lightning
- Training Models with PyTorch Lightning
- Best Practices and Tips for PyTorch Lightning

Key Benefits of Pytorch Lightning

Cleaner Code

PyTorch Lightning enforces a clear separation between the model's logic and the training process. In standard PyTorch, training code is often tightly coupled with model definition, making it difficult to read, reuse, and debug. By introducing the `LightningModule`, PyTorch Lightning helps developers organize their code by defining the model's architecture, forward pass, and loss calculation in a structured way, while the actual training loop is handled by Lightning's `Trainer`.

For example, a typical PyTorch training loop requires manually written optimization steps, backpropagation, and device management, leading to code that can be long and error-prone. PyTorch Lightning simplifies this by taking care of these steps under the hood, while still allowing full customization if needed.

Less Boilerplate

In standard PyTorch, tasks such as setting up optimizers, handling multiple devices (GPUs), and logging metrics often involve repetitive code. With PyTorch Lightning, much of this boilerplate is eliminated. The framework handles tasks such as saving checkpoints, early stopping, and logging through its built-in callbacks and configuration options. This allows for cleaner and more readable code that can be maintained easily.

By removing this boilerplate, PyTorch Lightning reduces the risk of errors and ensures that the code remains focused on the model logic, not the training mechanics.

Streamlining the Training Process

One of the standout features of PyTorch Lightning is how easily it scales models to multiple devices such as GPUs or even distributed training setups. Without Lightning, scaling PyTorch models to multi-GPU setups or distributed environments requires significant code changes and complexity. With PyTorch Lightning, this process is abstracted, allowing developers to scale their models with just a few lines of code.

Additionally, Lightning provides built-in support for features such as automatic mixed precision training, which can further optimize the training process, reducing memory usage while maintaining model performance.

Example: PyTorch vs PyTorch Lightning Training Loop

Let's look at a basic example of training a model in PyTorch and compare it with how PyTorch Lightning simplifies this process.

Standard PyTorch Training Loop:

```
import torch
import torch.nn as nn
import torch.optim as optim

# Define a simple model
class SimpleModel(nn.Module):
    def __init__(self):
```

```
        super(SimpleModel, self).__init__()
        self.fc = nn.Linear(10, 1)

    def forward(self, x):
        return self.fc(x)

# Training loop in PyTorch
model = SimpleModel()
optimizer = optim.Adam(model.parameters(), lr=0.001)
criterion = nn.MSELoss()

for epoch in range(100):
    for inputs, targets in dataloader:
        optimizer.zero_grad()
        outputs = model(inputs)
        loss = criterion(outputs, targets)
        loss.backward()
        optimizer.step()
```

In this standard PyTorch example, the training logic, including the forward pass, loss calculation, backpropagation, and optimization, is manually coded in the training loop. This can lead to duplication and complexity, especially when scaling.

PyTorch Lightning Version:

```
import pytorch_lightning as pl
import torch.nn as nn
import torch.optim as optim
class SimpleLightningModel(pl.LightningModule):
    def __init__(self):
        super(SimpleLightningModel, self).__init__()
        self.fc = nn.Linear(10, 1)
        self.criterion = nn.MSELoss()

    def forward(self, x):
        return self.fc(x)

    def training_step(self, batch, batch_idx):
        inputs, targets = batch
        outputs = self(inputs)
        loss = self.criterion(outputs, targets)
        return loss

    def configure_optimizers(self):
        return optim.Adam(self.parameters(), lr=0.001)

# Training with PyTorch Lightning
model = SimpleLightningModel()
```

```
trainer = pl.Trainer(max_epochs=100)
trainer.fit(model, train_dataloader)
```

In the PyTorch Lightning version, the model definition and training logic are distinctly separated. The **`training_step`** method defines how the model trains on a batch of data, while **`configure_optimizers`** sets up the optimizer. The training process is handled by the **`Trainer`** class, which manages the entire training loop, allowing developers to focus on the model itself without worrying about the low-level details of training.

By using PyTorch Lightning, developers can write more organized and efficient code, making it easier to scale their models while keeping the training process clear and concise. In the following sections, we will explore how to convert PyTorch code into PyTorch Lightning and how to train models effectively using this framework.

Converting PyTorch Code to PyTorch Lightning

One of the core benefits of PyTorch Lightning is how it simplifies the structure of code by separating the model logic from the training process. This clear separation not only makes the code cleaner but also makes it easier to scale and maintain. In this section, we will walk through the process of converting an existing PyTorch model into PyTorch Lightning, focusing on how to define a **`LightningModule`**, manage the forward pass, and handle training and validation logic.

Defining the `LightningModule`

The heart of any PyTorch Lightning model is the **`LightningModule`**, which organizes the key components of the model, such as the forward pass, optimizer configuration, and training steps. This modular approach allows you to keep your model logic separate from the training loop, making it easier to understand and reuse.

In standard PyTorch, the training process often involves a lot of manual coding, such as handling the forward pass, loss calculation, backpropagation, and optimization. In contrast, PyTorch Lightning abstracts these details into the **`LightningModule`**, allowing you to define your model and training steps in a more structured way.

Separating Model Definition from Training Logic

In PyTorch Lightning, the model definition is separated from the training loop. While PyTorch requires you to manage the optimizer, loss function, and data iteration manually, Lightning handles much of this behind the scenes, allowing you to focus on the architecture of your model.

Let's walk through a simple example of converting a PyTorch CNN model for MNIST classification into a PyTorch Lightning version. In standard PyTorch, the model and training loop are typically combined, with training steps written directly inside the loop. In Lightning, we'll refactor the code to organize these steps more efficiently.

Converting a PyTorch CNN Model for MNIST

Here's a simple CNN model for classifying MNIST digits in standard PyTorch:

Standard PyTorch Model and Training Loop:

```
import torch
import torch.nn as nn
import torch.optim as optim
from torchvision import datasets, transforms

# Define a simple CNN for MNIST
class CNNModel(nn.Module):
    def __init__(self):
        super(CNNModel, self).__init__()
        self.conv1 = nn.Conv2d(1, 32, kernel_size=3)
        self.conv2 = nn.Conv2d(32, 64, kernel_size=3)
        self.fc1 = nn.Linear(9216, 128)
        self.fc2 = nn.Linear(128, 10)

    def forward(self, x):
        x = torch.relu(self.conv1(x))
        x = torch.relu(self.conv2(x))
        x = torch.flatten(x, 1)
        x = torch.relu(self.fc1(x))
        return self.fc2(x)

# Initialize model, optimizer, and loss function
model = CNNModel()
optimizer = optim.Adam(model.parameters(), lr=0.001)
criterion = nn.CrossEntropyLoss()

# Training loop
for epoch in range(5):
    for inputs, targets in train_dataloader:
        optimizer.zero_grad()
        outputs = model(inputs)
        loss = criterion(outputs, targets)
        loss.backward()
        optimizer.step()
```

In this example, the model logic, forward pass, and training loop are tightly coupled, requiring manual management of each step. Now, let's convert this model into PyTorch Lightning to simplify and clean up the code.

Converting to PyTorch Lightning:

```
import pytorch_lightning as pl
import torch
import torch.nn as nn
import torch.optim as optim
from torchvision import datasets, transforms

# Define the CNN model using LightningModule
class LightningCNNModel(pl.LightningModule):
    def __init__(self):
        super(LightningCNNModel, self).__init__()
        self.conv1 = nn.Conv2d(1, 32, kernel_size=3)
        self.conv2 = nn.Conv2d(32, 64, kernel_size=3)
        self.fc1 = nn.Linear(9216, 128)
        self.fc2 = nn.Linear(128, 10)
        self.criterion = nn.CrossEntropyLoss()

    def forward(self, x):
        x = torch.relu(self.conv1(x))
        x = torch.relu(self.conv2(x))
        x = torch.flatten(x, 1)
        x = torch.relu(self.fc1(x))
        return self.fc2(x)

    # Training step defines a single iteration over the batch
    def training_step(self, batch, batch_idx):
        inputs, targets = batch
        outputs = self(inputs)
        loss = self.criterion(outputs, targets)
        return loss

    # Validation step (if needed) for performance evaluation
    def validation_step(self, batch, batch_idx):
        inputs, targets = batch
        outputs = self(inputs)
        loss = self.criterion(outputs, targets)
        return loss

    # Optimizer configuration
    def configure_optimizers(self):
        return optim.Adam(self.parameters(), lr=0.001)

# Initialize the model and Lightning trainer
model = LightningCNNModel()
trainer = pl.Trainer(max_epochs=5)
trainer.fit(model, train_dataloader)
```

Breaking Down the `LightningModule`

In this PyTorch Lightning version, the model logic is separated from the training loop:

- **`forward()`**: Defines the forward pass, just like in standard PyTorch. This remains unchanged.
- **`training_step()`**: Handles a single training iteration. It takes a batch of inputs and targets, performs the forward pass, calculates the loss, and returns it. This removes the need to manually write the training loop in every experiment.
- **`validation_step()`**: Optionally handles validation logic, keeping the training and validation steps consistent.
- **`configure_optimizers()`**: Returns the optimizer, which is automatically used by the PyTorch Lightning **`Trainer`**.

By using the **`Trainer`** class, PyTorch Lightning handles all the boilerplate code related to training loops, backpropagation, and optimization. As you can see, the Lightning version is more modular and easier to maintain. This approach also allows for easy scaling, as Lightning abstracts away the details of handling multiple devices (GPUs) and distributed training.

Benefits of Conversion

- **Cleaner Separation:** The training logic (for example, optimization, loss computation, and so on) is now separated from the model architecture. This makes the code more modular and easier to understand.
- **Scalability:** PyTorch Lightning's Trainer makes it easy to scale the training to multiple GPUs with minimal code changes.
- **Built-in Functionality:** With Lightning, features such as logging, checkpointing, and early stopping can be added with just a few lines of code, eliminating the need for custom code.

Converting existing PyTorch code into PyTorch Lightning is a straightforward process that brings immediate benefits in terms of code clarity, maintainability, and scalability. By organizing the model logic into a `LightningModule` and handling training steps via the Trainer class, PyTorch Lightning simplifies many of the repetitive tasks associated with training deep learning models, allowing you to focus on building and refining your models.

In the next section, we will explore how to train models with PyTorch Lightning in greater detail, including how to use the **`Trainer`** class to streamline the training process and handle common tasks such as validation and checkpointing.

Training Models with PyTorch Lightning

Training deep learning models can involve a lot of repetitive tasks, such as setting up training loops, managing devices like GPUs, and handling validation and checkpointing. PyTorch Lightning's Trainer class simplifies these tasks by managing the entire training process, allowing you to focus on the model. In this section, we will explore how to set up the `Trainer` for training, validation, and testing, handle multiple GPUs or distributed training, and use built-in features such as checkpointing and logging.

Setting Up the Trainer Class for Training, Validation, and Testing

The Trainer class in PyTorch Lightning abstracts away many of the manual tasks you would typically need to handle when training a model. It manages the training loop, backpropagation, and optimization. You can easily set up the **`Trainer`** with parameters such as the number of epochs, the frequency of validation, and whether to use early stopping. The **`Trainer`** also handles validation and testing phases seamlessly by calling the appropriate methods within your **`LightningModule`**.

Basic Configuration of the Trainer

To train a model, you need to instantiate the Trainer and call its fit() method. This handles all aspects of the training loop automatically.

Example: Basic Trainer Setup

```
import pytorch_lightning as pl

# Instantiate the Lightning model
model = LightningCNNModel()

# Set up the Trainer with basic configurations
trainer = pl.Trainer(max_epochs=10)  # Set to train for 10 epochs

# Train the model
trainer.fit(model, train_dataloader, val_dataloader)
```

In this example, the **`Trainer`** is initialized with **`max_epochs=10`**, indicating that the model will train for 10 epochs. The **`fit()`** method then takes the model and the training and validation data loaders as input, handling the entire training process.

Handling Multiple GPUs or Distributed Training

One of the key advantages of using PyTorch Lightning is how easily it handles multi-GPU and distributed training. In standard PyTorch, scaling models across multiple devices can be complex and require additional code to manually manage the GPUs and distribute the model. PyTorch Lightning abstracts this complexity, allowing you to train across multiple GPUs or even distributed systems with a few configuration changes.

Training on Multiple GPUs

To train your model on multiple GPUs, you simply need to specify the number of GPUs in the Trainer configuration. Lightning will automatically distribute the model across the specified GPUs, handle data parallelism, and manage backpropagation.

Example: Multi-GPU Training

```
trainer = pl.Trainer(max_epochs=10, gpus=2)  # Use 2 GPUs for training
trainer.fit(model, train_dataloader)
```

In this example, specifying `gpus=2` allows the `Trainer` to automatically distribute the model across two GPUs. This eliminates the need for complex manual GPU management.

Distributed Training

For distributed training across multiple nodes (that is, distributed data parallelism), Lightning simplifies the setup further. By setting the **`distributed_backend`** option, you can easily configure distributed training. This is especially useful for large models or datasets that need to be trained on multiple machines.

Example: Distributed Training

```
trainer = pl.Trainer(max_epochs=10, gpus=2, strategy='ddp')  # Use DDP
for distributed training
trainer.fit(model, train_dataloader)
```

In this case, the model is trained across multiple GPUs using the **Distributed Data Parallel (DDP)** strategy. Lightning handles the process of distributing the data and synchronizing gradients across the GPUs.

Common Tasks: Checkpointing and Logging

Two common tasks during training are saving model checkpoints and logging performance metrics. These are essential for tracking the progress of your model and for resuming training if it's interrupted. PyTorch Lightning makes both checkpointing and logging extremely simple through built-in features.

Model Checkpointing

With PyTorch Lightning, you can save the model's weights at regular intervals using a built-in callback called `ModelCheckpoint`. This callback automatically saves the model after every epoch or when specific criteria (for example, best validation loss) are met.

Example: Using Model Checkpointing

```
checkpoint_callback = pl.callbacks.ModelCheckpoint(monitor='val_loss',
save_top_k=1, mode='min')

trainer = pl.Trainer(max_epochs=10, callbacks=[checkpoint_callback])
trainer.fit(model, train_dataloader, val_dataloader)
```

In this example, the **ModelCheckpoint** callback saves the model only when the validation loss improves, keeping the best model during training. The **save_top_k=1** argument ensures that only the top model is saved based on the minimum validation loss.

Logging with PyTorch Lightning

Logging metrics such as loss, accuracy, or custom-defined metrics is straightforward in Lightning. You can log any metric during training, validation, or testing using the **self.log()** method within the **LightningModule**.

Example: Logging Validation Accuracy

```
class LightningCNNModel(pl.LightningModule):
    # Model definition here...

    def validation_step(self, batch, batch_idx):
        inputs, targets = batch
        outputs = self(inputs)
        loss = self.criterion(outputs, targets)

        # Calculate accuracy
        acc = (outputs.argmax(dim=1) == targets).float().mean()

        # Log accuracy
        self.log('val_accuracy', acc, prog_bar=True)

        return loss
```

In this example, the validation accuracy is calculated in the `validation_step()` method and logged using **self.log()**. The **prog_bar=True** argument ensures that the metric is displayed in the progress bar during training.

Using Early Stopping

Early stopping is a critical technique for preventing overfitting, especially in deep-learning models. PyTorch Lightning includes an **EarlyStopping** callback that monitors a specified metric such as validation loss and halts training if the metric stops improving.

Example: Early Stopping in PyTorch Lightning

```
early_stopping_callback = pl.callbacks.EarlyStopping(monitor='val_loss',
patience=3, mode='min')

trainer = pl.Trainer(max_epochs=20, callbacks=[early_stopping_callback])
trainer.fit(model, train_dataloader, val_dataloader)
```

In this example, training will stop if the validation loss does not improve for 3 consecutive epochs **(`patience=3`)**. This prevents the model from overfitting to the training data and saves time by halting unnecessary training.

Training models with PyTorch Lightning's `Trainer` class simplifies many of the repetitive tasks involved in training deep-learning models. By abstracting away details, such as backpropagation, optimization, multi-GPU management, checkpointing, and logging, Lightning enables developers to focus on building better models without worrying about the complexity of the training loop. The built-in functionality for handling common tasks, such as early stopping and model checkpointing, makes the training process more efficient and scalable.

Best Practices and Tips for PyTorch Lightning

Using PyTorch Lightning not only simplifies the training process but also helps you write more structured, scalable, and maintainable code. By adhering to best practices, you can ensure that your projects remain clean and easy to manage as they grow in complexity. This section will provide guidance on organizing your code, using callbacks effectively, and debugging or improving performance in PyTorch Lightning projects.

Code Organization: Separating Concerns

A key aspect of PyTorch Lightning is how it encourages you to separate different concerns of your model, training, and data processing logic. The **`LightningModule`** is where you define your model's architecture, training steps, validation steps, and optimization logic. However, Lightning also supports the use of **`DataModules`** which are dedicated classes for handling data loading and pre-processing. By separating these concerns, your code becomes easier to read, maintain, and scale.

Best Practice: Using DataModules

A **`DataModule`** in PyTorch Lightning is responsible for organizing the data pipeline. It handles downloading datasets, preparing and transforming them, and setting up data loaders for training, validation, and testing. Separating the data logic into its own module ensures that the **`LightningModule`** stays focused purely on the model's logic.

Example: Structuring Code with LightningModule and DataModule

```
import pytorch_lightning as pl
from torch.utils.data import DataLoader
from torchvision import datasets, transforms

# Define DataModule for organizing data
class MNISTDataModule(pl.LightningDataModule):
    def __init__(self, batch_size=32):
        super().__init__()
        self.batch_size = batch_size
        self.transform = transforms.Compose([transforms.ToTensor()])

    def setup(self, stage=None):
        self.train_data = datasets.MNIST(root='data', train=True,
download=True, transform=self.transform)
        self.val_data = datasets.MNIST(root='data', train=False,
download=True, transform=self.transform)

    def train_dataloader(self):
        return DataLoader(self.train_data, batch_size=self.batch_size)

    def val_dataloader(self):
        return DataLoader(self.val_data, batch_size=self.batch_size)

# LightningModule for model and training logic
class LightningCNNModel(pl.LightningModule):
    def __init__(self):
        super().__init__()
        self.conv1 = nn.Conv2d(1, 32, kernel_size=3)
        self.fc = nn.Linear(32 * 26 * 26, 10)
        self.criterion = nn.CrossEntropyLoss()

    def forward(self, x):
        x = torch.relu(self.conv1(x))
        x = torch.flatten(x, 1)
        return self.fc(x)

    def training_step(self, batch, batch_idx):
        inputs, targets = batch
        outputs = self(inputs)
        loss = self.criterion(outputs, targets)
        return loss

    def configure_optimizers(self):
```

```
        return torch.optim.Adam(self.parameters(), lr=0.001)

# Train model using both modules
data_module = MNISTDataModule()
model = LightningCNNModel()

trainer = pl.Trainer(max_epochs=10)
trainer.fit(model, data_module)
```

In this example, the **`DataModule`** handles all data-related logic, such as setting up data loaders and applying transformations, while the **`LightningModule`** is solely responsible for the model and training logic. This separation improves code clarity and maintainability.

Leveraging Callbacks for Logging and Checkpointing

PyTorch Lightning provides built-in support for callbacks that make it easy to add functionality, such as checkpointing, logging, and early stopping without cluttering your core training code. Callbacks are extremely useful for tracking metrics, saving model checkpoints, or stopping training early when the model's performance plateaus.

Using Model Checkpointing and Logging Callbacks

Callbacks such as **`ModelCheckpoint`** and **`EarlyStopping`** are essential tools for managing the training process. By using callbacks, you can ensure that your code remains clean while benefiting from automated logging and model saving during training.

Example: Using Callbacks for Checkpointing and Early Stopping

```
import torch
import torch.nn as nn
import torch.optim as optim

class EarlyStopping:
    """Early stopping class to stop training when validation loss does
not improve."""
    def __init__(self, patience=5, delta=0):
        self.patience = patience
        self.delta = delta
        self.counter = 0
        self.best_loss = None
        self.early_stop = False

    def __call__(self, val_loss):
```

```
        if self.best_loss is None:
            self.best_loss = val_loss
        elif val_loss > self.best_loss - self.delta:
            self.counter += 1
            if self.counter >= self.patience:
                print("Early stopping triggered")
                self.early_stop = True
        else:checkpoint_callback = pl.callbacks.ModelCheckpoint
(monitor='val_loss', save_top_k=1, mode='min')
early_stopping_callback = pl.callbacks.EarlyStopping(monitor='val_loss',
patience=3)

trainer = pl.Trainer(max_epochs=20, callbacks=[checkpoint_callback,
early_stopping_callback])
trainer.fit(model, data_module)
```

In this example, the **ModelCheckpoint** callback saves the model with the best validation loss, and the **EarlyStopping** callback halts training if the validation loss does not improve for 3 consecutive epochs. This keeps your training process efficient while ensuring that only the best models are saved.

Tips for Debugging and Improving Training Performance

When working with deep learning models, efficient debugging and performance optimization are crucial. PyTorch Lightning provides useful features that help simplify debugging and boost training performance.

Debugging Tips

Fast Development Cycles: Use the **limit_train_batches** and **limit_val_batches** parameters in the Trainer to quickly run through smaller batches of data when debugging or testing model changes. This speeds up the feedback loop without needing to wait for full training runs.

```
trainer = pl.Trainer(max_epochs=5, limit_train_batches=0.1, limit_val_
batches=0.1)
trainer.fit(model, data_module)
```

Sanity Checks: PyTorch Lightning automatically runs a sanity check of validation steps before training begins to ensure that the model works as expected. You can leverage this feature to catch potential issues early in the process.

Improving Training Performance

Mixed Precision Training: PyTorch Lightning supports automatic mixed precision training with the **precision** flag. This reduces memory usage and increases training speed without sacrificing model accuracy.

```
trainer = pl.Trainer(max_epochs=10, precision=16)  # Enable mixed
precision training
trainer.fit(model, data_module)
```

Profiling: PyTorch Lightning's built-in profiler helps you monitor and identify bottlenecks in your training process, allowing you to optimize performance by adjusting parameters such as batch size or learning rate.

By following best practices for PyTorch Lightning, you can keep your code clean, modular, and scalable. Organizing the data and model logic separately improves maintainability while leveraging callbacks for tasks such as logging and checkpointing keeps the training loop uncluttered. Additionally, using built-in debugging and performance features ensures that your training process remains efficient and easy to manage. These practices allow you to focus on the model development itself, rather than on repetitive code management.

Conclusion

In this chapter, we explored how PyTorch Lightning streamlines the training process by simplifying the code structure, reducing boilerplate, and offering powerful tools, such as the `Trainer` class for managing training, validation, and testing. By organizing code into **LightningModule** and **DataModule**, we ensured that our deep learning workflows were not only efficient but also clean and scalable. The use of built-in callbacks for logging, checkpointing, and early stopping further demonstrated how PyTorch Lightning enables you to manage essential training tasks with minimal effort.

We also touched on key best practices, such as leveraging callbacks, organizing code for maintainability, and utilizing performance improvements such as mixed precision training. With PyTorch Lightning, the focus shifts from managing the complexity of the training loop to refining the model itself, allowing for a more productive and less error-prone development cycle.

As we move into the next chapter, we will explore how to take your trained models and deploy them into production environments. Whether it's serving models via APIs or deploying them on cloud platforms, this next step is crucial for bringing your models to real-world applications.

CHAPTER 12
Model Deployment and Production-Ready Considerations

Introduction

Building and training machine learning models is an exciting and crucial part of any project, but the real value of these models comes when they are deployed and used in real-world applications. Transitioning a model from development to production involves a shift from experimentation and research to ensuring that the model can consistently deliver high performance in dynamic environments. In this chapter, we will explore how to effectively prepare and deploy models trained in PyTorch to production settings, highlighting the key considerations and tools that make this process smoother.

One of the biggest challenges in deploying machine learning models is ensuring that they remain **performant** under different conditions. In research and development, models are often optimized for accuracy or specific tasks, but once deployed, factors such as latency, resource consumption, and real-time performance become critical. A model that performs well in a controlled environment may struggle when deployed to handle live traffic, respond to user queries in real time, or scale to meet fluctuating demand.

Another major consideration is **scalability**. A production-ready model must be capable of scaling to accommodate growing amounts of data or increasing numbers of requests. Whether the model is deployed on a server, a cloud platform, or edge devices, it must be flexible enough to scale both vertically (increasing resources on the same machine) and horizontally (distributing the load across multiple machines). Balancing these requirements without sacrificing performance is often a challenging task, especially for larger models or those deployed in complex environments.

Maintenance and **robustness** are also critical factors. A production environment can introduce various risks, from hardware failures to changing data patterns. The deployed model needs to be easily maintainable, with clear logging, monitoring, and version control systems in place to ensure smooth updates, debugging, and the ability to roll back if necessary. Additionally, robustness is key to ensuring the model can handle unexpected inputs or conditions without crashing or degrading during their performance.

In this chapter, we will guide you through the essential steps for deploying PyTorch models, from using tools such as **TorchServe** to setting up models for real-time use. We'll also discuss **optimizations** such as quantization and pruning, which are critical for improving the efficiency of models in production environments. Lastly, we'll explore key **deployment considerations** such as managing latency, ensuring scalability, and building robust systems that can handle real-world demands.

By the end of this chapter, you'll have a clear understanding of how to take a model from development to production, ensuring it is ready for real-world use while maintaining the performance, scalability, and robustness necessary for long-term success.

Structure

In this chapter, the following topics will be covered:

- Streamlining Model Deployment for Production
- TorchServe: Simplifying PyTorch Model Deployment
- Optimizing Models for Production: Techniques for Efficiency
- Key Production Considerations: Scalability, Latency, and Robustness

Streamlining Model Deployment for Production

Deploying machine learning models into production environments involves several key steps, each aimed at ensuring that the model is ready to handle real-world scenarios efficiently and reliably. The transition from development to deployment requires not only packaging the model but also setting up the appropriate infrastructure to serve it effectively. In this section, we will provide an overview of the basic steps in the deployment process, focusing on the broader workflow rather than the low-level technical details.

Exporting and Packaging the Model

The first step in any deployment process is preparing the model for production. Once a model has been trained and validated, it must be exported in a format that can be easily loaded and served in the production environment. In PyTorch, this often involves exporting the model using **`torch.save()`** to save the trained model's state, which can then be loaded when the model is deployed. This aspect has been covered in detail in previous chapters, so we'll focus on how models fit into the bigger picture of deployment.

In a production setting, the model needs to be packaged in a way that allows it to be served reliably. This can include serializing the model into a format such as **`TorchScript`**, which is optimized for production inference and allows easy integration with deployment platforms. **`TorchScript`** models can be run in environments where Python may not be available, making them suitable for mobile or edge devices.

For more complex applications, models can also be containerized using Docker to ensure that the necessary dependencies and environment configurations are bundled together. This ensures that the model behaves consistently regardless of the underlying hardware or operating system.

Setting Up the Serving Environment

Once the model is exported and packaged, the next step is setting up the serving environment where it will run. The serving environment is responsible for loading the model, handling requests such as inference queries, and returning the results. Depending on the use case, this could involve deploying the model on a cloud service, an on-premise server, or even on edge devices for low-latency applications.

In modern machine learning workflows, models are often deployed as part of a microservice architecture, where the model is served through an API. This allows external applications to send data to the model, receive predictions, and integrate the model's outputs into broader workflows. Tools such as TorchServe (which will be covered in the next section) help simplify this process by providing a scalable, production-ready serving solution specifically for PyTorch models.

For cloud-based environments, services such as **AWS SageMaker**, **Azure ML**, or **Google AI** Platform offer managed platforms that automate much of the deployment process, from setting up scalable infrastructure to handling load balancing and versioning. These platforms allow for seamless scaling as demand for the model increases.

Managing Model Versioning and Updates

In production, it's common to iterate on models over time as new data becomes available or as the model is improved through retraining. Therefore, it's essential to have a strategy in place for model versioning and updates. Maintaining different versions of a model ensures that you can test new versions in a controlled environment (for example, A/B testing or shadow deployment) while continuing to serve the current production model.

When updating a model, it's important to have mechanisms for rollback in case the new model underperforms or causes unexpected issues. Having a robust versioning system allows you to quickly revert to the previous model without downtime, ensuring continuous service availability.

Monitoring and Maintaining Models in Production

Once deployed, models must be monitored continuously to ensure they perform as expected in the production environment. Unlike in development, where models are tested on curated datasets, real-world data can vary significantly, and changes in data patterns (known as data drift) can cause model performance to degrade over time.

Monitoring tools can track various performance metrics, such as response times, throughput, and prediction accuracy, allowing you to identify issues before they impact users. Alerts can be set up to notify you if the model's performance drops below a certain threshold, or if there are spikes in latency or errors. Tools such as Prometheus, Grafana, and cloud-specific monitoring services are commonly used to monitor deployed models.

It's also important to track the resource consumption of your model, particularly in environments with limited computing power or where cost efficiency is important. Monitoring GPU/CPU utilization, memory usage, and disk I/O can help identify bottlenecks and optimize the model's performance further.

Ensuring Scalability and Reliability

Finally, scalability and reliability are essential when deploying models in production. As demand for a model grows, the deployment must be able to scale to handle increasing traffic without sacrificing performance. This is where cloud-based platforms, load balancers, and auto-scaling tools come into play.

To ensure that the model remains reliable, redundancy and fault-tolerance mechanisms should be in place. For instance, deploying the model across multiple servers or data centers helps ensure that even if one server goes down, the model can continue to serve requests from another instance. Autoscaling can dynamically adjust the number of active instances based on traffic, ensuring that the model can handle peak loads efficiently.

By following these basic steps, exporting and packaging the model, setting up the serving environment, managing versioning, and monitoring its performance, you can ensure that your PyTorch models are well-prepared for production. The deployment process is not just about making predictions; it's about ensuring that your model is scalable, reliable, and easy to maintain over time. In the next section, we'll explore how TorchServe can simplify this process, providing a streamlined way to deploy and serve PyTorch models at scale.

Converting PyTorch Code to PyTorch Lightning

Deploying machine learning models can often be a complex and time-consuming process, especially when it comes to managing scalability, versioning, and performance monitoring. TorchServe is an open-source tool developed by AWS and Facebook to simplify the deployment of PyTorch models in production environments. TorchServe enables you to serve models as REST APIs, handle model versioning, and scale your deployment with minimal effort, making it a practical choice for both small and large-scale applications.

In this section, we will introduce TorchServe and explore how it can be used to streamline the deployment of PyTorch models, from serving models via APIs to monitoring and scaling in production environments.

Understanding TorchServe

TorchServe is a model-serving framework specifically designed for PyTorch models. It abstracts much of the complexity involved in deploying models by providing ready-made functionalities, such as API endpoints, multi-model support, scaling, and performance monitoring. TorchServe allows you to deploy models without needing to write extensive code to manage infrastructure, making it highly accessible to developers.

Some of the key features of TorchServe include:

- **Serving models as REST APIs:** This allows your model to receive input and return predictions through HTTP requests, making it easier to integrate into web services or applications.
- **Model versioning:** TorchServe allows you to manage multiple versions of a model so that you can easily roll back to a previous version if needed.
- **Scalability:** TorchServe can scale horizontally to handle increased traffic by deploying multiple instances of the model.
- **Logging and monitoring:** Built-in support for logging and monitoring lets you track performance metrics, such as inference time, request throughput, and model accuracy.

Serving Models as REST APIs

One of the most common use cases for deploying models is making them available through REST APIs. TorchServe simplifies this by automatically creating API endpoints that can be called with input data, returning model predictions in response. This functionality allows you to integrate your model into applications such as web services, mobile apps, or other systems that require real-time predictions.

To deploy a model with TorchServe, you need to package the trained model and provide a model handler that defines how the input data is processed and how the output is returned.

Example: Serving a PyTorch Model with TorchServe

Here's how you can package and serve a simple image classification model using TorchServe:

1. **Export the model:** Save the trained model using `torch.save()`, and create a `model_store` directory to store the model artifacts.

   ```
   torch-model-archiver --model-name mnist --version 1.0 --model-file
   model.py --serialized-file model.pth --export-path model_store
   --handler image_classifier
   ```

2. **Start TorchServe:** Launch the TorchServe server, which will load the model and expose an API for inference.

   ```
   torchserve --start --ncs --model-store model_store --models
   mnist=mnist.mar
   ```

3. **Send inference requests**: Once the model is served, you can send HTTP POST requests with input data (for example, an image) to the REST API and receive predictions in response.

   ```
   curl -X POST http://127.0.0.1:8080/predictions/mnist -T input_
   image.png
   ```

   In this example, TorchServe handles all the heavy lifting of serving the model as an API. This makes it easy to integrate the model into any production system that needs predictions on demand such as web applications or backend services.

Scaling and Monitoring the Model

TorchServe is designed to handle scaling efficiently. As traffic to your model increases, TorchServe can scale horizontally by deploying additional instances of the model to handle the load. This ensures that the model can serve requests without experiencing bottlenecks or downtime, making it suitable for both small applications and large-scale deployments.

Additionally, TorchServe provides built-in support for logging and monitoring, making it easier to track key metrics, such as latency, throughput, and resource usage. These metrics are essential for maintaining performance in a production environment, where it's crucial to monitor how well the model handles requests under different conditions.

Example: Scaling TorchServe for Increased Traffic

To scale TorchServe, you can configure the server to deploy multiple workers that process requests in parallel. This can be configured when starting TorchServe:

```
torchserve --start --ncs --model-store model_store --models mnist=mnist.
mar --gpus 2 --workers 4
```

In this example, TorchServe is configured to use 2 GPUs and 4 workers, ensuring that the model can handle a higher volume of requests. TorchServe automatically distributes incoming requests across the available workers, improving throughput and reducing latency.

Monitoring Model Performance

TorchServe includes a metrics API that provides real-time statistics about the model's performance. You can monitor these metrics to ensure that the model is responding within acceptable limits and adjust the infrastructure as needed.

```
curl http://127.0.0.1:8080/metrics
```

This command returns detailed metrics, such as request count, latency, and error rates, allowing you to keep track of the model's behavior in production and respond to any performance issues before they impact the user experience.

TorchServe is an invaluable tool for deploying PyTorch models in production environments. By simplifying the process of serving models as REST APIs, managing versioning, scaling, and monitoring performance, TorchServe makes it easier for developers to move their models from experimentation to real-world applications. Whether you're deploying a model for a small application or a large-scale service, TorchServe provides the necessary tools to ensure your model is ready for production.

In the next section, we will explore how to optimize models for production environments by applying techniques such as quantization and pruning, which help improve model performance and efficiency.

Optimizing Models for Production: Techniques for Efficiency

Deploying machine learning models into production environments comes with a set of challenges, especially when dealing with resource constraints, such as limited memory, processing power, or bandwidth. Optimizing models for such environments ensures they run efficiently while maintaining accuracy and performance. Two key techniques for optimizing models in production are **quantization** and **pruning**. These techniques help reduce the model size and improve inference speed, making them ideal for deploying models on devices with limited hardware, such as mobile devices or edge computing platforms.

In this section, we will discuss how quantization and pruning can be applied to optimize models for production environments, with practical examples of their usage in PyTorch.

Model Quantization

Quantization is a technique used to reduce the precision of the numbers (weights and activations) that the model uses during inference. Typically, models are trained with **32-bit floating point (FP32)** precision, but this high precision isn't always necessary during inference. By reducing the precision of these numbers, such as converting them to **8-bit integers (INT8)**, you can significantly reduce the model's memory footprint and speed up computation, all while maintaining similar levels of accuracy.

Quantization is particularly useful for deploying models on resource-constrained devices such as mobile phones or IoT edge devices, where memory and computational resources are limited. By quantizing the model, you can ensure that it runs efficiently while still providing the necessary performance for real-time tasks.

Types of Quantization

PyTorch offers several methods for quantization, each of which can be applied depending on the requirements and constraints of the deployment environment.

- **Post-training quantization:** This technique involves quantizing the model after it has been fully trained. This is the simplest approach and often achieves a good balance between performance and accuracy.
- **Quantization-aware training (QAT):** With QAT, the model is trained with quantization in mind, which typically results in better accuracy compared to post-training quantization but requires more training time.

Example: Post-Training Quantization in PyTorch

In PyTorch, post-training quantization is straightforward and can be applied to a trained model using the **`torch.quantization`** module. Here's how you can quantize a simple image classification model using post-training quantization:

```
import torch
import torch.quantization
from torchvision import models
```

```
# Load a pre-trained model
model = models.resnet18(pretrained=True)
model.eval()

# Fuse the model layers (required before quantization)
model.fuse_model()

# Apply post-training static quantization
model.qconfig = torch.quantization.get_default_qconfig('fbgemm')
torch.quantization.prepare(model, inplace=True)
torch.quantization.convert(model, inplace=True)

# Now the model is quantized and ready for deployment
```

In this example, we load a pre-trained ResNet-18 model, prepare it for quantization by fusing layers (a necessary step to combine certain operations for efficient execution), and then apply static quantization. The model is now in a quantized format, ready for deployment in environments with limited computational resources.

The key advantage of this approach is that it reduces the model's memory footprint and inference time, especially on CPUs or edge devices that support INT8 operations.

Model Pruning

Pruning is another effective technique for reducing the size and computational cost of a model by eliminating unnecessary parameters. Many deep learning models are over-parameterized, meaning they contain several weights that don't contribute significantly to the model's predictions. Pruning removes these redundant weights, resulting in a smaller, more efficient model without a significant loss in accuracy.

Pruning is especially useful when deploying models in environments where memory is a limiting factor, such as embedded systems or edge devices. By pruning unimportant connections in the model, you can reduce its complexity and inference time.

Types of Pruning

There are several approaches to pruning a model, including:

- **Global unstructured pruning:** This method removes individual weights across the entire model based on their importance, leading to a sparser model.
- **Structured pruning:** In structured pruning, entire neurons, channels, or layers are removed. This approach is more hardware-friendly, as it results in a model with a reduced structure that can be efficiently executed on modern hardware.

Example: Applying Unstructured Pruning in PyTorch

```
import torch
import torch.nn.utils.prune as prune
from torchvision import models

# Load a pre-trained model
model = models.resnet18(pretrained=True)

# Apply global unstructured pruning to all Conv2d layers
for module in model.modules():
    if isinstance(module, torch.nn.Conv2d):
        prune.global_unstructured(
            module, name="weight", amount=0.2
        )

# Remove the pruning reparameterization to make the model ready for
deployment
for module in model.modules():
    if isinstance(module, torch.nn.Conv2d):
        prune.remove(module, 'weight')
# The pruned model is now ready for deployment
```

In this example, we apply global unstructured pruning to the convolutional layers of a **ResNet-18** model, removing 20% of the least important weights. After pruning, the model's size is reduced, making it more efficient for inference in production environments. Structured pruning can also be applied similarly, depending on the hardware requirements.

Benefits of Quantization and Pruning

Both quantization and pruning offer significant benefits when deploying models in production environments:

- **Reduced Model Size:** Quantization and pruning can drastically reduce the model's memory footprint, making it suitable for deployment on devices with limited storage or memory.
- **Faster Inference:** Reducing the precision of weights through quantization and removing redundant parameters through pruning can lead to faster inference times, which is critical for real-time applications such as video processing or autonomous systems.
- **Energy Efficiency:** Optimized models consume less computational power, which is especially important for battery-powered devices or cloud environments where energy consumption is a key factor.

By applying these techniques, you can deploy models that are not only smaller and faster but also more energy-efficient, without sacrificing too much accuracy.

Optimizing models for production is essential when deploying them to environments with limited computational resources or strict performance requirements. Techniques such as quantization and pruning allow you to reduce the size and complexity of your models while maintaining high levels of accuracy and performance. Whether you're deploying models to mobile devices, edge computing platforms, or cloud environments, these optimization techniques ensure that your models run efficiently and can scale to meet the demands of real-world applications.

In the next section, we'll explore critical production considerations such as latency, scalability, and robustness, ensuring that your models not only perform well but also handle real-world demands reliably.

Key Production Considerations: Scalability, Latency, and Robustness

When deploying machine learning models into production environments, ensuring that they are ready to handle real-world demands is crucial. Production models must not only deliver accurate predictions but also meet performance requirements, such as **scalability**, **low latency**, and **robustness**. These factors are essential to ensure that the model can serve a largc number of users, process requests quickly, and handle unexpected failures or traffic surges without degrading performance.

In this section, we will explore the critical aspects of deploying models into production, focusing on practical tips for addressing scalability, minimizing latency, and ensuring robustness. These concepts will help you ensure that your models can function reliably in various production environments without the need for complex architectural setups.

Scalability

Scalability refers to the ability of a model to handle increasing workloads efficiently. In a production setting, traffic to your model may grow over time, or there may be sudden surges in demand. To avoid bottlenecks, it's important to ensure that your model can scale both vertically and horizontally.

- **Vertical scaling** involves increasing the computational power of the machine hosting the model, such as adding more memory, CPUs, or GPUs.
- **Horizontal scaling** involves distributing the workload across multiple machines or instances, allowing for parallel processing.

Practical Tips for Scalability

- **Use Autoscaling:** Most cloud platforms, such as AWS, Azure, or Google Cloud, offer autoscaling features that automatically spin up additional instances of your model as traffic increases. This helps ensure that the model can handle peak loads without manual intervention.

   - **Example:** If you deploy your model using a service such as AWS SageMaker or Kubernetes, configure autoscaling to add or remove instances based on real-time traffic.

- **Load Balancing:** When scaling horizontally, it's essential to use a load balancer to distribute incoming requests evenly across multiple model instances. Load balancers ensure that no single instance becomes a bottleneck and that traffic is spread efficiently.
   - **Example:** Using a service such as **Elastic Load Balancing (ELB)** on AWS or Google Cloud Load Balancing can help balance traffic and provide fault tolerance in case one instance fails.
- **Containerization for Portability:** By containerizing your model using tools such as **Docker**, you can easily deploy it across multiple instances, ensuring that the same environment is replicated consistently. This makes horizontal scaling more seamless.
   - **Example:** Package your model in a Docker container and deploy it on Kubernetes for automatic scaling and efficient resource management.

Latency

Latency refers to the time it takes for a model to process a request and return a prediction. In many real-world applications, such as real-time analytics, recommendation systems, or autonomous systems, low latency is critical to ensuring a smooth user experience. Reducing latency becomes even more important when models are deployed in edge environments, where real-time responses are required.

Practical Tips for Reducing Latency

- **Optimize Model Size:** Reducing the model's complexity can significantly lower inference time. As discussed in the previous section, techniques such as **quantization** and **pruning** can help reduce model size and improve processing speed, leading to lower latency.
   - **Example:** Apply post-training quantization to reduce the model's size and speed up inference, especially in environments where real-time predictions are crucial.
- **Deploy Models Closer to Users:** Use **edge computing** to deploy models closer to the end-user, reducing the time it takes for data to travel between the user and the server. This is especially useful for applications that require real-time processing, such as IoT devices or mobile applications.

   - **Example:** Deploy models using edge platforms such as **AWS Greengrass** or **Google Cloud IoT** to ensure low-latency responses.

- **Asynchronous Processing:** For non-real-time tasks, consider using asynchronous processing to batch requests and process them in parallel. This reduces the perceived latency by distributing the workload over time.
   - **Example:** For tasks that don't require immediate results (for example, batch processing for analytics), implement an asynchronous request-response system to handle multiple requests efficiently.

- **Caching Predictions:** For models that produce repeated predictions (for example, recommendations or static results), caching the results of previous inferences can reduce the need for repeated computation. Tools such as **Redis** or **Memcached** can be used to cache frequently requested predictions and serve them instantly.
   - **Example:** Use a caching system to store predictions for frequently queried inputs, reducing the need to run the model repeatedly for the same requests.

Robustness

In production environments, models must be robust enough to handle unexpected scenarios, such as hardware failures, network issues, or sudden traffic spikes. Ensuring robustness means that the model should continue to operate reliably, even in adverse conditions. This involves implementing failover mechanisms, monitoring the model's health, and ensuring that any issues are detected and resolved quickly.

Practical Tips for Ensuring Robustness

- **Health Checks and Monitoring:** Set up health checks to continuously monitor the status of the model and its environment. This helps ensure that the model is running smoothly, and any failures can be detected early. Tools such as **Prometheus** and **Grafana** are commonly used for monitoring machine-learning models in production.
   - **Example:** Implement health checks that track the model's response time, error rates, and resource consumption. If an issue is detected, alerts can be triggered to notify the appropriate teams.

- **Graceful Failover and Redundancy:** Implement redundancy by deploying multiple instances of the model across different servers or data centers. In the event of a failure, traffic can be redirected to a working instance, ensuring minimal downtime.

  - **Example:** Use multi-region deployment to ensure that if one region's infrastructure fails, requests are automatically routed to another region without service interruption.
- **Circuit Breakers and Retry Logic:** Introduce circuit **breakers** in your application to detect when the model or service is under strain. If the model is experiencing high error rates or slow responses, the circuit breaker can stop sending new requests and allow the system to recover. **Retry logic** can be implemented to automatically retry failed requests.
  - **Example:** Use a circuit breaker pattern to stop overloading the model with requests during peak times and allow it to recover, while retry logic handles transient failures gracefully.
- **Versioning and Rollbacks:** Always have a plan for rolling back to a previous version of the model in case the latest update introduces bugs or performance degradation. Keeping multiple versions of the model in production allows for quick rollbacks if needed.
  - **Example:** If a new model version shows performance issues in production, use your model versioning system to revert to the previous stable version immediately.

When deploying models into production, **scalability**, **latency**, and **robustness** are key considerations that ensure your model can handle real-world traffic, respond quickly, and remain resilient to failures. By using techniques such as autoscaling, load balancing, and failover mechanisms, you can ensure that your model is scalable and robust. Additionally, optimizing your model and infrastructure for low-latency responses ensures a smoother user experience, even in high-demand environments. Implementing these strategies will prepare your models for the challenges of production, ensuring they are ready to perform efficiently and reliably.

Conclusion

As this final chapter and the book conclude, let us reflect on the key takeaways from the journey of model development and deployment. In this chapter, we covered some important steps required to take a machine-learning model from the research phase to a production-ready environment, focusing on critical aspects, such as **scalability**, **latency**, and **robustness**. The techniques discussed ranged from using tools such as **TorchServe** for deployment to optimizing models with **quantization** and **pruning**. All are designed to ensure that models can perform efficiently in real-world settings.

Deploying machine learning models is more than just pushing code into production. It's about ensuring that the model continues to function effectively, even under changing data conditions and varying traffic loads. Scaling, both vertically and horizontally, is key to meeting growing demand while maintaining low latency ensures that users experience smooth, real-time interactions. Additionally, ensuring the robustness of models through monitoring and failover mechanisms helps mitigate risks and maintain continuous service in the face of unpredictable failures.

Throughout this book, we have built a strong foundation that covers all aspects of model development, from designing and training models to optimizing them for performance. We've explored advanced techniques, such as hyperparameter tuning, regularization, and ensemble methods to improve model performance, and in this final chapter, we've looked at how to prepare those models for deployment in real-world applications. Together, these techniques form a comprehensive toolkit that supports every phase of the machine learning lifecycle.

Now, equipped with the knowledge from this book, you are ready to take your models from experimentation to full-scale production. Whether you are deploying models on a cloud platform for millions of users or on edge devices for real-time inference, the principles and techniques you've learned will guide you through the challenges ahead. Remember, machine learning is an iterative process where each deployment is an opportunity to improve and refine, and each real-world application opens new possibilities for innovation.

Index

D

E

F

G

H

I

T